Jesus's Opening Week

JESUS'S OPENING WEEK

A Deep Exegesis of John 1:1—2:11

E. Ray Clendenen

WIPF & STOCK · Eugene, Oregon

JESUS'S OPENING WEEK
A Deep Exegesis of John 1:1—2:11

Copyright © 2019 E. Ray Clendenen. All rights reserved. Except for brief quotations in critical publications or reviews, no part of this book may be reproduced in any manner without prior written permission from the publisher. Write: Permissions, Wipf and Stock Publishers, 199 W. 8th Ave., Suite 3, Eugene, OR 97401.

Wipf & Stock
An Imprint of Wipf and Stock Publishers
199 W. 8th Ave., Suite 3
Eugene, OR 97401

www.wipfandstock.com

PAPERBACK ISBN: 978-1-5326-7507-2
HARDCOVER ISBN: 978-1-5326-7508-9
EBOOK ISBN: 978-1-5326-7509-6

Manufactured in the U.S.A.   MAY 8, 2019

To my wife, Gigi, whose uncritical acceptance of me as I am
has helped me to discover who that is,
and who has filled my life with laughter.

Contents

Permissions / ix
Preface / xi
Acknowledgements / xv
Abbreviations / xvii

1. Introduction / 1
2. Prologue (1:1–18) / 15
3. Introductions (1:19–51) / 53
4. Day Seven: Jesus's First Sign (2:1–11) / 101
5. Conclusion / 161

Bibliography / 169

Permissions

Unless otherwise noted, all Scripture quotations are taken from The Christian Standard Bible (CSB). Copyright © 2017 by Holman Bible Publishers. Used by permission. Christian Standard Bible®, and CSB® are federally registered trademarks of Holman Bible Publishers, all rights reserved.

Scripture passages marked ESV are taken from The Holy Bible, English Standard Version. ESV® Text Edition: 2016. Copyright © 2001 by Crossway Bibles, a publishing ministry of Good News Publishers.

Scripture passages marked GW are from the God's Word translation. Copyright © 1995 by God's Word to the Nations. All rights reserved.

Scripture passages marked HCSB are from the Holman Christian Standard Bible® Copyright © 1999, 2000, 2002, 2003, 2009 by Holman Bible Publishers, Nashville Tennessee. All rights reserved.

Scripture passages marked KJV are from the King James Version. Public domain.

Scripture passages marked NAB are from the New American Bible, revised edition © 2010, 1991, 1986, 1970 Confraternity of Christian Doctrine, Inc., Washington, DC All Rights Reserved.

Scripture passages marked NASB are from the New American Standard Bible®, Copyright © 1960, 1962, 1963, 1968, 1971, 1972, 1973, 1975, 1977, 1995 by The Lockman Foundation All rights reserved.

Scripture passages marked NET are from the New English Translation. NET Bible® copyright ©1996-2006 by Biblical Studies Press, L.L.C. http://netbible.com All rights reserved.

Scripture passages marked NIV are from The Holy Bible, New International Version®, NIV® Copyright ©1973, 1978, 1984, 2011 by Biblica, Inc.® All rights reserved worldwide.

PERMISSIONS

Scripture passages marked NIV84 are from The Holy Bible, New International Version®, NIV® Copyright ©1973, 1978, 1984 by Biblica, Inc.® All rights reserved worldwide.

Scripture passages marked NJB are from The New Jerusalem Bible, copyright © 1985 by Darton, Longman & Todd.

Scripture passages marked NKJV are from The New King James Version, copyright © 1982, Thomas Nelson, Inc., Publishers. All rights reserved.

Scripture passages marked NLT are from the Holy Bible, New Living Translation, copyright © 1996, 2004, 2015 by Tyndale House Foundation. All rights reserved.

Scripture passages marked NRSV are from the New Revised Standard Version Bible, copyright © 1989 the Division of Christian Education of the National Council of the Churches of Christ in the United States of America. All rights reserved.

Scripture passages marked REB are from the Revised English Bible, copyright © Cambridge University Press and Oxford University Press 1989. All rights reserved.

Scripture passages marked RSV are from the Revised Standard Version of the Bible, copyright © 1946, 1952, and 1971 the Division of Christian Education of the National Council of the Churches of Christ in the United States of America. All rights reserved.

Scripture quotation marked TEV are from Today's English Version, also known as the Good News Bible. Copyright © 1992 by American Bible Society.

All emphases in Scripture quotations have been added by the author.

Preface

I HAVE CHRISTIAN (YES, Christian) friends whose lives are in turmoil, who are severely depressed or even angry with God and struggling with their faith in the light of devastating illness, the pain and sorrow and even death of loved ones, the aftermath of being cheated and lied to by "friends" and family, or a sense of personal failure and hopelessness due to a lifetime of addiction. They are desperate for comfort and for peace. Others are paralyzed by loneliness and disappointment and fear of what the future may hold. They feel abandoned and useless and are desperate for companionship, wisdom, and guidance.

I've been there. Christ welcomed me into his family in 1967 when I graduated from high school, and I've been attending church regularly, studying the Bible every day, and trying to serve him since then. But I've also been intimately acquainted with sin, depression, anger, grief, disappointment, failure, hopelessness, loneliness, fear, and feelings of abandonment, uselessness, and desperation. I can say to my friends, "I've been there. God will see you through." But is that all I've got?

God sent me people to love me and help me, without whom I could not have come out of the darkness. Someday I hope to write a book called *God Is Not Enough*, unpacking and applying God's words in Genesis 2:18: "It is not good for the man to be alone." But if God is not enough, people are certainly not enough. God has also used the truth of his Word, ministered to me by his Spirit, to bring me and keep me out of the pit. A few years ago, God led me to a book about the incarnation to read during the Christmas season. It was *The Incarnation of God*, by John C. Clark and Marcus Peter Johnson. It opened for me new vistas of God's grace and mercy in the gospel. It also introduced me to many other wonderful books, especially those dealing with the biblical doctrine of the Christian's union with Christ. All these books inspired me to dig more deeply especially into the apostle Paul's letter to the Colossians and then into John's Gospel. The latter in particular

I've found to be an amazing source of insight into God's heart and the depth of his love, and I've felt compelled to share with others what I find there.

My education and ministry through the years have been mostly focused on the riches of the Old Testament, which I love. I believe that without it the Christian would be like the proverbial "one-armed paper hanger." Studying John's Gospel without the background of the Old Testament is almost like watching a baseball game through a knothole. But oh, what a game it is! God is in the Old Testament "abounding in faithful love and truth" (Exod 34:6). But John shows us that in Jesus Christ the creative Word of God has become flesh and come down to our level. He has looked us in the face, put his hand on our shoulder, and said "Follow me!" As John says in 1:17, whereas the law "was given" and could therefore be separated from Moses, "grace and truth *came*" and has made its home with us in the person of Jesus Christ. This and many other life-altering truths can be found in concentrated form in these opening verses of John's Gospel (1:1–2:11). Here I've found something I can share with my friends who are in pain and struggling with their faith.

I hope this book can be found useful for anyone struggling with the sorrows of life. But I'm writing especially for those who are called to minister the gospel of Christ to a hurting world. I hope that God's Spirit in their lives will use these thoughts and the results of my research on John's prologue and Jesus's opening week to bring healing, hope, and joy to those God has entrusted to them. But I also hope that God will use what I've written to speak words of love and comfort to ministers themselves who are discouraged and, perhaps, whose lives are in turmoil.

Since I'm writing primarily for those in ministry and not for scholars, I have left the thorniest technical issues to be handled by those more competent than I and have focused on John's message and its practical application. I have also included personal anecdotes, illustrations, and devotional thoughts. Since readers will probably vary in the depth of their knowledge of the Bible and of biblical languages, I have tried not to assume too much and will, at times, explain things that some readers already know quite well. I beg their pardon and indulgence.

On the other hand, I also hope readers who haven't studied Greek and Hebrew will forgive me for including a smattering of Greek and Hebrew words that I felt were necessary (I've used a simple transliteration style in the text I hope will aid pronunciation). Although there are many excellent English translations of the Bible (like the CSB, the Christian Standard Bible I used here), that language was not in use when Jesus entered the world, and God led the writers of the New Testament to use Greek. English Bible translators have selected the English words and phrases they believe best reflect the meaning of the Greek, and that's usually all we need to know. But in some cases, there is a richness and depth of meaning and significance in the Greek that the English cannot convey.

The purpose of the footnotes, in addition to letting the reader know my sources, is to address readers whose background in biblical studies and whose knowledge of biblical languages is more advanced than others. Greek and Hebrew fonts, therefore, are used there.

Finally a word about my subtitle, *A Deep Exegesis of John 1:1–2:11*. In Peter Leithart's book, *Deep Exegesis: The Mystery of Reading Scripture* (see the bibliography), he presents a model for getting "to the rich and richly varied *sensus plenior* [fuller meaning] of the sacramental word not by moving past the letter to a spiritual sense, not by treating the letter as a husk for removal. We get at the riches of Scripture precisely by luxuriating in the letter, by squeezing everything we can from the text as written."[1] He also argues that "interpretation is all about tracing out the crucial missing elements that make the text mean what it does."[2] I have tried to squeeze everything I could from John 1:1–2:11 as the apostle wrote it. I have also tried to demonstrate that by paying close attention to the words of the text, by opening ourselves to the unexpected, and by recognizing the gaps in the account and in the conversations, we can see how John presents Jesus against the backdrop of the whole Bible. It is often when we find the "crucial missing elements" of the New Testament account in the Old Testament that we see Jesus the Lamb of God (John 1:29, 36) most clearly, and are thereby ready to ingest his flesh and blood unto eternal life (6:53-56).

---

1. Leithart, *Deep Exegesis*, vii.
2. Leithart, *Deep Exegesis*, 112.

Acknowledgements

My thoughts here began as notes for a Bible study in our home for a small group of wonderful Christ-followers from the Seventh-Day Adventist church I've been attending since my marriage to Gigi a few years ago. They have accepted this Baptist with loving arms and offered kind and generous fellowship in service of Christ, forgiving my ignorance of the fine points of Adventist theology and also teaching me much about Christian love and service.

I must also acknowledge my debt to some friends who offered words of encouragement for my work here, such as Tom Schreiner and David Allen. Blessing me with many helpful comments and suggestions were also Craig Blomberg, Peter Gentry, and Tim Wiarda, whose amazingly gracious advice I'm sure I should have followed more often than I did. I will always have much to learn. Various friends such as George Carpenter, Dan Davis, and Pike Williams have also unwittingly furnished me with ideas and phrases I liked and have incorporated here, such as "in the weeds," "ready, fire, aim," and the enneagram personality test. My colleague and friend, Dave Stabnow, has been a wonderful sounding board and source of helpful ideas. As one friend said tongue-in-cheek to me once, "What good are friends if you can't use them?" I am grateful. I also feel I should express gratitude to the more than one hundred authors and editors, living and dead, listed in my bibliography and frequently cited in my comments. Most of what I have written I have gleaned from them, and I can only hope they would not disapprove of the use I have found for their comments.

I learned biblical interpretation long ago from outstanding scholars in several wonderful schools, and I continue learning through God's gifted teachers from their books and lectures (especially at the annual Evangelical Theological Society meetings). But much of my understanding of the Christian life came after and as a result of my experience of brokenness. It came and continues to come especially through my association with Celebrate Recovery, a ministry and fellowship of kind, welcoming, supportive believers with whom I serve. God's miraculous power to change lives is continuously in evidence, inspiring perseverance in the pursuit of godliness. I can never repay my sister in the faith, Julie Vega, for inviting me to Celebrate Recovery in 2011 and, as Celebrate Recovery pastor, serving as encourager and cheerleader for me and countless others on the road to recovery from life's hurts, hang-ups, and habits. I am also grateful to her husband, Dino, for an example of enthusiastic wonder at God's creation and especially God's grace in Jesus Christ. He is the epitome of Brennan Manning's "disciple who is truly poor in spirit," and I always leave him feeling, *"My life has been enriched by talking with you."*[1]

Finally, I must acknowledge the immense debt I owe God's gift to me of my wife, Gigi. No one but God knows me better than she does, and yet, like him, loves me with so much patience, kindness, and compassion anyway. I greatly admire her wisdom, insight, and spiritual maturity. Her thoughts and perceptive questions as she persevered in reading through these studies were of inestimable value to me.

---

1. Manning, *Ragamuffin Gospel*, 81 (emphasis original).

Abbreviations

AYBD	Freedman, ed. *Anchor Yale Bible Dictionary.*
BDAG	Danker, ed. *A Greek-English Lexicon of the New Testament and Other Early Christian Literature,* 2000.
ca.	circa
cf.	compare
chap(s).	chapter(s)
DBI	Ryken, et al., eds. *Dictionary of Biblical Imagery.*
DJG	Green and McKnight, eds. *Dictionary of Jesus and the Gospels,* 1992.
DJG2	Green, et al., eds. *Dictionary of Jesus and the Gospels,* 2013.
DLNT	Martin and Davids, eds. *Dictionary of the Later New Testament and Its Developments*
DNTB	Evans and Porter, eds. *Dictionary of New Testament Background.*
EBC	Gaebelein, ed. *Expositor's Bible Commentary,* 1984.
ed(s).	editor(s), edition, edited by
EDNT	Balz and Schneider, ed. *Exegetical Dictionary of the New Testament*
e.g.	for example

Gk.	Greek
Hb.	Hebrew
i.e.	that is
L&N	Louw and Nida, *Greek-English Lexicon of the New Testament*.
Lat.	Latin
LXX	Septuagint, Greek Old Testament
NIDNTT	C. Brown, ed., *New International Dictionary of New Testament Theology*, 1986.
NIDNTTE	Silva, ed. *Dictionary of New Testament Theology and Exegesis*, 2014.
p(p).	page(s)
rev.	revised, revised by, revision
TDNT	Kittel and Friedrich, eds. *Theological Dictionary of the New Testament, Abridged in One Volume*, 1985.
TDOT	Botterweck and Ringgren, eds. *Theological Dictionary of the Old Testament*.
trans.	translated by
vs.	versus
v(v).	verse(s)
vol(s).	volume(s)

1

Introduction

The Character of John's Gospel

JOHN'S GOSPEL IS OFTEN said to be shallow enough for an infant to wade in, but deep enough for an elephant to swim in.[1] The origin of the saying is uncertain and may derive from a statement by Pope Gregory I (Gregory the Great, ca. 540-604) about the Bible as a whole: "Scripture is like a river again, broad and deep, shallow enough here for the lamb to go wading, but deep enough there for the elephant to swim."[2] Even earlier, Saint Augustine (354-430) put it more prosaically in describing Scripture in his *Confessions* as "a text lowly to the beginner but, on further reading, of mountainous difficulty and enveloped in mysteries." The Bible, he said, "was composed in such a way that as beginners mature, its meaning grows with them."[3] Also in his *Confessions* (12.14.17) he wrote, "What wonderful profundity there is in your utterances! The surface meaning lies open before us and charms beginners. Yet the depth is amazing, my God, the depth is amazing. To concentrate on it is to experience awe—the awe of adoration before its transcendence and the trembling of love."

If the mysterious quality of Scripture's simplicity turning to unfathomable depths in response to growing maturity and experience is true of any Bible book, it is certainly true of John's Gospel. Countless new believers have been enthralled by John's portrayal of Jesus and have been led by its profundity into deeper and deeper understanding and experience of Jesus's

---

1. See Morris, *Gospel according to John,* 7. The quote has been attributed to various people.
2. Gregory the Great's commentary on Job (*Moral. inscr.* 4).
3. Augustine, *Confessions,* 3.5.9 (Chadwick translation, p. 40).

person and work. As Leon Morris wrote, the "simple words" of John's Gospel, which display for the sinner with such clarity the deity and saving power of Jesus Christ, also "carry such profound meaning that the wisest scholar or the holiest saint will scarcely feel that he has even begun to explore their significance. Accordingly we shall be able to see some of John's thought, but we must expect that the writer has greater depths of meaning than we can plumb."[4]

A couple of years ago, my wife Gigi introduced me to snorkeling. I have exulted in the amazing variety of incredibly beautiful and delightful sea creatures I've seen: green turtles, grouper, stingray, nurse shark, barracuda, angelfish, blue tang, snapper, lionfish, sergeant major, bar jack, and parrotfish, among others. But I have not yet learned to Scuba in order to plumb the depths and see even more amazing creatures of the sea. My experience of being awestruck by God's creation will only increase the deeper I go. The same is true of my awe at the wonders of God's Word and even more his character and our redemption. A sample of this experience can certainly be found in the study of John's Gospel.

As D. A. Carson points out,

> Perhaps more than any other [Bible book], the Gospel of John has been used by Christians in every age, and for the greatest array of purposes. University students distribute free copies to their friends in the hope of introducing them to the Saviour. Elderly Christians on their deathbed ask that parts of this Gospel be read to them . . . Children memorize entire chapters and sing choruses based on its truth. Countless courses of sermons have been based on this book or on some part of it. It stood near the centre of Christological controversy in the fourth century, and for the last 150 years it has been at the heart of debate about the relation between history and theology. Until recently, the best known verse in the Bible was John 3:16 (possibly displaced today by Mt. 7:1!).[5]

According to Paul Woodbridge, "If you really want to understand Jesus and why he came, this is the Gospel to read."[6]

This is the Gospel of love, where the term for love occurs fifty-seven times, more than in any other book. The second most frequent is in the little book of 1 John—forty-six times! The famous German theologian, Karl

---

4. Morris, *Cross in the New Testament*, 145.

5. Carson, *Gospel according to John*, 21.

6. Woodbridge, "'Kingdom of God' and 'Eternal Life,'" in Green, *God's Power to Save*, 55.

Barth, after a lecture at the University of Chicago in 1962, was asked if he could summarize his whole life's work in theology in a single sentence. He replied by quoting, "Jesus loves me, this I know, for the Bible tells me so."[7]

The prophet Isaiah prayed, "If only you would tear the heavens open and come down" (64:1). John describes how that happened. A famous nineteenth-century British biblical scholar, J. B. Lightfoot, wrote,

> I believe from my heart that the truth which [John's] Gospel more especially enshrines—the truth that Jesus Christ is the very Word incarnate, the manifestation of the Father to mankind—is the one lesson which duly apprehended will do more than all our feeble efforts to purify and elevate human life here by imparting to it hope and light and strength, the one study which alone can fitly prepare us for a joyful immortality hereafter.[8]

Judging from the number of Christian manuscripts left behind from the second and third centuries, the New Testament writings were, of course, the most popular among Christians (with more than sixty manuscripts), and the Gospel of John was the most popular New Testament book (with eighteen manuscripts).[9] So we may rightly expect that God will impart hope, light, and strength to us as we study the Gospel of John and that he will use it to "fitly prepare" us for heaven.

How Does John Differ from the Other Gospels?

One of the reasons even elephants find the Gospel of John challenging is the differences between John and the other three ("Synoptic") Gospels. First, many passages familiar to Christians from two or three of the other Gospels are missing from John: no parables (but many metaphors and symbols), no demon-casting (although John often speaks of Satanic opposition), no lepers or tax collectors, no Sermon on the Mount/Plain, no account of Jesus's birth in Bethlehem (only that the Word became flesh), no Gethsemane, no transfiguration, no Lord's baptism (although John the Baptist recounts part of that event in John 1:32–33), no institution of the Lord's Supper (although this is surely the supper referred to in John 13:2,[10] and it is the setting for chaps. 13–17), etc. One likely explanation for this is that other Gospels

---

7. "Did Karl Barth Really Say 'Jesus Loves Me, This I Know...?'" https://www.patheos.com/blogs/rogereolson/2013/01/did-karl-barth-really-say-jesus-loves-me-this-i-know.

8. Lightfoot, *Biblical Essays*, 43–44.

9. Kruger, *Canon Revisited*, 235.

10. See Burge, *John*, 364–67; Blomberg, *Historical Reliability of the New Testament*, 217.

were available at the time of John's writing. New Testament scholar Richard Bauckham argues, for example, "John presupposes that his readers know Mark's Gospel and deliberately does not repeat what could be read in Mark unless he has a specific reason for doing so."[11] As Craig Blomberg states, "John knew that he was choosing largely different material from his predecessors but did not see his emphases as conflicting with theirs."[12] His goal was not to correct or replace them but to accomplish his own purposes in his own way, with his own emphases. "Years of preaching to Jews, both in Palestine and in the diaspora, had given him some ideas about how it should be done."[13]

Second, many familiar stories about Jesus are *only* found in John: for example, changing water into wine, talking to Nicodemus and the Samaritan woman, the resurrection of Lazarus, and the upper room discourse. Also, only in John is Jesus *explicitly* identified as God, and only here does he use the well-known "I am" (*egō eimi*) statements. According to one calculation, in fact, the amount of overlap between the Synoptic Gospels and John is only about eight percent![14]

Third, there are passages that seem inconsistent with the Synoptic Gospels, such as John the Baptist denying that he is Elijah (1:21; cf. Mark 9:11–13) and Jesus's bestowal of the Spirit before his ascension (20:22; cf. Acts 2).

Fourth, some scholars have accused John of having a different theology of salvation from the Synoptic Gospels. In John the good news is the gift of eternal life and resurrection, referred to at least sixteen times in John but only two or three times in each of the Synoptics. The Gospels speak of salvation in terms of the kingdom of God or of heaven eighty times in Matthew, sixty times in Luke, and thirty times in Mark, but only four in John (3:3, 5; 18:36).[15]

Fifth, there are chronological differences, such as the temple cleansing occurring at the beginning rather than the end of Jesus's ministry (2:14–22), the number of Passovers during Jesus's ministry, and the chronology of events surrounding the cross.

11. Bauckham, *Gospel of Glory*, 104.

12. Blomberg, "John and Jesus," in McKnight and Osborne, *The Face of New Testament Studies*, 220. See also in the same volume, Klaus Scholtissek, "The Johannine Gospel in Recent Research," 455.

13. Carson, *Gospel according to John*, 93.

14. Woodbridge, "'Kingdom of God' and 'Eternal Life,'" 56.

15. This issue is thoroughly discussed in Woodbridge, "'Kingdom of God' and 'Eternal Life,'" 55–78. In the same volume see also his article, "Theological Implications of 'Eternal Life' in the Fourth Gospel," 79–103.

Finally, there are differences of style and also individual passages in John that strain the interpretive skill of even the most advanced Bible students. One thing that sets John apart from the other Gospels is its prevalent use of symbolism. Andreas Köstenberger concludes an extended discussion of this feature in this way:

> It is hard to overstate the interpretive significance of symbolism [in John]. It is virtually impossible to understand John's gospel without appreciating the meaning of the symbols it contains, and the gospel's "symbolic universe" renders it virtually impenetrable to outsiders who fail to grasp it. The discussion of water, bread, and light symbolism . . . illustrate the foundational nature played by symbolism in conveying John's theology, especially with regard to Jesus' messianic mission and the benefits it bestows on those who believe in him.[16]

The problem of inconsistencies between John and the other Gospels was felt even in the second century, when the Syrian theologian, Tatian, tried to solve it by weaving the Gospels together into a harmony that came to be called the *Diatessaron*. Charges from critics of Christianity that the Gospels contradict one another led Augustine to produce his *Harmony of the Four Gospels* in about AD 400. Many Gospel harmonies are available today. Another solution was offered at that time by Marcion, who used only a "corrected" version of Luke and rejected the other Gospels (as well as some of Paul's writings). Other solutions have been offered since then, such as the view that John's Gospel is only interested in theology, not history. Some scholars have also argued that, rather than being based on fact, the various Gospels were produced by different and competing Christian communities advancing their own beliefs and concerns. None of these solutions are ultimately satisfying. The historical accuracy and value of all the Gospels, including the Gospel of John, has been amply and solidly defended by many scholars.[17] Jonathan Pennington explains that "*focusing* on the differences gives one a distorted picture, for despite discrepancies such as those highlighted above, overall the picture of all four Gospels is amazingly consistent in terms of Jesus's character, tone, teaching emphases, and the general course of his life and death."[18] Carson speaks of "the interlocking nature of the diverse Gospel

---

16. Köstenberger, *Theology*, 167.

17. In addition to the recommended commentaries, see Wilkins and Moreland, eds., *Jesus Under Fire*; Bock, "Precision and Accuracy," 367–81; and especially Blomberg, *Historical Reliability of John's Gospel*, and his *Historical Reliability of the New Testament*. Also see Harris, "Major Differences between John and the Synoptic Gospels."

18. Pennington, *Reading the Gospels Wisely*, 59 (his emphasis). See also his brief discussion of the issues related to John versus the Synoptics on pp. 64–66.

presentations."[19] Each Gospel supplements the others. The reason that God chose to give us four unique biographies of Jesus rather than just one is that, as Bauckham has pointed out, "the real Jesus must be *more than* the Jesus of any of the Gospels."[20] Pennington echoes, "If it is indeed true that Jesus was God's Son incarnate, the Creator of the universe, and the consummation of all knowledge and wisdom, then it stands to reason that no one account—or a million—could begin to describe and plumb the depths of his person, teaching, and actions."[21] Finally, Michael F. Bird concludes, "The distinctive character of John need not be a source of historical or theological embarrassment; nor should we consider the tensions between John and Synoptics as necessarily problematic . . . The Fourth Gospel adds a richness and diversity to the fourfold Gospel testimony to Jesus Christ that enhances its appeal and its impact . . . As Calvin commented, John shows us not only the body of Jesus but also his soul."[22]

If the Christ who came to us were like a simple monolith rising from the earth, easily captured and comprehended by a single photograph, then we could get by with just one Gospel. But we do not have a monolithic Savior. The God we worship and the Jesus who came to save us are infinitely faceted. I am fascinated by Theodore Roosevelt. I have read several biographies of him and hope to read more. I would not argue that one is better than the others; they all add to my understanding and appreciation of the man. If that is true of a flawed human being, how much more is it true of the perfect Son of Man?

I've recently taken up photography. My wife Gigi and I love to travel to beautiful places and experience new aspects of God's creation, and I love to try to capture the beauty and excitement in photographs and even videos. When we return home and I load the pictures on my large-screen computer, we often gasp at the beauty and thank God for his creation and the experiences he gave us. But the audiovisual record only reminds us of what we saw and heard. The reality and even the memories are so much more! That is the case with Jesus. It took four Gospel biographies of Jesus to accurately and sufficiently (though not comprehensively) portray the person and work of our Creator, who embodies for us life and light and grace and truth.

In 2017 Gigi and I visited a hill in Provincetown, Massachusetts, to see an eighty-one-foot-tall monument called the "National Monument to the Forefathers." It is perhaps the world's largest solid granite monument and

---

19. Carson, *Gospel according to John*, 55.
20. Bauckham, *Gospel of Glory*, 187.
21. Pennington, *Reading the Gospels Wisely*, 70.
22. Michael F. Bird, "Synoptics and John," *DJG2*, 922.

was built in 1888 to commemorate the Mayflower pilgrims and to celebrate their ideals. On top is a statue of a woman representing faith, whose right hand is pointing up to heaven and whose left hand is holding a Bible. On four sides are smaller human statues representing liberty, education, law, and morality. How many pictures did I take? I actually took seven, including close-ups, but a minimum of four would be required. Each picture is an accurate portrayal of part of the monument, but at least four are necessary to capture the whole. If that's true of a human monument, all the more is it the case with the King of kings and Lamb of God who came to take away the sin of the world.

Who Was John's Primary Audience, and What Was His Primary Purpose?

Another issue we should consider before plunging into our study is the question of John's primary audience and purpose. He states his purpose in 20:30–31:

> Jesus performed many other signs in the presence of his disciples that are not written in this book. But these are written so that you may believe that Jesus is the Messiah, the Son of God, and that by believing you may have life in his name.

Some have argued that John wrote primarily to Christians and that his goal was to establish them in the faith. In some manuscripts of John, the verb *believe* is a present tense, perhaps meaning "continue to believe," whereas other manuscripts have a past (aorist) tense, perhaps meaning "come to believe." But Carson argues convincingly that John's primary purpose was evangelism (the difference in verb tense is not so clear and decisive) and that his initially intended audience was especially Jews (particularly those living outside Palestine) and Gentiles who had converted to or were attracted by Judaism. This is suggested by the great number of John's quotations and especially allusions to the Old Testament. Carson also argues that v. 31 should be translated "that you may believe that the Messiah, the Son of God, is Jesus."[23] The fundamental question John was answering, he says, is not "Who is Jesus?" but rather "Who is the Messiah?" Christians already know the answer.

Nevertheless, John *does* deal very thoroughly with the question "Who is Jesus?," and Christians have always found that the study of this book deepens their faith, clarifies their calling, and comforts them in their trials.

23. Carson, *Gospel according to John*, 662–63.

Besides, the ultimate goal of John's Gospel is not *belief*, but *life*—"that by believing you may have life in his name." And the life that Jesus provides is not only in abundance (John 10:10), but it is ever-increasing and ever-deepening. Some have argued that the "upper-room discourse" in John 14–17 is not evangelistic. But Carson points out that "the best evangelistic literature" explains not only the *why* and *how* of becoming a Christian, but "*what it means* to be a Christian," which John 14–17 addresses "rather pointedly."[24]

Who Wrote the Fourth Gospel?

Before we begin our study of this Gospel, we also need to consider the question of authorship. Unfortunately, all four of the Gospels are formally anonymous. None of them begins like Paul's letters, naming the author. But the earliest manuscripts of the four Gospels in the second century all have the title, "The Gospel of Jesus Christ according to ____."[25] This shows that as soon as they began to be copied and distributed, the title indicated the author. Although formally anonymous, everyone knew who wrote them. And everyone knew that the author of the fourth Gospel was the apostle John, even though his name never even appears in his book.

Although John, the son of Zebedee and the brother of James, is mentioned three times in Matthew, ten times in Mark, and seven times in Luke, he is never mentioned in John. He appears there only as "the one/disciple Jesus loved" (13:23; 19:26; 20:2; 21:7, 20). John the Baptist is referred to by name nineteen times in John's Gospel, but never with the title, "the Baptist." As Craig Blomberg points out, "Unless John the apostle were known to be the author of this document, surely this omission of any further clarification as to which "John" was in view would be surprising."[26]

Although John did not name himself as the author, someone might think that arrogance caused him to designate himself as "the one/disciple Jesus loved." But although this is usually the way the phrase is translated in English, suggesting perhaps that Jesus did not love the others the way he loved John, the Greek does not suggest this. It could more properly be rendered, "one of his disciples, whom Jesus loved" (13:23). The Greek does not actually say, "the one." Therefore, it may not be arrogance that John is expressing, but wonder that someone like he, a "son of thunder," could

---

24. Carson, *Gospel according to John*, 92 (his emphasis).
25. See Carson, et al., *Introduction to the New Testament*, 46.
26. Blomberg, *Jesus and the Gospels*, 197–98. I am grateful to Craig Blomberg for calling my attention to this.

become a beloved son of God, just as when I in faith echo God's Word and personalize the gospel that "God loves even me."

But how do we know that "the Beloved disciple" is the one who wrote the Gospel of John? He tells us in 21:20-24 (emphasis added),

> So Peter turned around and saw *the disciple Jesus loved* following them, the one who had leaned back against Jesus at the supper and asked, "Lord, who is the one that's going to betray you?" When Peter saw him, he said to Jesus, "Lord, what about him?" "If I want him to remain until I come," Jesus answered, "what is that to you? As for you, follow me." So this rumor spread to the brothers and sisters that this disciple would not die. Yet Jesus did not tell him that he would not die, but, "If I want him to remain until I come, what is that to you?" *This is the disciple who testifies to these things and who wrote them down. We know that his testimony is true.*

This disciple, "whom Jesus loved," was an *eyewitness* to all that he describes and tells us about in his Gospel (see 19:35). He knew Jesus personally from the very beginning of his ministry (cf. 15:27) and even had a close relationship with him. He was probably the anonymous companion of Andrew we will encounter in 1:35-40.[27] Jesus loved him and talked with him and told him things he wanted John to tell others. John is saying, "I was there. I saw it for myself. I know what I'm talking about. You can trust what I'm telling you. This is the truth, and you'd better believe it. Jesus really is the Messiah, and you can come to know him and be loved by him just like me. Just as I saw and believed, you can read and believe." In 1 John 1:1-3 the apostle wrote,

> What was from the beginning, what we have heard, what we have seen with our eyes, what we have observed and have touched with our hands, concerning the word of life—that life was revealed, and we have seen it and we testify and declare to you the eternal life that was with the Father and was revealed to us—what we have seen and heard we also declare to you, so that you may also have fellowship with us; and indeed our fellowship is with the Father and with his Son Jesus Christ.

So the Gospel of John is a *testimony*. At the weekly meeting of Celebrate Recovery that I attend, we have "testimony night" twice a month. Someone comes and recounts for us what Jesus has done in his or her life—how he has changed them, perhaps through the ministry of Celebrate Recovery. They

---

27. See Bauckham, *Gospel of Glory*, 151-52.

often tell us that God used someone's *testimony* to get their attention and to convince them that the Lord could help them. John's Gospel is intended as John's testimony, whose purpose is to allow God to transform its readers in some way.

The Approach to Be Followed

We'll be looking here at only the prologue and the first week of Jesus's ministry. We'll see how the prologue in 1:1–18 is a kind of overture, introducing us to the main themes to be encountered, not only in John's Gospel as a whole,[28] but also in 1:19–2:11. After the prologue, John structures the opening events of his account around the opening week of Jesus's ministry, which he describes in 1:19–2:11. If Richard Bauckham's argument is sound, as I think it is, and John 1:40–42 covers the events of the fourth day, then this opening section of John's Gospel helps tie together the whole Bible, reaching back to the week of creation and ahead to the week of new-creation fulfillment in Jesus's climactic passion week. It becomes an even more thunderous prelude to the Gospel, encapsulating the gospel message and preparing us for all that follows. As Bauckham explains,

> Given the biblical and Jewish significance of the week as a period of time, established by the Creator at the beginning (Gen. 1:1–2:4), there is an obvious appropriateness in beginning the Gospel's narrative of new creation with a week. But we should notice that there is one other week whose seven days are carefully enumerated by the writer of the Gospel, a week that is almost (though not quite) at the end of the narrative. This is the week that begins six days before the last Passover in the Gospel (12:1) and ends with the day of Jesus's resurrection on "the first day of the week" (20:1).[29]

---

28. Jörg Frey calls the prologue "reading instruction" for the following Johannine narrative (*Glory of the Crucified One*, 285).

29. Bauckham, *Gospel of Glory*, 133. We must note that not all scholars agree that John intended to present 1:19–2:11 as an account of Jesus's first week. See, for example, Ridderbos, *Gospel of John*, 102–3, and Brown, *John 1–XII*, 106. I believe, however, that Bauckham, 131–84, makes a compelling case that John probably did intend this. We should also note that 2:1 begins with the conjunction *kai*, which, according to Stephen Levinsohn, serves two functions in John's Gospel: "to associate information together in certain specific contexts" and "to add one or more events." This argues against those who begin a new main division at 2:1. See Levinsohn, *Discourse Features of New Testament Greek*, 84; Buth, "Οὖν, Δέ, Καί, and Asyndeton in John's Gospel," 144–61.

According to Bauckham, another clue that John intends us to set side-by-side these two weeks that begin and end Jesus's earthly ministry is that both weeks begin at a Bethany (1:28; 12:1).[30]

We often hear about Jesus's "passion week," the last week of his life on earth, which is described in John 12:1–20:23. But John also tells us about Jesus's first week. People keep track of the "opening weekend" or "opening week" of movies and how they rank in revenue. The record as of March 22, 2019 is held by *Avengers: Infinity War,* which grossed $640,521,291 in its opening week.[31] My son Jon has always been excited about opening week of NFL football, and other sports have equally exciting openings. Of course, the people in John's Gospel did not know this was Jesus's opening week, so their situation was a little different. The excited anticipation of the people of Israel returning from Babylon had waned over the years of foreign occupation, although many still hoped for and talked about a coming Messiah. It was somewhat like arriving at the airport, nervously excited that a much-needed vacation is about to start. But then there are long lines, forgotten items, and delays or even cancellations due to weather or mechanical failure. We begin to settle in and get bored as we wait at the airport, wondering whether our vacation will ever start, whether we will ever hear the good news that our plane is here and they are ready for us to board. Like people waiting for a plane, the people in Judea passed the time in different ways. Some were agitated and angry; some used various coping strategies to dull the pain, but most simply went about their lives, trying to survive. From the perspective of post-resurrection Christians, however, who know the rest of the story, Jesus's opening week is bursting with excitement. Nothing in our daily lives can touch the tremendous significance of the beginning of the earthly work of the Son of God, the Savior of the world. And no one describes its significance better than the apostle John.

Of course, with opening weeks in sports or live entertainment, we do not expect everything to go right. There are many uncertainties and "bugs" still to be worked out, rookies still to be cut from the roster who do not fit. Jesus's opening week, on the other hand, was divinely orchestrated and perfectly executed. Examining these opening sections of the Gospel not only prepares us for what is to follow, but it also reveals to us profound and life-changing truths.

---

30. Bauckham, *Gospel of Glory,* 138.
31. https://en.wikipedia.org/wiki/List_of_highest-grossing_openings_for_films.

Outline

Based in part on John's use of the word *sign*, which occurs sixteen times in chapters 2–12 and not again until 20:30, one common outline of John is to divide it into four sections:

> Prologue (1:1–18)
> Book of Signs (1:19–12:50)
> Book of Glory (13:1–20:31)
> Epilogue (21:1–25)[32]

Craig Blomberg sees the divisions somewhat differently:

> Introductory Testimony (1:1–51)
> Testimony of Signs and Discourses (2:1–11:57)
> Testimony of Death and Resurrection (12:1–20:31)
> Concluding Testimony (21:1–25)[33]

Use of the word *sign* in 20:30, however, suggests that the whole Gospel is a "book of signs." Certainly Jesus's resurrection is a sign, which John had just reported before saying in 20:30, "Jesus performed many other signs."[34] Edward Klink claims that "there is no warrant for dividing the Gospel into only two major sections or 'acts.'" He points out that there are all kinds of parallels and connections in the book.[35] D. A. Carson agrees: "Themes are so intricately interwoven in the Fourth Gospel that several quite different outlines of the book are possible."[36] Klink divides the book into ten major sections,[37] but this fails to appreciate some overall connections. Nevertheless, where we see the major divisions of the book depends on which features and themes we consider the most important. Carson's outline offers another helpful view of these connections:[38]

> Prologue (1:1–18)
> Jesus's Self-Disclosure in Word and Deed (1:19–10:42)
> Transition: Life and Death, King and Suffering Servant (11:1–12:50)
> Jesus's Self-Disclosure in His Cross and Exaltation (13:1–20:31)

32. See, for example, Brown, *John I-XII*, xi-xii.; Köstenberger, *John*, vii.
33. Blomberg, *Jesus and the Gospels*, 185–86.
34. However, see Köstenberger's argument regarding the signs in *Theology of John's Gospel*, 326–33.
35. Klink, *John*, 65–66.
36. Carson, *Gospel according to John*, 304.
37. Tasker also divides the book into ten sections, though in a different way. See Tasker, *St. John*, 39–40.
38. Carson, *Gospel according to John*, 103–8.

Epilogue (21:1-25)

Although most scholars agree that Jesus's first sign in Cana in 2:1-11 (or 2:1-12) begins a new section of the book, many would agree that John also uses the Cana incident to complete his account of Jesus's first week.[39] As we'll see, not only does it occur on the seventh day of that week, but it also picks up from chapter 1 the themes of Jesus's glory and the disciples' believing in him:

> 1:7—He came as a witness to testify about the light, so that all might believe through him.

> 1:12—But to all who did receive him, he gave them the right to be children of God, to those who believe in his name.

> 1:50—Jesus responded to him, "Do you believe because I told you I saw you under the fig tree? You will see greater things than this."

> 1:14—We observed his glory, the glory as the one and only Son from the Father, full of grace and truth.

Then after Jesus's miracle at Cana, John concludes in 2:11 (emphasis added), "He revealed his *glory*, and his disciples *believed* in him."

As a result, I've chosen to follow a slightly different outline and to focus only on 1:1-2:11:[40]

Prologue (1:1-18)

---

39. Köstenberger, for example, acknowledges that John 1:19-2:11 "narrates a week in Jesus' ministry," although he also argues that 2:1-4:54 is a narrative unit (*Theology*, 169; see also p. 147). Also see Klink's argument that 2:1-11 not only recounts the first of six specified "signs" in John's Gospel, but it also describes the events of the last of six specified "days" when Jesus's ministry began. Jesus's death and resurrection in John 18-20, he says, was the seventh sign that took place on the "seventh" day, "completing the first week of the old creation . . . , with the resurrection occurring 'on the first day of the week' (20:1), the first week of the new creation" (*John*, 825-27, especially p. 827). Although we have followed Bauckham in counting 2:1-11 as occurring on the seventh day of Jesus's first week (see comments on 1:40-42), it may be possible still to incorporate Klink's understanding if we don't count the day of travel, which John doesn't mention. The wedding, then, takes place on the sixth specified day, just as John specifies seven signs, though he acknowledges the fact of others.

40. Cf. Bruce, *Gospel of John*, 24. Guthrie, *New Testament Introduction*, 328-30, portrays 1:19-2:12 as recounting "introductory events." McHugh, *John 1-4*, 113, understands 1:19-2:12 as recounting Jesus's first week. Although not reflected in his outline, Köstenberger recognizes 1:19-2:12 as a unit (*John*, 89). Tasker (*St. John*, 39) includes the prologue in his first section, called "Jesus the Word of God, incarnate and revealed" (1:1-2:11).

- God's Preexistent Word (1:1–2)
- The Word as Creator, Life, and Light (1:3–5)
- John, the First Witness to the Light (1:6–8)
- Human Response to the Light (1:9–13)
- The Word Became Flesh (1:14)
- The Uniqueness of the Word (1:15–18)

Jesus's Ministry Begins (1:19–2:11)
- Introductions (1:19–51)
  - Day One: The Baptist Introduces the Jewish Leaders to Jesus (1:19–28)
  - Day Two: The Baptist Introduces His Disciples to Jesus (1:29–34)
  - Day Three: The First Two Disciples Follow Jesus (1:35–39)
  - Day Four: Peter Follows Jesus (1:40–42)
  - Day Five: Philip and Nathanael Follow Jesus (1:43–51)
- Day Seven: Jesus's First Sign (2:1–11)

Jesus Reveals the Father in the World (2:12–12:50)

Jesus Reveals the Father to His Disciples (13:1–17:26)

Jesus's Glory in the Hour of His Cross and Exaltation (18:1–20:31)

Conclusion (21:1–25)

2

Prologue (1:1–18)

It might be helpful to think of the prologue as a kind of foyer, vestibule, or lobby where someone entering a house, church, or some other building prepares in some way to enter the main part of the structure (removing hat and coat, etc.). Works of music such as musicals and operas always begin with a prelude called an overture, which previews music that will be heard in the main work. Literary works or plays often begin with a prologue, which prepares the readers or audience to understand and appreciate what they are about to read or see. Greek plays often began with a prologue that would give the audience vital information, often about the desires and plans of the gods, which they would see worked out in the human characters and plot of the play. John prepares his readers here by introducing us to some of the main themes he'll develop throughout the book, such as life, light, witness, world, glory, and truth. But, as in a Greek play, the opening scene takes place outside the earth, where we learn of the desires and plans of God that broke out on the stage of human history: in creation, then in the coming of John the Baptist, then in the coming of the eternal Word, the true light, who became flesh and came to dwell with us. Countless people throughout history have asked, "If there's a God, what's he like?" John's prologue gives us the short answer that the rest of his Gospel will elaborate on: God is like Jesus.

The prologue also has a certain poetic quality that suggests a purpose to *celebrate* God's sending of his Son into the world. If John's Gospel is "the pearl of great price among the NT writings," then, as Raymond Brown suggests, "one may say that the Prologue is the pearl within this Gospel . . . The choice [by the early church] of the eagle as the symbol of John the Evangelist was largely determined by the celestial flights of the opening lines of the

Gospel."[1] Because of all these factors, this section of John's Gospel deserves special care.

God's Preexistent Word (1:1–2)

> 1 *In the beginning was the Word, and the Word was with God, and the Word was God.* 2 *He was with God in the beginning.*

The many allusions to the Old Testament in John begin in the very first verse. The first two Greek words, translated *In the beginning,* are also the first two words of the Greek translation of Genesis.[2] They take us mentally to Gen 1:1, where we find God, creation, the world, darkness and light, the Spirit, and God speaking. But John even takes us *before* Gen 1:1, to the situation existing not on the earth or in the universe but in heaven before time began. He describes what "was" even before his story actually begins.

But why does John, whose purpose in his Gospel is to lead his readers to faith in Jesus as the Messiah and "life in his name," begin in Genesis? Is he giving us "too much information"? Shouldn't he rather just get to the point? We might answer that question by reflecting on the experience of being late for a movie and missing the beginning. Who are these characters? Why are they in this situation? What's going on? Part of what John is doing here is answering those questions by stitching the story of Jesus into the bigger story of the Bible, which is the story of God and his relationship to all that exists. John knew that we could only understand and appreciate the story of Jesus if we saw it in the light of the greater story. Richard Bauckham points out that "the one biblical book that, in its way, matches the span of the whole canon is the Gospel of John," not only beginning with "a deliberate echo" of Genesis, but also ending with "until I come" in 21:23.[3]

One of my favorite TV shows when I was ten to twelve years old was the sitcom, *The Many Loves of Dobie Gillis,* starring Dwayne Hickman, Bob Denver, Tuesday Weld, and Warren Beatty. It was the first TV show starring teenagers and was the model for *Scooby Doo*. It began with Dobie sitting beside and mimicking a famous Rodín sculpture popularly known as "The Thinker." I was intrigued by the question of what "The Thinker" was thinking about. Then, while teaching at a college in the eighties, I walked over to the Dallas Art Institute and saw a huge sculpture (twenty feet high by

---

1. Brown, *John I-XII*, 18.

2. The Greek translation of the Old Testament is called the Septuagint, abbreviated LXX.

3. Bauckham, "Reading Scripture as a Coherent Story," in Davis and Hays, *Art of Reading Scripture*, 41.

thirteen feet wide) by Rodín that contained "the Thinker." The larger context made clear what was his subject of contemplation. The sculpture, commissioned in 1880 and called "The Gates of Hell," was inspired by Dante's *Divine Comedy*. It showed "the Thinker" deep in thought, while scores of people were falling into hell. I was blown away by how context can fill something with meaning.

But when John takes us to heaven before time in Gen 1:1, what do we find there? Not initially "God" as in Genesis. Rather, John introduces us to someone called the *Logos*, "the Word." The phrase "the word" is used about 200 times in the Old Testament to describe what God says to people. Has anyone ever refused to talk to you? Or refused to tell you why they're upset or sad? That can be very frustrating and sometimes scary. We have literature from other religions describing people's frustration and insecurity because their god does not speak. A second-millennium BC Babylonian writer, for example, asks, "Where has befuddled mankind ever learned what a god's conduct is?"[4] The God of the Bible, however, speaks, and his words are not only reliable (Pss 33:4; 119:81, 114) but also powerful (Ps 33:6; Isa 11:4) and able to give life (Deut 32:47; Ps 119:25, 107). Sometimes in the Old Testament, God's "word" is personified—spoken of as if it were a person, as in Ps 105:19 ("The word of the LORD tested him [Joseph]"), Ps 107:20 ("He sent his word and healed them"), Ps 147:15 ("He sends his command throughout the earth; his word runs swiftly"). God's word is even described as eternal (Ps 119:89).[5]

But here in John "the Word" is not a personification[6]—it's a Person, who is described with three statements telling us the *when*, the *where*, and

---

4. Pritchard, *Ancient Near Eastern Texts*, 435.

5. The first century BC Jewish apocryphal book, The Wisdom of Solomon (9:1-2) has "God of our ancestors, Lord of mercy, who by your word have made the universe, and in your wisdom have fitted human beings to rule the creatures that you have made" (NJB). And Wisdom 18:14-15 declares, "When peaceful silence lay over all, and night had run the half of her swift course, down from the heavens, from the royal throne, leapt your all-powerful Word like a pitiless warrior into the heart of a land doomed to destruction, carrying your unambiguous command like a sharp sword" (NJB). In the Targums, the Aramaic translation of the Old Testament, "the LORD," is often rendered "the Memra," that is, the Word. It is a kind of messenger or manifestation of God, who takes God's place wherever what is said is not thought to conform to divine dignity or spirituality. For example, instead of God shielding Moses with his hand in Exod 33:22, the Targum reads, "And it will come about when My glory passes by, that I will set you in the cave of the rock, and I will protect you with My Memra until I pass by" (Clem, "Translation of Targum Onkelos and Jonathan").

6. Simon Gathercole reviews the predominant scholarly view that the concept of Jesus's preexistence was a late development in the early church, found mainly in John and perhaps some of Paul's letters (*The Preexistent Son*, 1-20). James Dunn confines Jesus's

the *who* of the Word. First, the Word already existed *in the beginning*, before time began. Second, the Word was a distinct Person in God's presence and in communion with God—*the Word was with God*. To understand that statement we must first know what John meant by "God." The term *God* is not a proper name, although we use it as one, like *Mom*, or *Dad*. In the context of the Old Testament, "God" could only refer to the God who created all things, chose Abraham, parted the Red Sea, and became the Father of the people of Israel. He is "the God of gods and Lord of lords, the great, mighty, and awe-inspiring God" (Deut 10:17) and "the Most High God" (Dan 3:26). But in John's Gospel, God is identified as the Father of Jesus (see also Col 1:3; 1 Pet 1:3; 1 John 1:3; 4:14; 2 John 3; Rev 2:28; 3:5, 21), who loved the world and sent his only (unique) Son to save it (3:16–18). The word "Father" occurs in John more than any other word (136 times), and God is referred to as "Father" 112 times in John.

The next thing we have to understand about the second statement, that *the Word was with God*, is the meaning of "with." Greek had four main words for "with." The less common one used here (*pros*) could also mean "toward," as in John 1:29 where it says, "John saw Jesus coming *toward* him." So John's second statement about the Word means more than just being in the Father's presence. It means that the Word is a distinct, personal being, who before the beginning of time was in communication and communion with the Father. And it means that not only is *the Word* a Person, but *God* is a Person too. Dale Bruner brings out the meaning by translating, "and the Word was in close fellowship with God." He also suggests that "this Father-Son relation is almost the key teaching in the Gospel according to John."[7]

John's third statement about the Word is the most shocking of all. *The Word was God*. Some, like Jehovah's Witnesses, resurrect the ancient Christian heresy of Arianism and claim that this statement should be translated "the Word was a god" or "the Word was divine." But Greek has another word for "divine" that is not used here. And the translation "a god" is based on a faulty understanding of Greek grammar. Greek has a "definite article," but it does not function exactly like the English article (there is no indefinite article like "a" in Greek). Words can be definite without the article. The word "beginning," for example, in the phrase "in the beginning," has no article; yet

---

preexistence to John (see Dunn, *Christology in the Making*, 33–64). As Gathercole explains, for Dunn "the other NT authors (including Paul) may have thought of Jesus as the embodiment of divine Wisdom, but of a divine Wisdom who was a personification of God rather than having actual prior existence" (*The Preexistent Son*, 5). Gathercole's book shows that Jesus's preexistence is also found in the rest of the New Testament, even in the Synoptic Gospels.

7. Bruner, *Gospel of John*, 11.

it is not "in a beginning." Also, in 1:49 the word "king" in the statement "You are the King of Israel" has no article expressing the word's clear definiteness.

The reason "God" has no article here is that it occurs first in the clause for emphasis: "The Word was *God.*" If it had the article, it would not be clear what was the subject, and John would be saying that *the Word* and *the Father* were identical, which would be nonsense in view of the fact that the Word was *with* the Father. "The Word does not by Himself make up the entire Godhead; nevertheless, the divinity that belongs to the rest of the Godhead belongs also to Him."[8] As Thomas would declare in John 20:28, the Word, who was Jesus, was "my Lord and my God" (literally, "*the* Lord of me and *the* God of me").

The Word as Creator, Life, and Light (1:3–5)

> *3 All things were created through him, and apart from him not one thing was created that has been created. 4 In him [the Word] was life, and that life was the light of men. 5 That light shines in the darkness, and yet the darkness did not overcome it.*

The verb translated "were created" is actually similar in meaning to the word for "was." But it more commonly means "to become," "to come into existence" or "to happen." It's found twenty-three times in the Greek translation (LXX) of Genesis 1. Genesis 1:3 could be translated from Greek, "Let light come into being, and light came into being." So after describing the Word before time began, here John tells us what the Word did at the beginning of time. He tells us emphatically that everything that exists outside of God was brought into existence by the Word. Other New Testament passages also make the point (emphasis added).

> For *everything was created by him*, in heaven and on earth, the visible and the invisible, whether thrones or dominions or rulers or authorities—*all things have been created through him and for him.* He is before all things, and by him all things hold together. (Col 1:16–17)

> Long ago God spoke to the fathers by the prophets at different times and in different ways. In these last days, he has spoken to us by his Son. *God* has appointed him heir of all things and *made the universe through him.* The Son is the radiance of God's glory and the exact expression of his nature, *sustaining all things by his powerful word.* (Heb 1:1–3)

---

8. Tasker, *St. John*, 45.

Existence itself depends on the divine Word. Bruner cites a poem by D. H. Lawrence (1885–1930) called "The Third Thing."

> Water is H2O—two parts hydrogen, one part oxygen.
> But there is also a third thing that makes it water,
> and no one knows what that is.[9]

Bruner also explains, "If we had a microscope powerful enough to see the most minute entities in creation, imagination suggests, we might detect on them something like the imprint—*Made by J.C.*"[10]

But why did John put so much emphasis on the Word as Creator of everything? One reason may be that the concept of *God* as *Creator* is so important in the Old Testament. It's the first thing we learn about God in Genesis 1–2. The distinctive Hebrew verb for "create" (*bārā'*) is found forty-one times in the Old Testament describing God. The term *Creator* is virtually a definition of God. Hear what Isaiah says about God:

> "To whom will you compare me, or who is my equal?" asks the Holy One. Look up and see! Who created these? He brings out the stars by number; he calls all of them by name. Because of his great power and strength, not one of them is missing. Jacob, why do you say, and, Israel, why do you assert, "My way is hidden from the LORD, and my claim is ignored by my God"? Do you not know? Have you not heard? The LORD is the everlasting God, the Creator of the whole earth. He never becomes faint or weary; there is no limit to his understanding. (Isa 40:25–28)

Isaiah tells us why we should listen to God:

> This is what God, the LORD, says—who created the heavens and stretched them out, who spread out the earth and what comes from it, who gives breath to the people on it and spirit to those who walk on it. (Isa 42:5)

> Now this is what the LORD says—the one who created you, Jacob, and the one who formed you, Israel— "Do not fear, for I have redeemed you; I have called you by your name; you are mine ... I am the LORD, your Holy One, the Creator of Israel, your King." (Isa 43:1, 15)

> For this is what the LORD says—the Creator of the heavens, the God who formed the earth and made it, the one who established it (he did not create it to be a wasteland, but formed it to be

---

9. Bruner, *Gospel of John*, 15.
10. Bruner, *Gospel of John*, 16.

inhabited) he says, "I am the Lord, and there is no other." (Isa 45:18)

John could have had these verses in mind in John 1. God sent "the Word," and we must listen to him because he is the Creator! Amos 4:13 also stresses God as Creator:

> He is here: the one who forms the mountains, creates the wind, and reveals his thoughts to man, the one who makes the dawn out of darkness and strides on the heights of the earth. The Lord, the God of Armies, is his name.

My friend Al Detter has written a booklet he calls *Creation and the Bible* in which he lists every verse in the Bible on creation. In the introduction he says,

> As I proofread the entire body of creation verses that follow in one sitting, it was as though something inside my creaturely heart was activated toward my Creator. I was moved, awestruck, and inspired to the point that I could actually feel an emotional lift before God. It was a worship experience of the creature—me—before the Creator—God. In the depths of my heart, I realized once again that He is the Potter and we are the clay; we are the work of His hands (Isa. 64:8). That it is He who made us and not we ourselves (Ps. 100:3). It took me a while to recover.

The apostle John is telling us that all the Old Testament says about God the Creator is true of the Word, whom he will reveal in v. 14 to be Jesus—the Creator and Sustainer of the universe, who became flesh and dwelt among us.

Another reason the Word as Creator is so important to John and the reason for so many parallels between John's prologue and the first chapter of Genesis may be that John understood the coming of the Son to mean the beginning of a new creation, as Isaiah prophesied (also see 48:6; 62:2; 66:22):

> Look, I am about to do something new; even now it is coming. Do you not see it? Indeed, I will make a way in the wilderness, rivers in the desert. (43:19)

> For I will create a new heaven and a new earth; the past events will not be remembered or come to mind. (65:17)

This new creation would eventually mean the end of darkness and the end of the curse. It would also mean the beginning of a new people, "the children of God" (John 1:12). The Word by his very nature is a Creator, and his work of creating is not over.

Then John further emphasizes the Word as Creator by declaring at the beginning of v. 4 that life itself exists only within the divine Word: "In him was life." As the one who created all things, he knows the nature and purpose of all things. Self-discovery is impossible without first acknowledging that who I am and why I exist must come in relationship with the one who made me. My identity and my very life can only be found in him. Furthermore, failing to recognize and welcome him into my life is irrational, because he made me to have fellowship with him and so to be God's child (vv. 10–11).[11] When John's two disciples begin to follow Jesus and ask him, "Rabbi, . . . where are you staying?" (John 1:38), they are fulfilling the purpose for which Jesus made them.

For many years I worked with and carpooled with a well-known Bible scholar named Trent Butler. He liked to go to work early, so we'd often watch the sunrise on our way downtown. Countless times we'd be driving along and suddenly he'd cry out, "Life!" That's what John does in v. 4. As Leon Morris wrote, "It is only because there is life in the *Logos* that there is life in anything on earth at all. Life does not exist in its own right."[12] And God did not just *create* life. It does not just come *from* the Word who was God. Life is *in him*! Jesus declared that the Father "has granted to the Son to have life in himself" (John 5:26). That's one of the most important things I've learned from John. We can only live if we are deeply connected to Jesus, the True Vine, because he *is* "the life" (11:25). Michael Reeves declares, "On our own we are but withered sticks."[13] Jesus expresses this in John 6:54 with the shocking statement, "The one who eats my flesh and drinks my blood has eternal life, and I will raise him up on the last day." But we must be careful here. Christ is not just a means to an end, the way to attain forgiveness, salvation, redemption, or eternal life.[14] He is himself the ultimate reality. I do not trust or love or follow Christ just in order to get something *else*. John Calvin wrote long ago that Christ "makes us . . . participants not only in all his benefits but also in himself."[15] As Frederick Godet said, our faith in Jesus must be faith in the One "beyond which it is impossible to go."[16] He is not just "the way." He is also "the truth and the life" (John 14:6). There *is* nothing

---

11. See R. W. L. Moberly, "How Can We Know the Truth? A Study of John 7:14–18," in Davis and Hays, *Art of Reading Scripture*, 248.

12. Morris, *Gospel according to John*, 82–83.

13. Reeves, *Rejoicing in Christ*, 98.

14. Richard B. Gaffin Jr., for example, complains of a "prevailing tendency . . . to be preoccupied with the various benefits of Christ's work," while "he, in his person and work, recedes into the background" ("Union with Christ," 280).

15. Calvin, *Institutes*, 3.2.24.

16. Cited by Bruner, *Gospel of John*, 6.

greater, nothing more worthy of our efforts to attain than Jesus himself. As Reeves puts it, union with Christ is not "the appetizer to the Christian life," nor is it

> the doorway that leads us through into a life that is about *something else*. It *is* the steak and the living room of the Christian life ... Bluntly, when not defined by Christ, I find myself as fragile as a puffed-up balloon. When I begin to define myself by success or popularity, they matter far too much to me: when I get them, my ego inflates preposterously; when I don't, I implode. That simply can't happen when the core of my identity is consciously found in Christ, for he is the same—yesterday, today and forever.[17]

Occupying ourselves only with Christ's *benefits* may result from focusing only on the cross and neglecting the incarnation. It has the effect of separating Christ's work from his person. We then treat salvation as a commodity for which Christ was just the agent or condition rather than being salvation himself.[18] Donald Fairbairn declares, "In salvation we receive the Logos (God the Son) himself. We do not simply receive something that he gives us, because the Son gives us his very self ... The essence of this gift of himself," he explains, and as we will see in John 1:12, "is that we become sons and daughters of God. We are adopted into the same relationship he has with God the Father—into his own sonship with the Father."[19] Richard Bauckham agrees:

> Eternal life is not just a divine gift to those who believe in Jesus; it is actual participation in Jesus's own life, made available through his death. This is the significance of [John 6] vv. 56–57. In v. 57 Jesus explains that he himself lives out of the eternal divine life of his Father, and so believers, participating in Jesus's life, are alive with this same divine life. In v. 56 he explains that faith in the crucified Jesus unites the believer with him in a union so intimate and enduring that it can be depicted as mutual indwelling and abiding.[20]

---

17. Reeves, *Rejoicing in Christ*, 97 (emphasis his).

18. See Clark and Johnson, *Incarnation of God*, 38. Also in his book *One with Christ*, 20, Johnson states, "Jesus is more than a provider *of* blessings such as eternal life, truth, living bread, living water, or resurrection life; He *is in himself* the blessings he provides ... They are not available to us except *by our participation in Christ's life*" (emphasis his).

19. Fairbairn, *Life in the Trinity*, 34.

20. Bauckham, *Gospel of Glory*, 102–3.

And this is not a new doctrine. The English puritan Rowland Stedman wrote in 1668, "If we will have life from the Son, we must have the Son; *that is,* we must be made one with him. No union with Jesus, and no communication of life and salvation from Jesus." The Lord blesses us in and through Christ, he said, by first planting us into him.[21]

These verses (1:4–5) introduce two major themes John will return to many times: *life* (*zoē* thirty-six times) and *light* (*phōs* twenty-three times): "that life was the light of men." Both are identified with Jesus, who declared himself to be not only "the bread of life" (6:35), but also "the light of the world" (8:12). And opposed to the theme of light, just as in Genesis 1, we find in v. 5, "That light shines in the *darkness*" (a term found eight times in John, seven times in 1 John). In John's writings, darkness represents evil. In 3:19 John says, "This is the judgment: The light has come into the world, and people loved darkness rather than the light because their deeds were evil." But why does John put *life* together with *light*?

For one thing, we find them together in the Old Testament (emphasis added). The scribe Ezra celebrated the Jews' return from Babylonian exile by saying, "But now, for a brief moment, the LORD our God has been gracious in leaving us a remnant and giving us a firm place in his sanctuary, and so our God gives *light* to our eyes and a little relief [Hb. *ḥāyāh*, "life"] in our bondage" (Ezra 9:8, NIV). The psalmist David thanked God that "the wellspring of *life* is with you. By means of your *light* we see light" (Ps 36:9). Job spoke of God blessing people with "the light of life" (33:30; also Ps 56:13). This could mean "the light that comes from life," although most interpreters think it refers to "the life that comes from light." Jesus picked up the phrase and used it of himself. When he declared himself to be "the light of the world," he explained, "Anyone who follows me will never walk in the darkness but will have the *light of life*" (John 8:12). However they are related, in him we have both.

But in v. 4 John does not say the *Word* was light. He says the *life* was light. In Genesis, God created light before he created life. But here he is *light* because he is *life*. We can only have the divine *light* if we have the divine *life*. The ancients worshiped the light of the sun and moon as givers of life and believed that there were two ultimate forces or entities in the universe at war with each other—the light of the sun representing order, life, and happiness versus the darkness representing chaos, death, and misery. But the Bible says that God does not need sun, moon, or stars to produce light or life. He did not create them until the fourth day! The modern world worships the light of knowledge, understanding, and insight. Historians refer to the eighteenth

---

21. Quoted in Letham, *Union with Christ*, 3 (emphasis his).

century in Europe as the Enlightenment or the Age of Reason, whose motto was "Have the courage to use your own intellect." But as Herman Ridderbos explains, "The light that the world needs and by which alone a person can escape the darkness is *Jesus,* and therefore . . . whoever follows *him* will not walk in darkness . . . [E]verything is concentrated on the person of Jesus."[22] If he were not the life, he could not be the light.

What significance does the Bible place on light? As the *Dictionary of Biblical Imagery* points out,

> The Bible is enveloped by the imagery of light, both literally and figuratively. At the beginning of the biblical narrative, physical light springs forth as the first created thing (Gen 1:3–4). At the end of the [Bible's] story the light of God obliterates all traces of darkness: "And night shall be no more; they need no light of lamp or sun, for the Lord God will be their light" (Rev 22:5 RSV). Between these two beacons [from Genesis to Revelation] the imagery of light makes nearly two hundred appearances, with light emerging as one of the Bible's major and most complex symbols.[23]

The Bible uses light as a symbol in several ways: (1) *Righteousness and holiness vs. evil.* In 2 Sam 23:3–4, God says to David, "The one who rules the people with justice, who rules in the fear of God, is like the morning light when the sun rises on a cloudless morning, the glisten of rain on sprouting grass." Light is said to represent a believer's life who is following the Spirit: "Let us discard the deeds of darkness and put on the armor of light. Let us walk with decency, as in the daytime: not in carousing and drunkenness; not in sexual impurity and promiscuity; not in quarreling and jealousy. But put on the Lord Jesus Christ, and don't make plans to gratify the desires of the flesh" (Rom 13:12–14).

(2) *Happiness of God's favor and blessing vs. distress and misery.* "When the Jews were rescued from Haman's planned genocide, they 'had light and gladness and joy and honor'" (Esth 8:16 RSV). "Light dawns for the righteous, gladness for the upright in heart" (Ps 97:11).

(3) *Truth, understanding, and guidance vs. falsehood, confusion, and hopelessness.* "Send your light and your truth; let them lead me. Let them bring me to your holy mountain, to your dwelling place" (Ps 43:3). God's Word is "a lamp for my feet and a light on my path" (Ps 119:105). The psalmist also declares, "Lord, you light my lamp; my God illuminates my darkness" (Ps 18:28). Isaiah urges Israel to "walk in the Lord's light" (2:5),

---

22. Ridderbos, *Gospel of John*, 293 (emphasis his).
23. *DBI*, 509.

and God promised his people a time when "I will turn darkness to light in front of them and rough places into level ground" (42:16). Peter says the prophetic word is "a lamp shining in a dark place, until the day dawns and the morning star rises in your hearts" (2 Pet 1:19). In Isaiah 51:4 God promised "my justice [or "just rule"] for a light to the nations." However, people tend to reject the light of divine truth. John Oswalt comments, "Instead of looking to the light of which Isaiah spoke twenty-seven hundred years ago, however, we have been willing to settle, as humans have for five thousand years or more, for the trappings of personal pleasure, comfort, and security, while human civilization crashes down around us. We have fastened a spurious light to ourselves, and it is rapidly devouring us (cf. 50:11)."[24]

(4) *God's splendor.* Since God is the ultimate source of holiness, joy, and truth, he is often represented by light, glory, and splendor that drives away darkness.

> "Though I have fallen, I will stand up; though I sit in darkness, the LORD will be my light" (Mic 7:8).

> "This is the message we have heard from him and declare to you: God is light, and there is absolutely no darkness in him" (1 John 1:5).

> "My soul, bless the LORD! LORD my God, you are very great; you are clothed with majesty and splendor. He wraps himself in light as if it were a robe" (Ps 104:1–2).

> "He is the blessed and only Sovereign, the King of kings, and the Lord of lords, who alone is immortal and who lives in unapproachable light, whom no one has seen or can see, to him be honor and eternal power" (1 Tim 6:15–16).

Isaiah prophesied, "The sun will no longer be your light by day, and the brightness of the moon will not shine on you. The LORD will be your everlasting light, and your God will be your splendor. Your sun will no longer set, and your moon will not fade; for the LORD will be your everlasting light, and the days of your sorrow will be over" (Isa 60:19–20). And about the new Jerusalem, John says, "The city does not need the sun or the moon to shine on it, because the glory of God illuminates it, and its lamp is the Lamb" (Rev 21:23), and "Night will be no more; people will not need the light of a lamp or the light of the sun, because the Lord God will give them light, and they will reign forever and ever" (Rev 22:5).

---

24. Oswalt, *Isaiah, Chapters 40–66*, 336.

(5) *The experience of God's children as his heirs.* God's nature and character shine on and through all who belong to him. The psalmist declares, "The LORD is my light and my salvation—whom should I fear? The LORD is the stronghold of my life—whom should I be dread?" (Ps 27:1). As the verse well-known from *The Messiah* declares, "The people walking in darkness have seen a great light; a light has dawned on those living in the land of darkness" (Isa 9:2). Isaiah also says,

> Arise, shine, for your light has come, and the glory of the LORD shines over you. For look, darkness will cover the earth, and total darkness the peoples; but the LORD will shine over you, and his glory will appear over you. Nations will come to your light, and kings to your shining brightness (Isa 60:1-3).

God's people, Peter says, have been called "so that you may proclaim the praises of the one who called you out of darkness into his marvelous light" (1 Pet 2:9). Jesus told his followers, "You are the light of the world ... let your light shine before others, so that they may see your good works and give glory to your Father in heaven" (Matt 5:14, 16). Paul tells Christians, "For you were once darkness, but now you are light in the Lord. Live as children of light" (Eph 5:8). He also says, "You ... are not in the dark ... For you are all children of light and children of the day. We do not belong to the night or the darkness" (1 Thess 5:4-5).

As the *Dictionary* points out, "Light in its varied meanings is at the heart of such central biblical themes as creation, providence, judgment, redemption and sanctification."[25] It also proposes that the passage best representing the range of meanings of light is 2 Cor 4:6, where creation and new creation meet: "For God who said, 'Let light shine out of darkness,' has shone in our hearts to give the light of the knowledge of God's glory in the face of Jesus Christ." Three times in Acts, Paul describes his conversion as an experience of an intense light from heaven, out of which Jesus spoke to him. R. V. G. Tasker quotes the nineteenth-century Scottish theologian and preacher James Denney: "In the light which flashed into his heart, he saw the face of Jesus Christ, and knew that the glory which shone there was the glory of God."[26] It was like the light that first shined into the darkness of creation and revealed a new world.

So in what sense does John speak of Jesus as "the light"?[27] He calls him "the light of men" because he is the gift from God that people need in order

---

25. *DBI*, 512.

26. Tasker, *Second Corinthians*, 71.

27. See the helpful study of how John develops his theme of Jesus as the light in Frey, *Glory of the Crucified One*, 126-37.

to live. People pursue other things they think give them light, but Jesus is "the true light that gives light to everyone" (1:9). As C. S. Lewis wrote,

> Christ will indeed give you a real personality: but you must not go to Him for the sake of that. As long as your own personality is what you are bothering about you are not going to Him at all. The very first step is to try to forget about the self altogether. Your real, new self (which is Christ's and also yours, and yours just because it is His) will not come as long as you are looking for it. It will come when you are looking at Him ... Look for yourself, and you will find in the long run only hatred, loneliness, despair, rage, ruin, and decay. But look for Christ and you will find Him, and with Him everything else thrown in.[28]

His light is available to all, though many prefer darkness (John 3:19–20). Light reveals or exposes what is (or would be) hidden in darkness, so the term *revelation* can be used of it. Jesus is light in that he reveals or displays the nature and character of the holy and loving God. But he also reveals the character of the wicked and, further, dispels or drives away darkness and evil. Malachi had prophesied, "For you who fear my name, the sun of righteousness will rise with healing in its wings" (4:2). That "sun of righteousness" was revealed to be Jesus. The verse describes the situation of those who have been living in devastating darkness and despair caused by sin and wickedness, when suddenly the light of God's glorious righteousness appears, and everything is set right. As Isaiah 9:2 (quoted in Matt 4:16) prophesied, when the Messiah appears, "The people walking in darkness have seen a great light; a light has dawned on those living in the land of darkness." God said he would make his Servant "a light for the nations, to be my salvation to the ends of the earth" (Isa 49:6; also 42:6). Thus, at the birth of his son, John the Baptist, Zechariah proclaimed, "Because of our God's merciful compassion, the dawn from on high will visit us to shine on those who live in darkness and the shadow of death, to guide our feet into the way of peace" (Luke 1:78–79). Jesus delivers us from the domain of darkness, makes us "children of light," and guides us along the path of blessing (John 11:9–10; 12:36, 46).

The verb in the last clause of v. 5 translated "overcome" (*katalambanō*) basically means "to seize." But it's used in the New Testament (fifteen times) in various contexts to mean either "to overpower, arrest, take control over," or to seize with the mind, "to comprehend, realize, gain information." John may have intended both senses, but translations must choose one or the other, so NRSV, ESV, NIV, CSB, and NLT render it "overcome"

---

28. Lewis, *Mere Christianity*, 226–27.

or "extinguish," but NASB, KJV, NKJV, NIV84 render it "comprehend" or "understand." Commentaries also usually line up on one side or the other. A couple of translations (NET, REB) try to preserve the ambiguity with "master." The world of darkness does not understand God's light but fears it and opposes it. Jesus's use of the verb in John 12:35, however, suggests that "overpower" might be the primary sense. He said, "Walk while you have the light so that darkness doesn't *overtake* you" (perhaps as a competitor might overtake you).

Bruner points out that before v. 5 all the previous verbs have been past tense. But the first verb in v. 5 ("that light *shines* in the darkness") is a present tense, which he calls attention to by translating "shines on still, even now." When Jesus died on the cross, it seemed that darkness had won. And when we hear of acts of violence and cruelty and of situations of deprivation, sorrow, and pain, it seems that darkness has won. But "the deepest fact in all of history" is that the Light of the Life shines on. As John wrote in 1 John 2:8, "the darkness is passing away and the true light is already shining."[29]

John, the First Witness to the Light (1:6–8)

> 6 *There was a man sent from God whose name was John. 7 He came as a witness to testify about the light, so that all might believe through him. 8 He was not the light, but he came to testify about the light.*

The first verb here translated "was" is the one used three times in v. 3, meaning "came into existence." Just as the invisible God created the visible universe as a witness to his "eternal power and divine nature" (Rom 1:20), so he also created the man John as a witness to the divine Light. The word translated "sent" (*apostellō*) is related to the English word "apostle." It can mean either to send a message or to send someone on a mission, that is, with an important task to perform on behalf of the sender. In the New Testament the sender is almost always God.

In the context of John's Gospel, it is interesting that John the Baptist is referred to as "a man sent from God." Jesus is said to be "sent" (*apostellō*) by God seventeen times in John. He is also called a "man" (*anthrōpos*) fifteen times. (In 8:40 Jesus says, "But now you are trying to kill me, a man who has told you the truth that I heard from God.") Their similarity sets up a contrast between Jesus and John. Although both were *men* "sent from God," Jesus was much more than that (see John 1:7–9, 19–23). Although Jesus was

---

29. Bruner, *Gospel of John*, 17–18.

to refer to John as "a burning and shining lamp" (5:35), meaning that John (like the moon) did give light, it was Jesus, not John, who was "the light."

Although this John is always referred to in the other Gospels as "John the Baptist [baptizer]," he is never called that in John's Gospel. He is always simply "John," partly because he is the only John who appears by name in the Fourth Gospel, but perhaps also because here he is not so much "the baptizer" as "the witness." Although John's Gospel presents ten different witnesses to Jesus (John the Baptist, Jesus himself, the Samaritan woman, Jesus's works, the Father, Scripture, those who witnessed Jesus raising Lazarus, the Holy Spirit, Jesus's disciples, and John the Apostle), John the Baptist is the first and most prominent (1:7, 8, 15, 19, 32, 34; 3:26, 32, 33; 5:32–33).

But this raises the question, Why did Jesus need a witness? Isn't light self-authenticating? Wouldn't Jesus's miracles and his own resurrection be sufficient testimony to who he was? In the Old Testament, the noun for "witness" often refers to someone who testifies to the truth of a matter.

> Boaz said to the elders and all the people, "You are witnesses today that I am buying from Naomi everything that belonged to Elimelech, Chilion, and Mahlon." (Ruth 4:9)

But more than one witness was required (see John 8:13–18).

> If anyone kills a person, the murderer is to be put to death based on the word of witnesses. But no one is to be put to death based on the testimony of one witness. (Num 35:30)

> The one condemned to die is to be executed on the testimony of two or three witnesses. No one is to be executed on the testimony of a single witness. (Deut 17:6)

> One witness cannot establish any iniquity or sin against a person, whatever that person has done. A fact must be established by the testimony of two or three witnesses." (Deut 19:15)

Bauckham explains that according to Jewish tradition "it was not for the Messiah to claim for himself his messianic role and status."[30] In the Old Testament God himself even comes down to the level of human society and submits to the rules of evidence and testimony. In Isaiah, God speaks as if he and the foreign idols are on opposite sides in a courtroom drama. As with Elijah on Mount Carmel, the question is, Who is God? It will be answered by determining who is able to predict the future and then bring it about. Through his prophets, God had announced the future exile and also the future restoration. God calls human witnesses to testify concerning what

---

30. Bauckham, *Gospel of Glory*, 150.

he has said and done. "The Israelites themselves are the living evidence that their God is the only one."[31]

> All the nations are gathered together, and the peoples are assembled. Who among them can declare this, and tell us the former things? Let them present their witnesses to vindicate themselves, so that people may hear and say, "It is true." "*You are my witnesses*"—this is the Lord's declaration—"and my servant whom I have chosen, *so that you may know and believe* me and understand that I am he. No god was formed before me, and there will be none after me. I—I am the Lord. Besides me, there is no Savior. I alone declared, saved, and proclaimed—and not some foreign god among you. So *you are my witnesses*"—this is the Lord's declaration—and I am God." (Isa 43:9–12; emphasis added)

> "Do not be startled or afraid. Have I not told you and declared it long ago? *You are my witnesses!* Is there any God but me? There is no other Rock; I do not know any. All who make idols are nothing [*tohu*, "elemental chaos" in Gen 1:2], and what they treasure benefits no one. Their witnesses do not see or know anything, so they will be put to shame." (Isa 44:8–9; emphasis added)

So John the Baptist was a very special one of these human witnesses to God's saving work. But he was also prophesied as an individual in the Old Testament on the model of a royal herald (Isa 40:3–5; Mal 3:1).

Earlier, Isaiah had heard a disembodied voice announcing to "all flesh" the Lord's coming in glory like a king, and it called on people to prepare a way for him in the desert (Isa 40:3–5). All four Gospels apply this passage to John's ministry. But only in the Fourth Gospel do we learn that John himself said, "I am a 'voice of one crying out in the wilderness: Make straight the way of the Lord'—just as Isaiah the prophet said" (1:23). Malachi had also prophesied that the Messiah's coming would be preceded by his "messenger," who would "clear the way before" him (Mal 3:1), and he called that messenger "the prophet Elijah" (Mal 4:5). The other Gospels and even an angel and Jesus himself identified John the Baptist with that prophet (Matt 11:14; 17:12–13; Mark 1:2–4; 9:11–13; Luke 1:16–17), although John refused to identify himself with Elijah (John 1:21). He would only admit to being "a voice crying out in the wilderness," calling people's attention to "the one coming after" him, "whose sandal strap I'm not worthy to untie" (1:27). As John Calvin wrote, "The sum of it is that he wants to abase himself

---

31. Oswalt, *Isaiah, Chapters 40–66*, 149.

as much as he can lest any degree of honour wrongly given to him should obscure the superiority of Christ."[32]

Although Jesus was "the light" in that he revealed the Father, conquered darkness, and brought "the light of life" to people, he temporarily laid aside his clothing of majesty and splendor when he became flesh (17:5, 24). This is why we needed the witness of John and the others to the light. Sometime in my distant past I saw a newspaper photograph from WWII that Donald Barnhouse, former pastor of Tenth Presbyterian Church in Philadelphia, used to describe the resurrection of Christ. I think it applies even better to the ministry of John the Baptist. The photograph was of British King George VI and a group of people visiting the site where a German bomb had destroyed a building during the blitz. The king was dressed in street clothes, so the newspaper had added an arrow pointing to the king. John the Baptist was God's arrow "so that all might believe through him."

Human Response to the Light (1:9–13)

The World He Created Turned Him Away (1:9–11)

> 9 The true light that gives light to everyone, was coming into the world.
> 10 He was in the world, and the world was created through him, and yet the world did not recognize him. 11 He came to his own, and his own people did not receive him.

The word translated "world" (*kosmos*) occurs seventy-eight times in John. Although v. 9 could be taken to mean just that Jesus came from heaven to earth, the term "world" is negative in John about half the time (thirty-eight times according to Klink[33]), and v. 10 indicates that is the case here. "The world" refers to created humanity in rebellion against God. When John 3:16 says that God loves the world, the point is not the expanse of God's love because the world is so big, but the grace of God's love because the world is so bad.[34] Craig Koester vividly portrays the significance of "world" in John:

> John's ominous portrayal of "the world" gives depth to his understanding of the love of God and the work of Jesus. The "world" in John's Gospel is not characterized by soft summer breezes and the graceful light of dawn, by meadows filled with flowers or gentle waves upon the shore. It requires little effort to

32. Calvin, *St. John 1–10*, 30–31.
33. Klink, *John*, 103.
34. Carson, *Gospel according to John*, 123.

love a world like that. But in John's Gospel God loves the world that hates him; he gives his Son for the world that rejects him. He offers his love to a world estranged from him in order to overcome its hostility and bring the world back into relationship with its Creator (3:16).[35]

The world hates Jesus and his followers; they are not of the world because he has taken them out of it (John 15:18-19). Bauckham points out that although the world's opposition to Jesus is introduced here and reappears in 7:7; 8:23; and 9:39, "it really comes into its own" in the upper room discourse of chaps. 14-16 and especially Jesus's prayer in chap. 17 (where "world" occurs eighteen out of seventy-seven times in John).[36]

Jesus is the "true light" in two senses. He does not just claim to be true, like the café in the movie *Elf* that advertises "the world's best cup of coffee." The world is full of false gods and false prophets who lead people out into the darkness and then leave them there. But he is the Truth, the *genuine* light. Jesus is also the *ultimate* light.[37] The manna in the wilderness was truly from God (Exodus 16), but it was only a taste that anticipated the "true bread from heaven" (John 6:32). Israel was truly God's chosen vine (Psalm 80; Isaiah 5), but Jesus is the "true vine" that gives life and fruitfulness to all those connected to him (John 15).

The verb translated "gives light" (*phōtizō*) can mean to "give light to" people so that they can see (Eph 1:18; Heb 6:4; Rev 22:5) or to "illuminate" them so that they can be seen (Luke 11:36; 1 Cor 4:5; 2 Tim 1:10). According to John, Jesus's coming does both. The light that is the Word offers truth and understanding to all, but it also reveals people's true character by how they respond to it (John 3:19-21).

John says that the world Jesus brought into existence did not even "recognize" him, even though he entered into the world. The verb for "recognize" means "to know" and could also be translated "acknowledge." It is extremely important in John's Gospel (the two verbs for "know" occur about 140 times in John). This verse is reminiscent of Isa 1:2-3 (the reason a cow and a donkey are usually found in the nativity?):

> Listen, heavens, and pay attention, earth, for the Lord has spoken: "I have raised children and brought them up, but they have rebelled against me. The ox knows its owner, and the donkey its master's feeding trough, but Israel does not know; my people do not understand.

---

35. Koester, *Word of Life*, 81.
36. Bauckham, *Gospel of Glory*, 128.
37. Carson, *Gospel according to John*, 122.

The world's failure to acknowledge or know the light is the world's own fault. They did not recognize it because they *refused* to do so.³⁸ As Paul the apostle wrote, the world "suppress[es] the truth" even though "what can be known about God is evident among them, because God has shown it to them" (Rom 1:18–19).

Verse 11 refers twice to "his own." Greek has three genders: masculine, feminine, and neuter. The first "his own" is neuter and refers to what belongs to him—his property, personal possessions, or *home* (as when the disciple John took Mary into "his home" in John 19:27; also 16:32; Acts 21:6; and LXX Esth 5:10; 6:12; 3 Macc 6:27; 7:8). The second "his own" is masculine and refers to his own *people* or *family* (as in 1 Tim 5:8), that is, the Jewish people, Israel, who was God's "own possession out of all the peoples, although the whole earth is mine" (Exod 19:5), the sheep of his pasture, whom he had rescued, guided, and cared for (Pss 79:13; 95:7; 100:3). But when the Jews refused to welcome him and take him in (the idea of the verb rendered "receive"; 14:3), they showed themselves to be part of "the world" that hated him despite his love.³⁹

The Welcoming Children of God (1:12–13)

> 12 But to all who did receive him, he gave them the right to be [become] children of God, to those who believe in his name, 13 who were born, not of natural descent, or of the will of the flesh, or of the will of man, but of God.

F. F. Bruce suggests that v. 11 might furnish a title to John 1–12: "His own people did not receive him." Verse 12, he says, might furnish a title to John 13–17, which begins, "Having loved his own who were in the world, he loved them to the end" (13:1b).⁴⁰ Verses 12–13 offer a qualification to what is otherwise a dismal situation. As Klink says, "In this verse the prologue shifts from tragedy to triumph."⁴¹ The coming of the divine light was not futile. Some who were in darkness did recognize his authority, welcome him, and find light. In other words, they *believed in his name* (also 2:23; 3:18). According to 3:18, to "believe in his name" is to "believe in him."

In the Bible a person's *name* could refer to his or her character, person, or reputation. God's name, recorded as YHWH but probably pronounced as

---

38. See Bruner, *Gospel of John*, 27.
39. See Klink, *John*, 103.
40. Bruce, *Gospel of John*, 37–38.
41. Klink, *John*, 103.

Yahweh (or shortened to Yah), is the most frequent word in the Old Testament, occurring about 6,800 times. But references to God's "name" (Hb. *shēm*; Gk. *onoma*) or the name of his Son occur about 500 times in the Bible. To bless, praise, magnify, glorify, rejoice in, thank, fear, love, remember, proclaim, or seek God's "name" is to do so to God *as he has revealed himself*. God's "name" could also be a term referring to his *presence*. Jerusalem was the place God chose "to put his *name* for his dwelling" (Deut 12:5). According to 2 Sam 6:2, "The ark bears the *Name*, the name of the Lord of Armies who is enthroned between the cherubim" (emphasis added; see also Jer 3:17). Isaiah 30:27 says, "The name of the Lord comes from afar" (ESV). The phrase "the name of the Lord" occurs eighty-seven times in the Old Testament, beginning with "call on the name of the Lord" five times in Genesis, which means to summon and depend on his power and presence. The psalmist says, "May the name of Jacob's God protect you" (Ps 20:1) and "Our help is in the name of the Lord, the Maker of heaven and earth" (Ps 124:8). According to Prov 18:10, "The name of the Lord is a strong tower; the righteous run to it and are protected" (see also Zeph 3:12). To praise his name means to praise him for who he is (Ps 113:1–3). To speak or act in the name of the Lord means to do so in dependence on and by his power and authority (Ps 118:10: "All the nations surrounded me; in the name of the Lord I destroyed them"). John may well have had this verse from Isaiah in mind: "Who among you walks in darkness, and has no light? Let him trust in the name of the Lord; let him lean on his God" (50:10). He may also have been thinking of this verse from Micah, which follows the prophecy of the Messiah's birth in Bethlehem: "He will stand and shepherd them in the strength of the Lord, in the majestic name of the Lord his God. They will live securely, for then his greatness will extend to the ends of the earth" (Mic 5:4).

The verb "to believe" occurs ninety-eight times in John's Gospel, ten times more than in any other Gospel and more than any other New Testament book. It is one of the five most common verbs in the book (the others being "speak," "be," "come/go," and "do/make") and is from the same root as the noun for "faith" and the adjective for "faithful" (*pisteuō* = "believe"; *pistis* = "faith"; *pistos* = "faithful"). It means either (1) to consider something to be true or that someone is telling the truth, or (2) to trust/have confidence in or rely on something or someone. A major lexicon of New Testament Greek expresses the second meaning like this: "to entrust oneself to an entity in complete confidence," to believe in or trust, with "implications of total commitment to the one who is trusted . . . God and Christ are objects of this type of faith that relies on their power and nearness to help, in addition to being convinced that their revelations or disclosures are true."[42]

The result of placing such confidence in the Word (Jesus Christ), welcoming him into one's life and making such a "total commitment" to him is the gift from him of the "right" or "authority" (Gk. *exousia*) to become "children of God." Although God created everyone, the idea that all people are "God's children" is unbiblical. In the Old Testament, God used the father/son relationship to describe the covenant relationship he formed with Israel when he brought them out of Egypt. He called Israel, "my firstborn son" (Exod 4:22; see also Hos 11:1) and "sons of the Lord your God" (Deut 14:1), whom he formed from the womb (Isa 44:2). But in Isa 1:2 God says, "I have raised children and brought them up, but they have rebelled against me."

So being a member of God's covenant people in the Old Testament was not the same as having a personal relationship with God. Now membership in God's family is the result of being related by faith to Jesus Christ. The nature of that relationship is clarified elsewhere by the concept of adoption (Rom 8:15; Gal 4:5; Eph 1:5). Whereas Jesus is the natural and eternal Son of God, the one receiving and believing him becomes the adopted son or daughter of God.[43] As John made clear in 1:4, however, becoming God's child involves more than just a change in role or legal status: "*in him* was life." It involves being united with Christ and infused with his immortal life. As Richard Gaffin explains, the "decisive difference between old and new covenant believers . . . is the Spirit-worked *union* New Testament be-

---

42. BDAG, 817.

43. David B. Garner makes a compelling case, however, that this distinction between Christ's sonship and ours is not as strict as is often portrayed. See his argument in *Sons in the Son*, 173–218. Although Rom 1:4 is often translated to say that Jesus was "declared" to be the Son of God by his resurrection (see KJV, NKJV, NASB, NRSV, ESV, GW, REB, HCSB), the verb ὁρίζω is better rendered "appointed" (CSB: "Jesus Christ . . . was appointed to be the powerful Son of God according to the Spirit of holiness by the resurrection of the dead"; also NIV, NET). As C. E. B. Cranfield declares, "No clear example, either earlier than, or contemporary with, the New Testament, of its use in the sense 'declare' or 'show to be' has been adduced" (*Romans*, 1:61). While emphatically affirming the essential and eternal Sonship of Christ, Garner argues that "Paul's declaration of Christ's sonship in Romans 1:3–4 is an epochal designation of historically attained sonship rather than an ontological one concerning the hypostatic union" (p. 195). Although forever the eternal Son of God in essence, it was necessary for our salvation that Jesus become the adopted Son of God at his resurrection in fulfillment of Ps 2:6–8, thus entering "a personally, historically, cosmically, and therefore soteriologically different stage of sonship" (p. 196). "For divine covenant purpose to be attained on earth, the eternal Son had to become the resurrected and adopted Son. And Christ brings *no* privilege of eschatological sonship (adoption) to believers if *he himself* has not attained to eschatological sonship (adoption) himself . . . [F]ailing to appreciate Christ's historical adoption undermines biblical soteriology" (p. 194; emphasis original).

lievers have with the *exalted* Christ."[44] Johnson defines our adoption like this: "Adoption is that benefit of being united to the Son of God through which we share in his sonship with the Father, become the beloved children of God, and enjoy all the privileges and rights of being included in God's family."[45]

So our becoming God's children (see also 1 John 3:1-2) involves more than a declaration from God or an *as if* status. Comparison to ancient or modern practices of adoption is only figurative and therefore imperfect. As Johnson says, "We *really are* his children."[46] In 1 John 3:1 the apostle marvels, "See what great love the Father has given us that we should be called God's children—and we are!" As John says in John 1:13, our adoption involves being "born . . . of God" (see also 1 John 4:7; 5:1). According to the stunning statement in 2 Pet 1:4, the believer is able to escape the world's corruption by coming to "share in the divine nature." This does not involve deification, however. Rather, as Fairbairn describes it, "Christians become adopted sons and daughters of God, thus sharing by grace in the fellowship the Son has with the Father by nature."[47]

Being God's child also entails the privilege of living with him. As Jesus says in John 14:23, "If anyone loves me, he will keep my word. My Father will love him, and we will come to him and make our home with him." This is not just a *possibility* for believers, however. The one who loves Jesus and keeps his word is the same as the one who has received him and become a child of God by being joined to the Son of God, who is life and love. As Jesus says in 14:19-20, "In a little while the world will no longer see me, but you will see me. Because I live, you will live too. On that day you will know that I am in my Father, you are in me, and I am in you." Johnson explains, "The relationship of love we have with Jesus includes a sharing in the love the Father has for his Son, so much so that the Father and the Son dwell within us."[48] Jesus prays in John 17:23, "You have sent me and have loved them as you have loved me." That word "as" (Gk. *kathōs*, "just as, even as, to the degree that") must not be missed. Keener says this is "one of the most remarkable statements of the Gospel, given the enormity of God's love for

---

44. Gaffin, "The Holy Spirit," 71-72 (emphasis his).

45. Johnson, *One with Christ*, 147. Johnson also argues that although there are different nuances in their thought, Paul and John "shared a basic, underlying conviction: we are included in God's family by virtue of being incorporated into God's own Son, Jesus Christ" (p. 150). Note also his remark that "Paul's understanding of our 'sonship' in Jesus Christ is remarkably (and understandably) similar to John's" (p. 158).

46. Johnson, *One with Christ*, 162.

47. Fairbairn, *Life in the Trinity*, 9.

48. Johnson, *One with Christ*, 153.

his uniquely obedient Son (3:35; 5:20; 10:17)."[49] God the Father even created all things "through him and *for him*" (Col 1:16). Carson calls it "breathtakingly extravagant" and goes on to point out that "Christians themselves have been caught up into the love of the Father for the Son, secure and content and fulfilled because loved by the Almighty himself (*cf.* Eph. 3:17b-19), with the very same love he reserves for his Son. It is hard to imagine a more compelling evangelistic appeal."[50] The Father's love for the Son cannot fail to "hit" us as well because we are *in him*.

Being God's *child*, however, may also suggest something else. Although the term does not necessarily imply a certain age, the Bible sometimes uses the image of a child as one who is weak, ignorant, foolish, dependent, and endearing. Being God's child means looking to him for strength, instruction, guidance, help, and love.

According to v. 13, that family relationship is also the result of being *born*. But John qualifies in three ways the kind of birth involved. First, we are not God's children through physical birth (literally, "not from bloods"). Neither our race (Jewish or not), nor our ancestors, our heritage, or our parents attracts God's attention or gives us any privileged position at God's table. The Jewish leaders in John 8 believed they were God's children because of their descent from Abraham. But Jesus says they were not children of God but of the devil (8:44). So John is not referring to a physical birth but a spiritual birth, or rebirth, as in John 3:3. Second, John says our birth into God's family does not result from "the will of the flesh." This may refer to sexual desire. Third, it isn't the result of "the will of man [or "a man/husband"]." The word translated "man" here is not the word that means "human" (*anthrōpos*) but the word for a male (*anēr*). John is emphasizing that the kind of birth that brings us into God's family is a spiritual birth that is an act of God, just like creation. The word translated "be" in "be children of God" is again the word for "come into existence" that has occurred five times before in this chapter. Becoming God's child involves a divine act of new creation.

We should not take John's references to the "will," however, as a denial of the importance of the human will in salvation. In the first place, we saw in vv. 10–11 that the world and his own people in general refused to acknowledge the authority of the divine light who came. That involved an exercise of will. Then v. 12 says that becoming God's child requires receiving or acknowledging him and his authority. That, too, is an exercise of the will. Finally, it is interesting that v. 12 does not say that those who received

---

49. Keener, *Gospel of John*, 1063.
50. Carson, *Gospel according to John*, 569.

him he *made children of God*. Rather, it says that he gave them the *right* to *become* children of God. John is not saying that an additional human act is required beyond receiving/believing, but neither is he removing the human will from the equation. Becoming God's child requires a divine, creative act. But it also requires an act of the human will, which we exercise when we "receive him."

To whom is this gift available? The first word in v. 12 in the Greek text is the word translated "all." It means "everyone" or "anyone." In the neuter gender, it means "everything" or "whatever." At Jesus's "all-you-can-eat" buffet of bread and fish in John 6:11, it means "as much as they wanted." When I was young, a cheap substitute for ice cream was something called "Mellorine" (as margarine is to butter). My mother and I loved it. Sometimes stores would have a sale: "Mellorine—half gallon 29¢—limit 2." Since two was not enough for us, however, she'd send me in to buy two, then she'd go in and buy two more. There are no limits, however, to the availability of God's gift of adoption in his Son. It is for "all."

The Word Became Flesh (1:14)

> *14 The Word became flesh and dwelt among us. We observed his glory, the glory as the one and only Son from the Father, full of grace and truth.*

After occurring three times in v. 1, "the Word" has not appeared in John's prologue until here. So we are reminded here at "the high point of the Prologue"[51] that John is speaking of the Word, who existed in the beginning and was with God and was God. This is the one who "became flesh." The verse begins in Greek with the word *kai*, "and," left untranslated in the CSB and NIV. Frey interprets it as an affirmative, accentuating and substantiating the previous statement about becoming God's children: "Yes, the Logos became flesh . . ." It marks v. 14 as "a further intensification, a new level, a climax."[52]

Clark and Johnson speak of the "grave state of affairs that many modern Christians are unable to think and speak about the incarnation with any considerable sense of competency, let alone any particular sense of wonder and delight."[53] Celebrating Christmas every year is wonderful, but it puts us at risk of treating the incarnation as just a sweet but old story about a

---

51. Frey, *Glory of the Crucified One*, 278.

52. Frey, *Glory of the Crucified One*, 278. A confirmation of the "new level," he says, is that the first person plural occurs for the first time in this verse.

53. Clark and Johnson, *The Incarnation of God*, 39.

humdrum event—like people who live and work every day in sight of Niagara Falls, the Grand Canyon, or Mount Rushmore. They stop really seeing the wonder of it. But when we think about it, humanity and deity are more incompatible than matter and antimatter, the north and south poles of a magnet, or the two posts of a car battery. J. I. Packer declared, "Nothing in fiction is so fantastic as is this truth of the Incarnation."[54] C. S. Lewis called it "the Grand Miracle," saying that "the Central Miracle asserted by Christians is the Incarnation."[55] Michael Reeves writes, "My mind goes quite giddy and I get goose bumps as I write this: *God has come to be with us!*"[56] Ed Welch marvels that the King of the universe has sought us out.

> Kings *receive* people. They consent to give you a five-minute audience, then off you go. Kings do not show up at your home or go out of their way to help you. But everything changes when King Jesus comes. This King leaves the palace precincts and finds you.[57]

How could the most superbly exotic and astonishing event in history be reduced to mundane language without losing most of its shocking quality? Trying to capture the mystery and wonder of it with the word *incarnation* still fails, but it's the best we can do. The Latin word *incarnatio* means "enfleshment" or "embodiment," that is, the joining of human and divine in Christ. It was invented in the early Christian centuries to describe what happened to the Son of God in Bethlehem. Yet John did not just say the Word "became man/ human"—a term that could smack of dignity; rather, the Word "became flesh"—our flesh—humanity in its "most vulnerable, the most corruptible, the most easily destructible, part of the human being."[58] The barrier between God and sinful flesh has been broken.[59] And this "'condescension' of God," Frey points out, which is "already signaled" by the use of "flesh" in 1:14, "is intensified in the Gospel of John all the way to the cross of Jesus."[60]

The mystery of the incarnation, that God in Jesus Christ "participates unreservedly in the same human nature that we ourselves possess, is at the

---

54. Packer, *Knowing God*, 52–53.
55. Lewis, *Miracles*, 143.
56. Reeves, *Rejoicing in Christ*, 47.
57. Welch, *Caring for One Another*, 18.
58. McHugh, *John 1–4*, 53. He points out, however, that σάρξ "stands, by synecdoche, for ἄνθρωπος, that is, for the whole human being, not merely for the flesh, but for the bones and blood and soul as well" (pp. 51–52).
59. Carson, *Gospel according to John*, 134.
60. Frey, *Glory of the Crucified One*, 284.

very center of the Christian faith."[61] This is more than clothing himself in humanity as with "a removable robe."[62] It involved *becoming* (the seventh use of this word in John) something new. The one who brought everything into existence (Jesus even created his own mother!) "became" part of that creation, something he had never been. Yet this is not on the order of a puddle of water becoming ice, a caterpillar becoming a butterfly, or even a boy becoming a man, which involve ceasing to be one thing (perhaps temporarily) as one becomes something else. The becoming of the Son of God involved addition, not substitution. As the word of God to Moses and the prophets became tablets of stone placed in the ark of the testimony in the most holy place, where God dwelt, so the eternal Word of God became flesh and blood and dwelt among us. God the Word with God became Man the Word with man. If we want to know the invisible God, we have only to look to the Word who became flesh. As Bauckham explains, John no longer calls Jesus "the Word" after this because "the audible word became visible flesh."[63] The eighteenth-century theologian John Williamson Nevin said that in the statement, the Word became flesh, "we have the whole gospel comprehended, ... the key that unlocks the sense of all God's revelations, ... all God's works, and brings to light the true meaning of the universe ... The incarnation forms thus the great central fact of the world."[64]

The word translated "dwelt" (*skēnoō*) is a verb found only here and in Rev 7:15; 12:12; 13:6; 21:3. It is related to the word for "tent" (*skēnē*), whose Hebrew equivalent (*'ōhel*) is often translated in the Old Testament as "tabernacle." The tabernacle in the Old Testament was also called "the tent of meeting" and "the tent of testimony," as in Exod 40:34: "The cloud covered the tent of meeting, and the glory of the Lord filled the tabernacle." The verbs related to this noun can mean to "pitch a tent," to "camp," or to "encamp." In Num 35:34 God says to Israel, "Do not make the land unclean [by bloodshed] where you live and where I dwell ["camp"]; for I, the Lord, reside ["camp"] among the Israelites." In Josh 22:19 Joshua instructs the tribes across the Jordan, "But if the land you possess is defiled, cross over to the land the Lord possesses where the Lord's tabernacle stands ["where the Lord's tent encamps"]." In 1 Chr 23:25, David says, "The Lord God of Israel has given rest to his people, and he has come to stay ["camp"] in Jerusalem forever." But the word did not always refer to a temporary dwelling. Solomon used it of God's dwelling in the temple (2 Chr 6:2), and it's used in

---

61. Clark and Johnson, *Incarnation of God*, 19.
62. Frey, *Glory of the Crucified One*, 281
63. Bauckham, *Gospel of Glory*, 50.
64. Quoted in Clark and Johnson, *Incarnation of God*, 12.

Ezra 6:12 for God's dwelling in the rebuilt temple (see also Ezra 7:15; Neh 1:9). The Hebrew verb usually translated by this Greek one is the common verb meaning "to set up a tent." Occasionally, however, the Hebrew verb translated by Greek *skēnoō* is *shakan*, meaning "dwell," related to another Hebrew word for "tabernacle," *mishkan*, "dwelling," and from which was later derived the noun "Shekinah." In post-biblical Hebrew this word was used of God's glory that visibly manifested itself in the tabernacle or temple by means of the cloud.

As the tabernacle or temple had been the place where God had displayed his glory in the Old Testament and where humans met with and worshiped God, that place would now be the incarnate Word, Jesus Christ, to whom the temple had pointed, and which he came to replace.[65] Jesus also referred to his body as the temple (John 2:19–21; Matt 26:61; 27:40; Mark 14:58; 15:29). In Rev 21:3, John reported a loud voice from the throne declaring, "Look! God's dwelling ["tent"] is with humanity, and he will live with them. They will be his peoples, and God himself will be with them and will be their God." In *The Message*, Eugene Peterson rendered John 1:14, "The Word became flesh and blood, and moved into the neighborhood." That expresses it pretty well, but that was only a start. Revelation 7:15 says that those coming out of the great tribulation, who are washed in the blood of the Lamb, will also reside in and serve/worship God in that temple and tent, which will be their "shelter." But we do not have to wait for that. As we saw in John 14:23 (one of the most remarkable verses in the book), Jesus promised his disciples, "If anyone loves me, he will keep my word. My Father will love him, and we will come to him and make our home ["dwelling place"; the word used in 14:2] with him." Because I'm his child, he lives in my home! But even more than that, he lives in me and I in him. As Johnson explains, "The incarnation tells us that the Word took on human flesh in order to incorporate us into his life. And because Christ is the natural Son of God, when we are joined to him, we become adopted sons of God through him, truly and really sharing in his relationship to the Father through the Spirit."[66]

---

65. See the discussion in Köstenberger, *Theology*, 425–35. Following Oscar Cullmann, he asserts that Jesus's replacement of the temple "constitutes a fundamental axiom of Johannine Christology" that can especially be seen in the first four chapters of the Gospel (p. 425). According to Frey, the "becoming flesh of the Logos in Jesus Christ" fulfills the "eschatological promises that God would one day 'tent' in the midst of his people (Ezek 37:27; Joel 4[ET 3]:17; Zech 2:14)" (*Glory of the Crucified One*, 283).

66. Johnson, *One with Christ*, 155. As previously noted, Garner considers Jesus's *adoption* as Son to be as vital to our salvation as his *eternal* sonship. See *Sons in the Son*, 145.

The word "observed" translates *theaomai*, the least common of four Greek words for "see" (six times in John; the others being *blepō* [seventeen times], *theōreō* [twenty-four times, but related to *theaomai*], and *horaō* [sixty-seven times). This is the word from which English gets the word "theater." It means to watch, to be a spectator, especially of something sensational (1:32), and can figuratively mean to "reflect on, notice [1:38; 6:5], understand, or comprehend."[67] It could be used of scientific observation. We might say it means to "really see" something (John 4:35: "open your eyes and look at the fields"), the kind of seeing that can result in faith (11:45). What are the most amazing things you have ever personally witnessed? Aretha Franklin in concert? An elephant giving birth? A total eclipse of the sun? The birth of your first child? Nothing compares to the thrill of the first disciples being spectators at the glory of the incarnate Son of God, "full of grace and truth."

The words translated "glory" (*doxa*) and "glorify" (*doxazō*) occur forty-two times in John's Gospel, making it one of the most prominent concepts in the book, almost as much as "life/live" (fifty-three times). In classical Greek the word *doxa* meant "opinion," and the word *doxazō* meant "to think, suppose." But the meanings changed for Jews when the Jewish translators of the Hebrew Bible into Greek used them to render Hebrew words related to *kavōd*, "be heavy." The Hebrew term could have one of three categories of meaning: (1) importance, wealth, or power (Gen 13:2: Abraham was very "heavy" in livestock, silver, and gold), (2) honor, prestige, or reputation, or (3) visible splendor or glory.[68] *Doxa* in the Septuagint and then the New Testament came to mean either (2) or (3). And *doxazō* came to mean either "to honor, to praise" ("give glory to God"), or "to endow with visible splendor."

These words for glory become especially prominent in the second half of John's Gospel. Richard Bauckham defines "glory" as "the visible manifestation of God." In John it is "the visible revelation of God's character, what one would see if one could see the very face of God."[69] We gauge a person's thoughts and feelings, in part, by looking at her face. Sometimes this is more reliable than hearing her words, which sometimes lie. We often try to "mask" our thoughts and feelings, which is seldom completely successful. Then after years of practice, honing our skills at being an imposter, it's almost impossible to unlearn and begin to live a life of transparency and

---

67. K. Dahn, "See, Vision, Eye," *NIDNTT*, 3:512. For a favorable summary of G. L. Phillips's argument that these words form "a hierarchy of various levels of 'seeing,'" see Miller, "'They Saw His Glory,'" 134-37, though Miller also cites John Painter's rejection of such a semantic hierarchy.

68. See Bauckham, *Gospel of Glory*, 44-45.

69. Bauckham, *Gospel of Glory*, 72-73.

genuineness. Like Aslan pulling the scales off the dragon in C. S. Lewis's *The Voyage of the Dawn Treader*, it requires a painfully redemptive act of God. The face of God, however, is a cloudless window into his glorious essence. We can only experience it in Jesus Christ. Bauckham explains that "Jesus uses the language of glory especially as he approaches and contemplates his own glorification and God's glorification in the event of his death-and-exaltation."[70] John uses the term *glory* to highlight "the extraordinary nature of the love of God for the world in going to the lengths of Jesus's abject dying in the pain and shame of crucifixion."[71] According to Frey, John's message that "the crucified one," who in fact is "the one clothed with glory by God and as such is the basis of faith and salvation, . . . is already signaled in an anticipatory way in the collocation of [*sarx*] and [*doxa*] in the Prologue."[72]

Whereas John reflects on Genesis in the first thirteen verses of the prologue, in vv. 14–18 he reflects on the book of Exodus.[73] What God began at Mount Sinai, he is finishing in Jesus Christ. God first began to reveal his glory to Israel hidden in a cloud—in the wilderness, then on Mount Sinai (Exod 16:10; 19:16; 24:16–17), then at the tent of meeting and the tabernacle (Exod 29:43; 33:8–11). Later, after the golden calf incident, Moses asked God not only to "teach me your ways," but he boldly requested, "Please, let me see your glory" (Exod 33:18). In response, God announced that he would reveal a new dimension of his character: "I will cause all my goodness to pass in front of you and I will proclaim the name 'the Lord' before you. I will be gracious to whom I will be gracious, and I will have compassion on whom I will have compassion." He would not show Moses his face, which would have meant Moses's death, but he hid Moses while *his glory* passed by; then he showed Moses his back (Exod 33:19–23). Then, when God had Moses bring two tablets up the mountain, God appeared to him in a cloud and declared (Exod 34:6–7; emphasis added),

> The Lord—the Lord is a compassionate and gracious God, slow to anger and *abounding in faithful love and truth*, maintaining faithful love to a thousand generations, forgiving iniquity, rebellion, and sin. But he will not leave the guilty unpunished, bringing the fathers' iniquity on the children and grandchildren to the third and fourth generation.

Moses cannot see the essence and totality of God, but he can hear of "all [his] goodness," which God equates with his glory, and he can catch a glimpse of

---

70. Bauckham, *Gospel of Glory*, 46.
71. Bauckham, *Gospel of Glory*, 43.
72. Frey, *Glory of the Crucified One*, 284.
73. See Bauckham, *Gospel of Glory*, 50.

him, what F. F. Bruce calls God's "afterglow,"[74] especially in his actions. This list of divine attributes is found many times later in Scripture (Pss 86:15; 103:8; 145:8; Joel 2:13; Jonah 4:2; Neh 9:17), and portions of it occur in many more (Num 14:18; Deut 4:31; Pss 25:6; 78:38; 111:4; 112:4; 116:5; 2 Chr 30:9; Neh 9:31; Nah 1:3).[75]

But John and the other eyewitnesses of the incarnate Word had a totally new experience with God's glory as they were spectators of it in Jesus. They still did not see God in the totality of his nature and radiant splendor, although Peter, James, and John approached it on the Mount of Transfiguration (Matt 17:1-8, Mark 9:2-8, Luke 9:28-36; also see 2 Pet 1:16-18). For the most part, they saw him veiled in flesh through the eyes of faith as they saw his works and listened to his words. But they really saw and experienced his glory in a new and very personal way. And the God they saw in Jesus was the same God who spoke with and revealed his glory and goodness to Moses. John's explanation that Jesus's glory was "full of grace and truth" is the Greek equivalent of God's "abounding in faithful love and truth" in Exod 34:6. Jesus's "glory" is the glory of God himself, which was revealed in Jesus's miracles (2:11), but especially in his death and resurrection, as John will make clear to us. As Carson explains, "The glory revealed to Moses when the Lord passed in front of him and sounded his name, displaying that divine goodness characterized by ineffable grace and truth, was the very same glory John and his friends saw in the Word-made-flesh."[76]

The terms *glory* and *truth* that occur together in this verse are two of what Bauckham calls "the four big theological words" of John's Gospel, the others being *life* and *love* (the latter appearing first in 3:16). "As windows on the meaning of Jesus's death and resurrection, they open vistas to contemplate."[77] And the reason the glory of God can be seen in Jesus is that Jesus is the unique, "one and only," Son of God the Father.

The phrase "one and only Son" translates just one word in Greek, *monogenēs*. It used to be translated "only begotten" (KJV, NKJV, NASB). But most scholars today are convinced that the term refers not to "begottenness," that is, the quality of being born, but to the uniqueness of an only son who is incomparable, irreplaceable, and supremely loved. The term actually means "one of a kind" and is related to the Greek word *genos*, which can refer to a "group" or "kind" of something. *Monogenēs* occurs nine times in the New Testament: three times in Luke (7:12 and 9:38 of a son, 8:42 of a

---

74. Bruce, *Gospel of John*, 44.
75. See the excellent study in Boda, *Heartbeat of Old Testament Theology*, 27-51.
76. Carson, *Gospel according to John*, 129.
77. Bauckham, *Gospel of Glory*, 64.

daughter), five times in John's writings referring to Jesus's relationship to the Father (1:14,18; 3:16,18; 1 John 4:9), and in Heb 11:17 of Isaac's relationship to Abraham. The fact that Abraham had also fathered Ishmael indicates that *monogenēs* did not mean "only begotten." According to G. Pendrick, the term was used in extrabiblical sources for an only child who was not the only begotten. "The father might have begotten other children who died young and so the preservation of his name rests on the only surviving son."[78] John's use of the term may have God's instructions to Abraham in Gen 22:2 in the background: "Take your son, . . . your only son, whom you love—Isaac." The Septuagint translated the Hebrew word for "only son" (*yāchid*) there as "the beloved one" (*agapētos*; also in Gen 22:1, 12, 16; Jer 6:26; Amos 8:10; Zech 12:10). The Hebrew word (which only occurs twelve times) was also used of Jephthah's daughter in Judg 11:34 (*monogenēs* in the Septuagint): "She was his only child; he had no other son or daughter besides her." *Yāchid* is used in three passages describing the deepest mourning: "mourn as you would for an only son" (Jer 6:26; cf. Amos 8:10; and the Messianic passage in Zech 12:10: "they will look at me whom they pierced. They will mourn for him as one mourns for an only child and weep bitterly for him as one weeps for a firstborn"). So the words "unique," "irreplaceable" and "supremely loved" fit both *monogenēs* and *yāchid*.

Finally, the phrase "the one and only Son from the Father" points back to v. 1 and further identifies the characters. There "the Word was with God." Now we know not only that "the Word" refers to the Son, but that the "God" he was with is his Father. John has introduced us to the first two Persons of the Trinity. But with the phrase "from the Father" John also introduces us to the theme that God the Father has sent his one and only Son on a mission (especially prominent in chaps. 5–8, 17). The British clergyman and hymnologist H. R. Bramley (1833–1917) celebrated the fact in a song:

> A Babe on the breast of a Maiden he lies,
> Yet sits with the Father on high in the skies;
> Before him their faces the Seraphim hide,
> While Joseph stands waiting, unscared, by his side . . .
> O wonder of wonders, which none can unfold,
> The Ancient of Days is an hour or two old;
> The Maker of all things is made of the earth,
> Man is worshiped by Angels, and God comes to birth.[79]

---

78. Pendrick, "*Monogenēs*," 590.

79. H. R. Bramley, "The Great God of Heaven Is Come Down to Earth," no. 29 in *The English Hymnal*, 51; quoted in Clark and Johnson, *Incarnation of God*, 42.

The Uniqueness of the Word (1:15-18)

> 15 *(John testified concerning him and exclaimed, "This was the one of whom I said, 'The one coming after me ranks ahead of me, because he existed before me.'") 16 Indeed [or "for"], we have all received grace upon grace from [or "out of"] his fullness, 17 for the law was given through Moses; grace and truth came through Jesus Christ. 18 No one has ever seen God. The one and only Son, who is himself God and is at the Father's side—he has revealed him.*

John the Baptist is like a thread woven through this chapter. The parenthetical v. 15 connects to and echoes the introduction of John the Baptist in vv. 6-8 and anticipates his testimony in vv. 19-36 (v. 30 repeats v. 15). Verse 15 serves to clarify that the Light about whom John the Baptist testified in vv. 6-8 was one and the same with the Word made flesh, Jesus Christ, introduced in vv. 14-18.

The first two verbs of v. 15 indicate that the testimony of John the Baptist continues to serve as God's arrow pointing to Jesus. "Testified" (Gk. *marturei*) is present tense and could be rendered "testifies"; "exclaimed" (Gk. *kekragen*) is perfect tense and could be rendered "has exclaimed," possibly suggesting that the cry continues to ring out. The word translated "exclaimed" is elsewhere rendered "cried out." In John it emphasizes the importance of what is said. The phrase "ranks ahead of me" is more literally, "has become ahead of me."[80] It's sometimes translated "has surpassed me [in importance]." John is not complaining, though, but telling us that the one following him is actually "the point of it all."[81] The last clause of the verse, literally "because he existed first of me," the REB translates, "before I was born, he already was."

These verses connect to v. 14, where John tells us Jesus's glory is "full of grace and truth." Here we learn that those who have received him and become God's children (v. 12) also receive "grace upon grace" from the

---

80. I use the term "(more) literal/literally" in these studies with hesitation. "Literal" is a slippery term that differs in meaning in different contexts and is often misunderstood and misused. As opposed to "figurative," it can indicate the less abstract use of a word: "sacrificial *lamb*" versus "sacrificial *Lamb*." Here and in Bible translation discussions, the term is often set against a more "idiomatic" rendering of a phrase as a whole, usually in a way that best suits the present context. A "more literal" rendering would be one that takes each word (usually in order) in its more common sense, without necessarily any attention given to context. Such a "literal" rendering is often interesting and sometimes enlightening, especially when it discloses the repeated use of a Hebrew or Greek word that has previously occurred with another translation. The "literal" should never be understood, however, as the "true," "real," or "actual" meaning, or necessarily even the "better" translation.

81. Ridderbos, *Gospel of John*, 55.

infinitely vast reservoir of his glorious grace, just as one might fill bucket after bucket of water from the ocean "without ever diminishing its content."[82] The preposition translated "upon" in the phrase "grace upon grace" more commonly means "instead of." Bible translations render it in various ways as they attempt to convey the sense: "grace after grace," "grace in place of grace," "grace for grace," "one gracious gift/blessing after another," and "gift after gift after gift." As F. F. Bruce explains, "What the followers of Christ draw from the ocean of divine fullness is grace upon grace—one wave of grace being constantly replaced by a fresh one. There is no limit to the supply of grace which God has placed at his people's disposal in Christ."[83] That's why his grace is sufficient for us (2 Cor 12:9) and "his mercies never end. They are new every morning; great is your faithfulness!" (Lam 3:22–23).

Verse 17 explains by means of a mild contrast how that never-ending grace comes to us. Two statements are placed side by side without an explicit indication of their relationship. Moses and the law are not being set *against* Jesus and "grace and truth." As we saw from v. 14, John's statement that Jesus's glory is "full of grace and truth" alludes to Exod 34:6 where God declares to Moses that he is "abounding in faithful love and truth," the equivalent expression. John's point is that a greater grace, the grace and truth in Jesus Christ, is superseding the former grace displayed in the law.[84] As Jay Sklar declares, "If what we see in the Old Testament is an acorn, what we see in Jesus is a magnificent oak."[85] John described Jesus in v. 9 as the "true light," not only in the sense that he is the *genuine* light, but also that he is the perfect and *ultimate* light, which will never need to be superseded (like iPhone 4, 5, 6, 7, 8, 10, ad infinitum). The manna in the wilderness was only a taste that anticipated the "true bread from heaven"; and John the Baptist was only a voice crying out in the wilderness, testifying about the light that became flesh. So the grace and truth available in the law of Moses were a foretaste, a shadow, an opening or warm-up act, to the grace and truth now embodied in Jesus, God's Son. Whereas the law "was given" and could, therefore, be separated from Moses, grace and truth—grace upon grace—"came" in the person of Jesus, who is *in himself* their only perfect and ultimate source. They cannot be detached from him as things he brought with him from heaven and then left behind.[86]

---

82. Bruce, *Gospel of John*, 43.
83. Bruce, *Gospel of John*, 43.
84. Carson, *Gospel according to John*, 133.
85. Sklar, *Leviticus*, 73.
86. Tasker, *St. John*, 49.

PROLOGUE (1:1-18) 49

Finally, the phrase "we . . . all" in v. 16 points to the universality of the experience "we all" have had with Jesus. Have you ever talked with or even prayed with Christians from another country and culture, or read Christian books, perhaps written centuries ago, in another country, culture, and language? Weren't you amazed that their experience with the Savior was just the same as yours? That's because *we all* have received "grace upon grace" out of his fullness.

In this final verse, John's prologue picks up the opening notes of 1:1, that "the Word was with God and the Word was God," and reaches its stunning crescendo. Bruner illustrates this verse with a story from Donald McCullough. There was a tower in the middle of Trafalgar Square in London with a statue at the top. The statue was of Lord Admiral Nelson, the hero of the Napoleonic wars. But the monument was so high that "viewers below could not see what the honored admiral looked like." So about fifty years ago a six-foot replica was placed at eye level so people could see it close up. This is what "the high, invisible God" did by sending the eye-level Jesus.[87] God told Moses in Exod 33:20, 23, "You cannot see my face, for humans cannot see me and live . . . you will see my back, but my face will not be seen." The point seems to be that humans cannot directly encounter the essence and totality of God. There seem to be exceptions to this. We speak of *theophanies* in the Old Testament, that is, appearances of God. But, as Carson points out, they are all qualified in some way. When God confronted Moses at the burning bush, "Moses hid his face because he was afraid to look at God" (Exod 3:6). Then after Israel's terrifying encounter with God at Mount Sinai, the elders came to Moses pleading that he serve as mediator in any future visitations:

> Look, the LORD our God has shown us his glory and greatness, and we have heard his voice from the fire. Today we have seen that God speaks with a person, yet he still lives. But now, why should we die? This great fire will consume us and we will die if we hear the voice of the LORD our God any longer. For who out of all mankind has heard the voice of the living God speaking from the fire, as we have, and lived? (Deut 5:24-26)

Yet after wrestling with the angel (identified as such in Hos 12:4), Jacob had said, "I have seen God *face to face*, . . . yet my life has been spared" (Gen 32:30; emphasis added). We are told in Exod 24:9-11,

> Moses went up with Aaron, Nadab, and Abihu, and seventy of Israel's elders, and they saw the God of Israel. Beneath his feet

---

87. Bruner, *Gospel of John*, 40-41.

was something like a pavement made of lapis lazuli, as clear as the sky itself. God did not harm the Israelite nobles; they saw him, and they ate and drank.

In Num 12:6–8, God tells Moses's rebellious sister and brother,

> "If there is a prophet among you from the LORD, I make myself known to him in a vision; I speak with him in a dream. Not so with my servant Moses; he is faithful in all my household. I speak with him directly ["mouth to mouth"], openly, and not in riddles; he sees the form ["appearance, likeness, shape"] of the LORD."

Even after Israel's rebellion with the golden calf at Mount Sinai, when Moses had to set up a tent outside the camp to meet with God, in Exod 33:11 we are told, "The LORD would speak with Moses *face to face*, just as a man speaks with his friend." After Samson's father realized he had been talking with God's angel, he declared, "We're certainly going to die, . . . because we have seen God!" (Judg 13:22). These cases all describe a personal but "limited-scale" encounter with a *manifestation* of God rather than his full glorious splendor, that is, his "face."[88] The phrase "face to face," like "mouth to mouth," is evidently not the same as seeing God's face but is an idiom meaning something like "personally" or "directly."

We might suppose that the statement in John 1:18 that no one has ever seen God means that before Jesus came no one *had* ever seen God. But the statement is repeated in 1 John 4:12: "No one has ever seen God." Also, in 1 John 3:2 John wrote, "We know that when he appears, we will be like him because *we will see him as he is.*" In the future when Jesus returns, God's children will experience an even more complete encounter with God, perhaps as the angels do. Jesus says that they "continually view the face of my Father in heaven" (Matt 18:10; also see Matt 5:8, "Blessed are the pure in heart, for they will see God"; Heb 12:14, "Pursue peace with everyone, and holiness—without it no one will see the Lord"; see also John 17:24).

What, then, is John's point in 1:18? As in v. 17, the question arises, Is a contrast intended here or not? Does he mean that no one had seen God before, but now we have? The verb translated "revealed" is used elsewhere only in Luke and Acts and means to "describe at length" or "report in detail." Our term *exegesis* comes from this word. *Exegesis* is the practice of expounding the meaning of Scripture. One Greek lexicon says it means to "make fully and clearly known."[89] Leon Morris says, "It is a suggestive thought that Christ

---

88. See Stuart, *Exodus*, 709.
89. L&N, 28.41.

is the 'exegesis' of the Father."⁹⁰ Outside the Bible the word often meant to describe something that could not otherwise be known, such as a dream, or to interpret something difficult to understand, such as an obscure oracle of the gods. But didn't Moses and the other Old Testament writers make God known to us? Is Jesus just giving us further revelation about God, just as the later prophets added to the revelation given by their predecessors?

No. With the coming of Jesus, something radically different has occurred. The contrast implied in this verse is not so much that we can see God, whereas people in the Old Testament could not. The point is that unlike Moses, Isaiah, and the rest of the Old Testament prophets, Jesus not only *has* seen God in the totality of his essence (John 6:46: ". . . not that anyone has seen the Father except the one who is from God. He has seen the Father"), but Jesus has an intimate relationship with him (7:29: "I know him because I am from him, and he sent me"; cf. 8:55). Jesus, in fact, is the one and only, beloved Son of God! He is even *himself* God! Alone of anyone who has ever lived, Jesus has a perfect and total knowledge of God. Clearly, something unprecedented happened when the Word, "the one and only Son, who is himself God and is at the Father's side," became flesh.

The phrase "at the Father's side" is literally "in/on the Father's bosom/chest/lap." The word for "side" (*kolpos*) is only found six times in the New Testament, such as the reference to "Abraham's bosom" in Luke 16:22–23 and John the apostle leaning on Jesus's chest ("bosom" in KJV, NKJV, NASB) at the Last Supper (John 13:23). It might help to know that the term could also refer to a portion of the sea partially enclosed by land, as in Acts 27:39, where Paul's ship "sighted a *bay* with a beach." It speaks of protection, closeness, friendship, and affection, and "refers to the unmatched intimacy of Jesus' relationship with the Father, which enabled him to reveal the Father in an unprecedented way."⁹¹ Anthony Thiselton explains, "The Logos declared the Father with a precision which could only be exhibited by one whose dwelling was in the bosom of the Father."⁹² A second-century BC sage named Ben Sira, author of the work called Sirach or Ecclesiasticus (among the apocryphal books), wrote, "Lift up your voices to glorify the Lord, though he is still beyond your power to praise; For who can see him and describe him? or who can praise him as he is?" (Sir. 43:30–31, NAB). John the apostle here gives him the answer. Doug Stuart commented on Exod 3:6, "The fact that God eventually made himself visible *in human form* represents the highest earthly experience of seeing God (John 14:9), far

---

90. Morris, *Gospel according to John*, 114.
91. Köstenberger and Swain, *Father, Son and Spirit*, 78.
92. Anthony C. Thiselton, "ἐξηγέομαι," *NIDNTT*, 1:575.

surpassing even Moses' unusual opportunity."[93] Christ alone is "the image of the invisible God" (Col 1:15). Recordings and photographs can suffer from distortion and noise. But this new revelation of the Father that Jesus in his person has brought into the world is so effective, complete, and reliable that Jesus could tell his disciples in John 14:7–9,

> "If you know me, you will also know my Father. From now on you do know him and have seen him." "Lord," said Philip, "show us the Father, and that's enough for us." Jesus said to him, "Have I been among you all this time and you do not know me, Philip? The one who has seen me has seen the Father."

As the author of Hebrews begins, "In these last days, [God] has spoken to us by his Son," who is "the radiance of God's glory and the exact expression of his nature" (Heb 1:2–3). T. F. Torrance does a good job of capturing the melody of John's prologue:

> There is in fact no God behind the back of Jesus, no act of God other than the act of Jesus, no God but the God we see and meet in him. Jesus Christ is the open heart of God, the very love and life of God poured out to redeem humankind, the mighty hand and power of God stretched out to heal and save sinners. All things are in God's hands, but the hands of God and the hands of Jesus, in life and in death, are the same.[94]

The importance of this fact cannot be overestimated. When Torrance was an army chaplain serving in Italy during World War II, he came across a dying soldier. When he knelt beside him, the soldier asked him, "Padre, is God really like Jesus?" "I assured him that he was—the only God that there is, the God who had come to us in Jesus, shown his face to us, and poured out his love to us as our Saviour. As I prayed and commended him to the Lord Jesus, he passed away."[95]

---

93. Stuart, *Exodus*, 116 (emphasis original).
94. Torrance, *Passion for Christ*, 17; quoted in Reeves, *Rejoicing in Christ*, 15.
95. From McGrath, *Thomas F. Torrance*, 73–74, cited in Letham, *Union with Christ*, 37.

3

Introductions (1:19–51)

John's account of Jesus's ministry begins with the seven days of Jesus's first week, his "opening week." I've divided our study of Jesus's opening week into two parts. Chapter 3 will look at John's account of the introductions of Jesus and his first disciples in John 1:19–51, which spans days one through five. John gives us no information about the happenings on day six. Rather, he skips ahead to day seven, the account of the wedding in John 2:1–11. We'll look at these verses in chapter 4. According to Jörg Frey, this section I am calling "introductions" serves not only as "the entryway of the narrative," but also as an "introduction" to Johannine Christology. He even calls it a *vade mecum*, a handbook or manual to John's Christology that should be kept constantly at one's side.[1] He also explains that "by narratively presenting [to his readers] the experiences of the disciples and their reactions, in combination with various interpretive elements from the Prologue and the narrative text, the readers themselves are meant to be brought into a reading encounter with Jesus and to an understanding of his person."[2]

The rules and practices of social interaction have been revolutionized since I was born seventy years ago. We used to search the mailbox every day for a letter from a loved one or friend. Now we just check email or some other ethereal social medium. Even when I was born, the requirement of a letter of introduction for social engagement with a person of higher status had become rare. Another means of introduction common in the eighteenth and nineteenth centuries does have vestiges today: the business card, formerly referred to as a "visiting" or "calling card." A visitor to an

---

1. Frey, *Glory of the Crucified One*, 287.
2. Frey, *Glory of the Crucified One*, 288.

elegant home would be met at the door by a butler holding a silver tray on which the visitor would place his card. Only after the master of the house had accepted the card could the visitor be granted an audience.[3] During my second or third year of college, I met a freshman named William Jennings Bryan III, who presented me with his card—rather odd, I thought, but then I wasn't descended from a famous person.

Introductions in first-century Judea were pretty informal among most people. Nevertheless, John describes here several instances of introductions. First, John the Baptist has inserted himself into Judean society without approval of the Jewish leaders, so they send a delegation to obtain his credentials (1:19–28). The Baptist, in turn, introduces his audience and, in particular, two of his disciples, to the Messiah, "the Lamb of God," and they begin following Jesus (1:29–39). Andrew then introduces his brother Simon to Jesus (1:40–42). After the two brothers probably introduce their friend Philip to Jesus (1:43–44), Philip introduces his friend Nathanael, who joins Jesus's followers (1:45–51).

The first principle of a healthy Christian life might be the realization that "I'm not God."[4] I have limited abilities, responsibilities, and even worth. Even at my best, apart from him I am helpless, useless, and worthless. But in him, as an instrument in his hands and a treasured child in his family and in his heart, I can do whatever he assigns to me. Dale Bruner points out that in 1:19–28 John the Baptist declares three things that he is not, three things that he is, and then six things that Jesus is. We would do well to follow John's example. We must remember what we are not, what we are, and who he is.

Day One: The Baptist Introduces the Jewish Leaders to Jesus (1:19–28)

19 This was John's testimony when the Jews from Jerusalem sent priests and Levites to ask him, "Who are you?"
20 He didn't deny it but confessed: "I am not the Messiah."
21 "What then?" they asked him. "Are you Elijah?"
"I am not," he said.
"Are you the Prophet?"
"No," he answered.

---

3. See http://sagemedia.ca/articles/the-history-of-business-cards-four-centuries-of-introductions/ (accessed 7/8/2018).

4. This is the first of Rick Warren's "eight principles on the beatitudes," called "The Road to Recovery." This is a vital part of the Celebrate Recovery program. See https://www.celebraterecovery.com.

INTRODUCTIONS (1:19–51)

22 "Who are you, then?" they asked. "We need to give an answer to those who sent us. What can you tell us about yourself?"

23 He said, "I am a voice of one crying out in the wilderness: Make straight the way of the Lord—just as Isaiah the prophet said."

24 Now they had been sent from the Pharisees. 25 So they asked him, "Why then do you baptize if you aren't the Messiah, or Elijah, or the Prophet?"

26 "I baptize with water," John answered them. "Someone stands among you, but you don't know him. 27 He is the one coming after me, whose sandal strap I'm not worthy to untie." 28 All this happened in Bethany across the Jordan, where John was baptizing.

Here the curtain goes up and the story, whose themes are introduced in the prologue, begins. John the Baptist has been attracting quite a following (Matt 3:5), which brings the Jewish officials to check him out. In those days of Roman oppression, which was inspiring many Jewish revolutionary movements that were met with vicious military reprisals, Jewish leaders had to be on their toes.

> When the Roman army occupied a land, it was accompanied by thousands of civilians (wives, children, doctors, merchants, etc.). The army lived off the occupied country, pilfering its natural resources, enslaving members of its population, raping women and generally terrorizing the populace. The gentry of Palestine collaborated with the occupying forces and, in exchange for personal safety and affluence, aided Israel's oppressors. This collusion led to class conflict between the rich and the poor, the faithful and the unfaithful, the rulers and the people ... After the death of Herod in 4 B.C. the Jews pressed Herod's son and heir apparent, Archelaus, for a number of reforms. During the Passover, when the demands reached a feverish pitch, Archelaus sent his armies into Jerusalem and massacred thousands of worshiping pilgrims. This action catalyzed revolt in every major area of Herod's kingdom, and some of these revolts took the form of messianic movements.[5]

The Jewish leaders have sent their henchmen, lower ranking clergy John refers to as "priests and Levites." The background for the question, "Who are you?" might be furnished by Luke 3:15—"Now the people were waiting expectantly, and all of them were questioning in their hearts whether

---

5. W. J. Heard and C. A. Evans, "Revolutionary Movements, Jewish," in *DNTB*, 937-38.

John might be the Messiah." So the Jews came asking, "Who do you think you are?" John "vigorously repudiated" the rumors about himself (lit. "he confessed and did not deny and confessed"), but he did it in such a way that confirmed the rumors that there *was* a Messiah. His statement in v. 20 means, "It is not *I* who am the Messiah."[6] The term for "Messiah" here is *christos*, from the verb *chriō*, "to anoint." The Septuagint used it to translate the Hebrew word *mashiach*, "the anointed one" (whether a priest, king, or the Messiah). Like the NIV, when *christos* has the article, the CSB usually translates it "the Messiah" in the Gospels and Acts, rather than the traditional "the Christ."

After the true-false question, the Jews try a multiple-choice. The questions confirm the scholarly view that although messianic expectations were high at this time, confusion was deep regarding what *kind* of messiah to look for.[7] Would he be divine or human; a Davidic king, a reforming priest, or some kind of prophet? Many, but not all, believed he would be a warrior who would drive out the Romans. John the Baptist's denial that he was *Elijah* is surprising. Malachi had prophesied that Elijah would precede the Messiah.

> "See, I am going to send my messenger, and he will clear the way before me. Then the Lord you seek will suddenly come to his temple." (3:1)

> Look, I am going to send you the prophet Elijah before the great and terrible day of the LORD comes. And he will turn the hearts of fathers to their children and the hearts of children to their fathers." (4:5–6)

Although Jesus's statements are sometimes ambiguous, he seems to consider John to be the fulfillment of Malachi's prophecies, and the angel's message to John's father seems to confirm this.

> "And if you're willing to accept it, he is the Elijah who is to come." (Matt 11:14)

---

6. Morris, *Gospel according to John*, 133. As Frey explains, "Jesus is not only what the Baptist rejects for himself, but he is also much more" (*Glory of the Crucified One*, 287–88).

7. Daniel I. Block, for example, states, "Because the Old Testament sources span a period of one thousand years, derive from a wide geographic range, and come in a variety of literary forms (e.g., narrative, prophetic oracles, poetic verse), one doubts whether we may even speak of *an* Old Testament messianic vision, as if there were a single, universally accepted view of the messiah" ("My Servant David," in Hess and Carroll, *Israel's Messiah*, 19).

> "Elijah is coming and will restore everything," he replied. "But I tell you: Elijah has already come, and they didn't recognize him. On the contrary, they did whatever they pleased to him. In the same way the Son of Man is going to suffer at their hands." Then the disciples understood that he had spoken to them about John the Baptist. (Matt 17:11–13)

> "[John] will turn many of the children of Israel to the Lord their God. And he will go before him in the spirit and power of Elijah, to turn the hearts of fathers to their children, and the disobedient to the understanding of the righteous, to make ready for the Lord a prepared people." (Luke 1:16–17)

Several reasonable answers to this seeming inconsistency have been suggested. One is that John was denying that he was *literally* Elijah returned from heaven, as perhaps some were expecting. Also, John did not consider himself to be that important. It's at least possible he did not *know* he was the fulfillment of the Elijah prophecy. Finally, C. F. D. Moule proposes, "The Baptist humbly rejects the exalted title, but Jesus, on the contrary, bestows it on him. Why should not the two both be correct?"[8] After all, as Morris says, "No man is what he is in his own eyes. He really is only as he is known to God."[9]

The next option the Jews give John is that he is "the Prophet." This likely refers to Moses's prophecy that "the LORD your God will raise up for you a prophet like me from among your own brothers" (Deut 18:15). There was considerable debate about the kind of person(s) this referred to: Messiah, Jeremiah, a prophet in the last days, etc.[10]

Since John had answered "none of the above," the Jews finally gave him a discussion question: "Who are you then?" John knew that his purpose was to point to the Messiah, not to himself, and to urge people to prepare for his coming. So he answered with a quote from Isa 40:3, which speaks of an unidentified voice calling on a distressed and discouraged people to believe that the God of all comfort is coming to them: "I'm no more than a voice crying out in the wilderness." John is the poster child for a Christian witness to Jesus. Katie Barclay Wilkinson was a British hymn writer born in 1859. Little is known of her life except that she ministered to young women in

---

8. Cited in Morris, *Gospel according to John*, 135.
9. Morris, *Gospel according to John*, 135.
10. See Block, "My Servant David," in Hess and Carroll, *Israel's Messiah*, 26–32, and responses in the same volume by J. Daniel Hays, "If He Looks Like a Prophet and Talks Like a Prophet," 57–69; and M. Daniel Carroll R., "New Lenses to Establish Messiah's Identity?" 72–78.

London. She is primarily known for one hymn she wrote, based on Phil 2:5: "May the Mind of Christ My Saviour." We might imagine John the Baptist singing it every morning in the shower.

> 1. May the mind of Christ my Saviour
> Live in me from day to day,
> By his love and power controlling
> All I do and say.
>
> 2. May the word of God dwell richly
> In my heart from hour to hour
> So that all may see I triumph
> Only through his power.
>
> 3. May the peace of God my Father
> Rule my life in everything
> That I may be calm to comfort
> Sick and sorrowing.
>
> 4. May the love of Jesus fill me
> As the waters fill the sea;
> Him exalting, self abasing,
> This is victory.
>
> 5. May I run the race before me
> Strong and brave to face the foe,
> Looking only unto Jesus
> As I onward go.
>
> 6. May his beauty rest upon me
> As I seek the lost to win
> And may they forget the channel
> Seeing only him.[11]

Verse 24 is a bit ambiguous. Verse 19 had said "the Jews from Jerusalem" had sent some "priests and Levites." Verse 24 can be translated "Now they had been sent from the Pharisees" (CSB, NASB, NRSV, ESV, TEV). But another way to understand v. 24 is that the "priests and Levites" who were *sent* were Pharisees (KJV, NKJV, NJB) or that *some* of them were (NIV, NAB, GW). This last understanding probably fits best the historical situation.[12]

---

11. https://hymnary.org/text/may_the_mind_of_christ_my_savior#media (accessed 1/28/2019).

12. See Klink, *John*, 130–31, for this understanding.

Pharisees appear eighty-five times in the Gospels, including nineteen times in John, so a word about them might be helpful.[13] They were a religio-political reform party originating during the "intertestamental period" in Judea. When the Old Testament closes, Judah was a Persian province. Then Philip of Macedonia united Greece, and his son Alexander conquered the Persian empire from the eastern Mediterranean all the way to India. He spread Greek language and culture everywhere he went. When he died in 323 BC, his generals fought over the empire and split it into a northern part ruled from Syrian Antioch by the Seleucids, and a southern part ruled from Alexandria in Egypt by the Ptolemies. The Ptolemies ruled Palestine at first and didn't cause the Jews much trouble. But when the Seleucids took over in 198 BC, things began to change.

When Antiochus IV became king in 175 BC, he severely increased taxation and demanded that the Jews adopt Greek culture (Hellenization). He even proclaimed himself God and started calling himself "Epiphanes" ("divine manifestation"). He began selling the high priesthood to the highest bidder. A group of pious Jews called *Ḥasidim* began to speak out and agitate against the Seleucids. In retribution, in 167 BC Antiochus massacred about 40,000 Jews on the Sabbath (when they wouldn't fight back). He also entered the Jewish temple, looted it, and renamed it, dedicating it to Zeus. He even set up a pagan altar there and sacrificed a pig on it. He also prohibited circumcision and Sabbath observance and banned and burned copies of the Torah.

This led to the Maccabean Revolt in 167 BC, which resulted in eighty years of Jewish independence from 142 to 63 BC. But the descendants of Judas Maccabeus set up a dynasty of priest-kings, known as the Hasmoneans, who became corrupt and power hungry and gave up their opposition to Hellenization. So the *Ḥasidim* arose again, and probably out of that movement came the Pharisees ("separatists"). One of the Hasmonean rulers, Alexander Jannaeus (103–76 BC), even had more than 800 Pharisees crucified for protesting his policies. Eventually, an internal power struggle resulted in the Romans taking over in 63 BC.

One religio-political party known as Sadducees supported the Hasmoneans and later the Romans. They were wealthy aristocrats, and such collusion was to their advantage. This set them against the more numerous Pharisees (perhaps about 6,000 at the time of Jesus, compared to a population of about 500,000), who were laymen and were very popular with the common people. Many Sadducees, on the other hand, were from priestly families (their name is related to "Zadokites"), and they were in charge of

---

13. See Blomberg, *Jesus and the Gospels*, 15–20, 48–52.

the temple. They also held a large majority on the Sanhedrin, the Jewish legislative and judicial body ideally comprising seventy-one members and led by the high priest, who was appointed by the Romans.

The Pharisees controlled most of the synagogues and also had members on the Sanhedrin. Although somewhat diverse in views and practices (for example, the more lenient Hillelites and the hard-liner Shammaites), they aimed at achieving God's favor by purifying the people and getting them to follow the law meticulously, in preparation for a messianic teacher of the law and for divine intervention. They believed the law covered every area of life, if properly interpreted, and that they were the authoritative interpreters of it through their knowledge of the oral law ("the tradition of the elders"). This oral law came from Moses, they claimed, and provided "a fence around the Torah." The scribes (mentioned fifty-seven times in the Gospels, though only once in John) were their Torah scholars. According to the *Mishnah* (a collection of the oral laws written down about AD 200), "It is more culpable to teach against the ordinances of the scribes than against the Torah itself" (*Sanh.* 11.3). In general, the Pharisees "sought to live as if they were priests and as if the laws that applied to the priests in the temple applied to ordinary Jews in their homes."[14] They were especially zealous about dietary laws, the Sabbath, circumcision, and tithing. The Pharisees believed in the bodily resurrection, future rewards and punishments according to one's works, angels and demons, etc. Later Rabbinic Judaism arose primarily from the Pharisees.

The Sadducees, on the other hand, who are mentioned only nine times in the Gospels and not at all in John, rejected the oral law and believed that doctrine must come only from the Pentateuch. So they rejected immortality and bodily resurrection, future rewards and punishments, and angels and demons.

It was the Pharisees who asked John about his baptizing in v. 25. Notice that the writer assumes his readers know about John's baptizing, although he hasn't mentioned it. What John was doing was evidently extraordinary for at least two reasons. One is that the kind of baptism people were most familiar with was for Gentiles converting to Judaism. Why was John baptizing *Jews*? The second reason is that in other baptism practices the person baptized *himself*. The Pharisees reasoned, therefore, that John must be claiming to be some kind of messianic teacher of the Law, who was announcing the last days.[15] So his denials puzzled them.

---

14. Witherington, *New Testament History*, 46.
15. See Carson, *Gospel according to John*, 145.

John's answer in vv. 26-27 dismisses the importance of his own ministry of water baptism and directs attention to another, about whom he says four things: (1) this person stands (lit.) "in the middle of you"; (2) the Jews did not recognize him; (3) he is the one whom John came to announce; and (4) John's importance relative to him is like that of the lowest slave to his master. Among the Jews a student was to serve his teacher like a slave—with the exception of taking off his shoes.[16]

An interesting illustration of Jesus's lack of recognition occurred in Washington, D.C., on a Friday in January 2007. During the morning rush hour, world famous violinist Joshua Bell, who, according to composer John Corigliano, "plays like a god," played six classical masterpieces for forty-three minutes in a subway station. He was playing on a violin handcrafted in 1713 by Antonio Stradivari that was worth 3.5 million dollars. Bell played beside a trash basket at the top of an escalator dressed as a homeless man. Three days before, he had played at a sold-out concert at Boston's Symphony Hall where tickets averaged $100. Here more than a thousand people passed by Bell, but only seven stopped to listen. A three-year-old boy named Evan was one of many children who were intrigued and tried to stop. But his mother was in a hurry and dragged him off. One man who passed four feet from Bell didn't even hear him. He had buds in his ears, listening to his iPod. Only one person recognized Joshua Bell. Stacy Furukawa had seen him play three weeks earlier at the Library of Congress. She didn't come until near the end, but she planted herself ten feet from Bell and listened to the rest of the concert with a huge grin on her face. Twenty-seven people dropped money into Bell's violin case that morning, and he collected $32.17 for his efforts—$20 of that came from Stacy Furukawa.[17] If Jesus, the Savior of the world, had been preaching in that subway station, would the response have been different? Would I have stopped to listen? Did I stop to listen to him speaking to me this morning?

We might be tempted to skip over v. 28 as having little significance beyond concluding the account of John and the Jewish leaders. The events that John's Gospel is relating happened "in Bethany across the Jordan." So what? In the first place, Bethany was a real place, probably the region of Batanaea, called Bashan in the Old Testament, although a more precise location is not given.[18] The Bible stories never start with "Once upon a time, in a land

---

16. See Carson, *Gospel according to John*, 146.

17. https://www.washingtonpost.com/lifestyle/magazine/pearls-before-breakfast-can-one-of-the-nations-great-musicians-cut-through-the-fog-of-a-dc-rush-hour-lets-find-out/2014/09/23/8a6d46da-4331-11e4-b47c-f5889e061e5f_story.html?utm_term=.25de2ad25c5b (accessed 8/22/2018).

18. See Rainer Riesner, "Bethany beyond the Jordan," *AYBD*, 1:703-5.

far, far away." They also never end, "And they lived happily ever after." We are dealing with real people and real history and geography that could have been verified by going to the place.

In the second place, unlike the Bethany near Jerusalem where Lazarus lived and where Jesus ended his ministry, this Bethany was outside Israel proper, on the east side of the Jordan River, in the region known as Transjordan (see John 10:40). John the Baptist refers to it as the wilderness where Isaiah had prophesied that a voice would cry out for repentance (1:23). The word translated "wilderness" occurs about 250 times in the Old Testament and often represents a place of suffering and exile, where no one wanted to go. But it was also often a place of redemption and renewal.[19] It was a place where many people—like Hagar, Jacob, Moses, the nation of Israel, David, Elijah, Paul the apostle—met with God. In Hos 2:14-23, God says he is going to move adulterous Israel into the wilderness where he could "persuade her . . . and speak tenderly to her . . . There she will respond as she did in the days of her youth, as in the day she came out of the land of Egypt . . . I will take you to be my wife in faithfulness, and you will know the LORD." Israel's hope was sometimes described as a wilderness becoming a garden:

> For the palace will be deserted, the busy city abandoned. The hill and the watchtower will become barren places forever, the joy of wild donkeys, and a pasture for flocks, until the Spirit from on high is poured out on us. Then the desert will become an orchard, and the orchard will seem like a forest. Then justice will inhabit the wilderness, and righteousness will dwell in the orchard. The result of righteousness will be peace; the effect of righteousness will be quiet confidence forever. Then my people will dwell in a peaceful place, in safe and secure dwellings. (Isa 32:14-18)

Many of God's people in the present as well as the past can testify to how God sustained them in a time of "wilderness wandering" and accomplished a great work of redemption and rebirth in their life. As Ed Welch points out, "This desert is where water comes from rocks and manna appears every morning. It is also where the Lord tests and trains his royal children."[20] Jesus's redemptive work, in fact, began with his entering our wilderness to initiate his battle with the devil (Matt 4:1-11//Luke 4:1-13). Such redemptive resonances are surely part of the background for John calling on the Jews to leave their homes in Israel and cross the Jordan into the wilderness to rediscover their God and experience cleansing and a new creation.

---

19. See Garrett, *Hosea, Joel*, 88-91.
20. Welch, *Caring for One Another*, 53.

Bauckham points out another significance of the mention of Bethany in v. 28. It suggests a parallel between Jesus's opening week, which began in a "Bethany across the Jordan," and his passion week, which began in the other Bethany near Jerusalem, "the village of Mary and her sister Martha" (John 11:1). Jesus's return to Bethany across the Jordan, "the place where John had been baptizing earlier" (John 10:40), a place of relative safety in the region under Philip's control, marks the end of his time of what Carson calls "Self-Disclosure in Word and Deed" (1:19–10:42), and "many believed in him there" (10:42). Following this time, Jesus's movement to the other Bethany began his journey to the cross.[21]

Day Two: The Baptist Introduces His Disciples to Jesus (1:29–34)

> 29 *The next day John saw Jesus coming toward him and said, "Here is the Lamb of God, who takes away the sin of the world! 30 This is the one I told you about: 'After me comes a man who ranks ahead of me, because he existed before me.' 31 I didn't know him, but I came baptizing with water so he might be revealed to Israel." 32 And John testified, "I saw ["watched"] the Spirit descending from heaven like a dove, and he rested ["remained"] on him. 33 I didn't know him, but he who sent me to baptize with water told me, 'The one you see the Spirit descending and resting ["remaining"] on—he is the one who baptizes with the Holy Spirit.' 34 I have seen and testified that this is the Son [or "Chosen One"] of God."*

Bruner calls v. 29 "the Mount Everest of John's witness to Christ."[22] Yet it's precipitated not by John taking people to Jesus, but by Jesus coming to him. When the Baptist saw Jesus, he pointed. That's the significance of the term *ide*, translated "Here is." It occurs fifteen times in John and only fourteen times elsewhere. The Greek lexicon says it's "a marker of strong emphasis" and might be paraphrased, "Look! What do you know! Of all things! Wonder of wonders!"[23] Pilate uses it when he parades Jesus's beaten, humiliated figure before the crowd and says, "Here is your king!" (19:14). But how did John know this was Jesus the Messiah? Verses 31, 33 stress that John only learned it when he baptized Jesus earlier, although John's Gospel does not describe the event. In fact, the Baptist says that the main reason God sent

---

21. See Bauckham, *Gospel of Glory*, 138–39.
22. Bruner, *Gospel of John*, 80.
23. BDAG, 468.

him to baptize was so that he might baptize Jesus and so reveal Jesus to Israel.

Prior to this, John the apostle has already given us an amazing set of terms describing Jesus: the Word, God, life, (the true) light, the one and only Son, Jesus Christ, the Lord, and the one coming after John the Baptist. In fact, twelve of John's nineteen Christological titles for Jesus occur in this first chapter.[24] But the understanding of the first disciples was not so elaborate. Besides someone coming after John, they were first introduced to him as the Lamb of God. But what did the Baptist mean by "the Lamb of God"? The phrase occurs nowhere else but this passage. Our understanding of it is based on much more information than the Baptist probably had. His discouragement and doubt described in Matt 11:2-15 suggest that he did not expect Jesus's sacrificial death on the cross. Carson comments, "Not only may the Baptist have become demoralized, like his namesake Elijah, but the Baptist had preached in terms of imminent blessing and judgment. By contrast Jesus was preaching in veiled fulfillment terms and bringing much blessing but no real judgment, and as a result the Baptist was having second thoughts."[25]

Several suggestions have been made on the possible background to the Baptist's phrase, "the Lamb of God." The first two are probably the most widely held: (1) the Passover lamb (Exodus 12); (2) the "lamb led to the slaughter" from Isa 53:7; (3) the lamb of the daily sacrifices; (4) "docile lamb led to slaughter" of Jer 11:19; (5) the scapegoat; (6) the lamb substituted for Isaac in Genesis 22; (7) the guilt offering that was sometimes a lamb; and (8) the triumphant lamb of Revelation (5:6-13; 6:1, 16; 7:9-17; 12:11; 13:8; 14:1-10; 15:3; 17:14; 19:7-9; 21:22-23; 22:1-3). Morris proposed a "composite" view of all these.[26] Ridderbos suggests that coming after John's meeting with the temple authorities, he might be implying that "in place of and as the fulfillment of the continual sacrificial lamb in the temple service, God himself is now, once and for all, providing the true ("eschatological")

---

24. See Bauckham's chart in *Gospel of Glory*, p. 161.

25. See Carson, "Matthew," comments on Matt 11:2-3.

26. See Morris, *Gospel according to John*, 144-48. Elsewhere, he wrote, "I am convinced that the term is vague of set purpose, so that the allusion is not to be tied down to any one sacrifice, be it passover, or sin offering, or any other. It is a way of bringing before the mind the sacrificial system as a whole" (*Cross in the New Testament*, 175). Peter M. Head agrees: "It seems likely that John has deliberately used an ambiguous term, in order to maintain that Jesus' death fulfils and displaces all the OT sacrifices, by dealing finally with sin" ("Christ as Sacrifice in Gospels and Acts," in Beckwith and Selman, *Sacrifice in the Bible*, 122).

Lamb."²⁷ Carson's view is that John likely had the triumphant lamb of Revelation in mind.

> The impression gleaned from the Synoptics is that he thought of the Messiah as one who would come in terrible judgment and clean up the sin in Israel. In this light, what John the Baptist meant by "who takes away the sin of the world" may have had more to do with judgment and destruction than with expiatory sacrifice. Certainly the verb *airō* normally means "remove," "take away," not "bear away in atoning death,"

for which another more common verb was used.²⁸ Nevertheless, Carson notes that John used the same word for "lamb" found in the LXX of Isa 53:7 and that John's Gospel quotes from Isaiah several times. Carson also proposes that, like the high priest Caiaphas in John 11:49-52, John "spoke better than he knew." So, with Morris, we may understand Jesus as the fulfillment of all those "lambs" that have been proposed. Bauckham, on the other hand, argues on the basis of verbal links that the primary Old Testament passages alluded to by the Baptist are Exod 12:3; Isa 53:7, 11-12; and also Gen 22:8. The latter connection is intriguing. Bauckham points out that although Abraham assures Isaac, "God himself will provide the lamb for the burnt offering" (using the word *seh*, "lamb," as in Exod 12:3 and Isa 53:7), what God actually provided (v. 13) was "a ram caught in the thicket by its horns," using the term *'ayil*, "ram." This was the animal that Abraham offered "as a burnt offering in place of his son." As Bauckham says, "Only one lamb in the Hebrew Bible is said to be provided by God: the lamb of Gen. 22:8." And only Jesus is said to be "the lamb of God," "the ultimate substitute for Isaac on the altar."²⁹

We should also not miss four additional facts expressed by the Baptist in vv. 29-30. First, Jesus came not just for the Jewish race but for "the world" that was in rebellion against him. Second, Jesus did not just happen to deal with sin while he was here on other business. He was the Lamb *of God*, sent

---

27. Ridderbos, *Gospel of John*, 73.

28. See Carson, *Gospel according to John*, 148-51, especially p. 150. Bauckham notes that "he bore the sin of many" in Isa 53:12 uses the Hebrew verb נָשָׂא, which can mean either "lift up" or "take away." Although the Septuagint translated it with ἀναφέρω, "offer up, bear," John used αἴρω, which was a better match for the ambiguity of נָשָׂא. Bauckham thinks it "likely that John intends both meanings." He also notes the use of נָשָׂא in Isa 52:13: the suffering Servant will be "*lifted up* and greatly exalted." The lifting up of Jesus in John describes both his literal lifting up on the cross and his exaltation (3:14; 8:28; 12:32-34). Thus, "the Lamb of God will remove the sin of the world by lifting it up with him when he is lifted up on the cross" (*Gospel of Glory*, 157).

29. Bauckham, *Gospel of Glory*, 156.

for that very purpose. Third, Jesus did not come to deal with "sins" but with "sin"—the whole thing once and for all. He won't stop until sin itself is gone. And fourth, the Baptist confirms that Jesus really is "a man."

Verses 32–33 contain the first three of nineteen references to the Spirit in this Gospel. Jesus will talk about the Spirit being God's gift who brings new birth, life, and truth, as well as encouragement, exhortation, and help as our Paraclete. Here we learn of the Spirit's work of pointing to Jesus and working through Jesus. The other Gospels add that the Spirit would also lead (Matt 4:1) and empower Jesus (Matt 12:28; Luke 4:14; Acts 10:38). Luke 1:35 tells us the Spirit was even responsible for Jesus's becoming flesh.

G. R. Beasley-Murray suggests that John's baptizing "was viewed by him in a manner comparable to the acts of prophetic symbolism performed by the prophets who were before him."[30] Jesus's baptism by John, he says, "demonstrated and effected his solidarity with sinful men." It also gave opportunity for the opening of heaven and the divine voice to indicate that the Messianic kingdom and the age of the Spirit had dawned.

The Baptist's statement in v. 32, "I saw [or "watched"] the Spirit" is striking, and that the Spirit "rested" (better "remained") on him is puzzling. How could he see the Spirit, and what did he mean by "remain"? What exactly did the Baptist see? Did he see a dove fly down and light on Jesus's shoulder like Captain Flint, the parrot who perched on Long John Silver, the pirate in *Treasure Island*? The Spirit remaining on Jesus at least suggests the theological truth that Jesus's possession of the Spirit was permanent. It also fulfilled Isaiah's prophecies about the Messiah in 11:2; 42:1; and 61:1:

> The Spirit of the LORD will rest on him—a Spirit of wisdom and understanding, a Spirit of counsel and strength, a Spirit of knowledge and of the fear of the LORD. (11:2)

> This is my servant; I strengthen him, this is my chosen one; I delight in him. I have put my Spirit on him; he will bring justice to the nations. (42:1)

> The Spirit of the Lord GOD is on me, because the LORD has anointed me to bring good news to the poor. He has sent me to heal the brokenhearted, to proclaim liberty to the captives and freedom to the prisoners. (61:1)

John 3:34 ("For the one whom God sent speaks God's words, since he gives the Spirit without measure") probably means that "Jesus utters the words of God *because* God gives *him* the Spirit without measure" (contrasted with

---

30. G. R. Beasley-Murray, "βάπτω," *NIDNTTE*, 1:463.

the prophets on whom the Spirit rested "only by measure").[31] Matthew 3:16, Mark 1:10, and Luke 3:22 tell us "the heavens opened/split," although John only tells us the Spirit descended "from heaven." The opening of the heavens signifies a literally earth-shaking divine intervention. Israel had prayed for just this to happen (Isa 63:18–64:1):

> Your holy people had a possession for a little while, but our enemies have trampled down your sanctuary. We have become like those you never ruled, like those who did not bear your name. If only you would tear the heavens open and come down, so that mountains would quake at your presence.

As John Oswalt explains in his commentary on Isaiah,

> Although the Creator is other than his creation, he can break into it at any point, and when he does lightning flashes, thunder rolls, and the earth shakes. In the voice of his deeply discouraged people, Isaiah cries out for God to do it again. Nothing else but God's direct intervention can break the power of the people's sin and make them a witness to the nations instead of a laughingstock.[32]

Yet for 400 years, God had been silent and hidden. Then suddenly at Jesus's baptism, God showed up. Whatever people saw and heard that day, we must not miss the significance of what happened. Matthew and Mark tell us *Jesus* saw the Spirit descending or coming "upon him like a dove," but that does not mean no one else saw something. Luke just says that the Spirit descended "in a physical appearance like a dove" (3:22), perhaps suggesting that everyone saw it. The comparison to a dove, however, could be either to the way the Spirit descended or to his appearance. Gerhard Hasel suggested that the reference to a dove alludes to Gen 1:2. He based this on a rabbinical tradition that "the Spirit of God was brooding on the face of the waters like a dove which broods over her young but does not touch them."[33] Others suggest the dove alludes to Noah's dove in Gen 8:11 and symbolizes "a herald or trustworthy messenger . . . and bearer of good tidings."[34]

The other Gospels also tell of an audible message from the Father. Mark and Luke give the message as "You are my beloved Son," suggesting that perhaps only Jesus heard it, but Matthew's "This is my beloved Son" suggests that perhaps others heard it too, especially the Baptist, although

---

31. M. M. B. Turner, "Holy Spirit," *DJG*, 347 (emphasis original).
32. Oswalt, *Isaiah Chapters 40–66*, 620–21.
33. Cited by Carson, *Gospel according to John*, 153.
34. Turner, "Holy Spirit," 345.

John's Gospel does not mention it at all. The only message from God in this account came directly to the Baptist earlier: "The one you see the Spirit descending and resting on—he is the one who baptizes with the Holy Spirit" (v. 33).

Verse 33 strongly contrasts John's water baptism with Jesus's Spirit baptism, explaining that Jesus is "the one who baptizes," a phrase used elsewhere only of John (Mark 1:4; 6:14, 24).[35] Klink points out, "John, unlike the Synoptics, never calls John 'the Baptist.' . . . For the Gospel of John, only Jesus is the Baptist. And true baptism can only be performed with the Holy Spirit. Jesus is the one who baptizes, and he will do so 'with the Holy Spirit.'"[36] According to Beasley-Murray, "The baptism of John had, therefore, two focal points: it marked the 'turn' (repentance means conversion) of a Jew to God, associating him with the penitent people and assuring him of forgiveness and cleansing, and it anticipated the Messianic baptism with Spirit and fire, assuring him a place in the Kingdom."[37]

Morris points out that whereas John's baptism was essentially negative, involving cleansing, Jesus's baptism with the Spirit would be positive, involving "the bestowal of new life in God."[38] Although the Spirit worked in people in Old Testament times, bestowing abilities (Exod 31:3; Num 11:17; 24:2; 27:18; Judg 3:10; 6:34; 14:6; 1 Sam 16:13; Neh 9:30), because of Jesus the Spirit has brought an infinite supply of "divine spiritual resources." As the Lamb removes our main problem—sin—the Dove provides our main resource—the Spirit.[39] Other than its external features, then, there seems to be very little similarity between John's baptism and that of the church after Jesus's death and resurrection.

A baptism by Jesus with the Holy Spirit (and fire) is also referred to in Matt 3:11; Mark 1:8; Luke 3:16; Acts 1:5; 11:16; 1 Cor 12:13. In John 7:38–39 Jesus would compare the coming Spirit to "streams of living water" flowing from "deep within." The Gospel writer explained, "Those who believed in Jesus were going to receive the Spirit, for the Spirit had not yet been given because Jesus had not yet been glorified." In Acts 1:4–5 Jesus described the coming baptism with the Spirit as "the Father's promise," perhaps referring to Ezek 36:26–27 and Joel 2:28–29. This baptism happened for the first time on the day of Pentecost when the Spirit "came on" believers with power,

---

35. The Greek phrase, ὁ βαπτίζων, used here, however, is not the usual phrase (found in Matthew, Mark, and Luke) translated "the Baptist," which is ὁ βαπτιστὴς, meaning "the baptizer."

36. Klink, *John*, 136.

37. Beasley-Murray, "βάπτω," *NIDNTTE*, 1:463.

38. Morris, *Gospel according to John*, 153.

39. See Bruner, *Gospel of John*, 88.

making them Jesus's witnesses (Acts 1:8). The Spirit is also said to have "filled" the believers that day (2:4), but also later (4:8, 31). Evidently, baptism with the Spirit happens only once, but filling can be repeated.[40]

The question of when the baptism of the Spirit occurs in the life of a believer is a bit unclear in Acts due to "Luke's desire to highlight groundbreaking historical events rather than describe normative patterns for receiving the Spirit."[41] On the basis of Acts 19:2 ("Did you receive the Holy Spirit when you believed?"), some believe Spirit baptism occurs after salvation, perhaps at water baptism. The situation there, however, is unique in that Paul was addressing a group of followers of John the Baptist who were still anticipating the coming Messiah. Some also argue from Peter's sermon in Acts 2, where he said, "Repent and be baptized, each of you, in the name of Jesus Christ for the forgiveness of your sins, and you will receive the gift of the Holy Spirit" (Acts 2:38). Some claim this implies that water baptism is necessary for receiving the Spirit. But what he says only amounts to an exhortation and a promise. He does not say when the promise will be fulfilled. If the Spirit only comes after water baptism, then that would apply also to forgiveness. The fact that both the command to "repent" and the promise, "you will receive," are plural, whereas the exhortation to be baptized is singular ("let each of you be baptized") suggests the promise actually follows from the *command* to repent. Also, in Acts 10 when Peter preached the gospel of Christ to some Gentiles, they believed and were baptized with the Spirit "while Peter was still speaking" (Acts 10:44). Then Peter said, "Can anyone withhold water and prevent these people from being baptized, who have received the Holy Spirit just as we have?" (v. 47). Clearly water baptism is not required for a person to receive the Spirit.

Paul seems to indicate even more clearly that Spirit baptism occurs at the time of conversion and new birth when a person first trusts Christ for salvation. He says in 1 Cor 12:13, "For we were all baptized by [better "with"] one Spirit into one body—whether Jews or Greeks, whether slaves or free—and we were all given one Spirit to drink." This could only be true if "we all," that is, believers, were baptized with the Spirit at the moment we exercise saving faith. Otherwise, there would have been some in Paul's audience of readers who had not yet been baptized by the Spirit. Bruner charges that withholding the gift of the Spirit for a later "second blessing" is "simply the circumcision heresy in new dress."[42]

---

40. See Stott, *Baptism and Fullness*, 48.
41. Personal communication from Timothy J. Wiarda.
42. Bruner, *Gospel of John*, 89.

The final verse of this section (John 1:34) reads like the Baptist's epitaph from his own lips: "I have seen and testified that this is the Son of God." Again he displays the divine assignment given to every follower of Christ merely to testify to what we have seen and heard (Acts 1:8). This is what John the apostle has done (John 19:35; 1 John 1:2) and what Paul the apostle was to do (Acts 22:15; 26:16).

We must recognize a significant difference among the manuscripts in how this verse is worded. Although the majority have "the Son [*huios*] of God," some of the earliest manuscripts have "the Chosen One [*eklektos*] of God," a Messianic term also found in Luke 23:35 (also Isa 42:1; Matt 12:18; Luke 9:35; 1 Pet 2:4). The question of which word is original is not easy to answer. Although most translations follow the majority and have "Son," the NIV, NLT, and a few others (NJB, NET, REB) have "Chosen One." The term is clearly an appropriate one for Jesus and could have been what the Baptist said. Bauckham argues that it alludes to the messianic prophecy in Isa 42:1 (emphasis added): "This is my servant; I strengthen him, this is *my chosen one*; I delight in him. I have put my Spirit on him; he will bring justice to the nations."[43] Certainly, the identity of Jesus as the Son of God does not rest on this verse, so a lack of certainty on the issue should not disturb us.

Day Three: The First Two Disciples Follow Jesus (1:35–39)

> 35 The next day, John was standing with two of his disciples. 36 When he saw Jesus passing by, he said, "Look, the Lamb of God!"
>
> 37 The two disciples heard him say this and followed Jesus. 38 When Jesus turned and noticed them following him, he asked them, "What are you looking for?"
>
> They said to him, "Rabbi" (which means "Teacher"), "where are you staying?"
>
> 39 "Come and you'll see," he replied. So they went and saw where he was staying, and they stayed with him that day. It was about four in the afternoon.

As Carson points out, these first disciples of Jesus represent those who received him, believing in his name and becoming children of God (John 1:12).[44] This account of Jesus meeting his first disciples, however, should not

---

43. See Bauckham, *Gospel of Glory*, 158.
44. Carson, *Gospel according to John*, 157.

be confused with the account of Jesus calling his disciples in the Synoptic Gospels (Matt 4:18-22; 9:9; Mark 1:16-20; 2:13-14; Luke 5:1-11, 27-28). The accounts there make the most sense if Jesus has met these men previously. That seems to be what is taking place in John.

The verb "follow" is used four times in this chapter, in vv. 37, 38, 40, and finally in v. 43 when Jesus tells Philip, "Follow me." The Christian life of faith and discipleship is called "following Jesus" in the Gospels many times (about thirty times in Matthew and fifteen times in John), although it only occurs outside the Gospels in Rev 14:4 ("These are the ones who follow the Lamb wherever he goes"). Jesus uses the image of sheep following their shepherd in John 10:4, 5, 27, and elsewhere of a servant following his master (12:26). In the Old Testament the idea of "following" is expressed as "going after."[45] It's used of servants attending their masters (1 Kgs 19:20-21; Ruth 1:16) and many times of people looking for help from other gods by serving and worshiping them (Deut 4:3; 6:14; 8:19; Judg 2:19; 2 Kgs 17:15; Jer 2:5; 8:2; 13:10; 16:11; 25:6; 35:15; Hos 2:5, etc.). Less frequently, Israel is exhorted to follow the Lord (Deut 13:4; 1 Kgs 14:8; 2 Kgs 23:3; 2 Chr 34:31-33). It describes a life of submission, dependence, and devotion. As Bauckham points out from John 13:36-38, however, these first disciples could not fully "follow" Jesus until after his death and resurrection, for to do so would mean that the disciple "hates his life in this world" (John 12:25). Although these men began to follow Jesus in one sense during his opening week, they could not yet follow Jesus fully until after his final week, as reflected in Jesus's echoing call to Peter in the epilogue to "follow me" (21:19, 22). Bauckham, however, notes that in 6:66, John does not use the term "follow" of the disciples who "turned back," but rather says that they had just been "accompan[ying] him" (the verb *peripateō*).[46]

When Jesus notices Andrew and his friend (probably John the author) behind him, he asks them a question we all hear often when we enter a store or restaurant. It takes many forms that all mean something like, "Why are you here?" They say, "What can I do for you?" "Can I help you?" "What can I get started for you?" "Are you finding what you need?" A restaurant host/hostess usually asks, "How many?" I was a bit offended when my wife and I recently entered a somewhat upscale, artsy restaurant and were asked "Can I help you?" as if they thought we were in the wrong place! But on the lips of Jesus the question probably carries more weight than that in a store or restaurant. Like God's question in the garden of Eden ("Where are you?"), Jesus, the epitome of the skilled investigator fishing for the truth or

---

45. Hb. הָלַךְ, "go, walk," with אַחַר, "after."
46. Bauckham, *Gospel of Glory*, 145-47.

inspiring self-examination, asks, "What are you looking for?" The answer seems obvious to us, as when Jesus walks by some blind men pleading for mercy and stops to ask them, "What do you want me to do for you?" But Jesus seems to be probing.

My friend and editor colleague, David Stabnow, gives the example of a homeless man begging at a bus station. When someone hands him a twenty-dollar bill, he goes to the vending machines only to discover they don't accept twenties. An angel comes up behind him and says, "Can I help you?" The man replies, "Can you make change?" The angel could have "changed" him for the better, but all he was looking for was to break a twenty. Here's another example from Dave:

> A guy was totally convicted. He realized that for his whole life he had only lived for himself and what pleasure he could find, with no concern for the feelings of others. He had cheated in school to get good grades, and he lied on his resume to get a good job. He had put on a facade of respectability to marry a nice girl, and then he cheated on her. Now his conscience was attacking him, and he saw that his whole life was a lie, a sham. The only solution he could think of was suicide. So he was down by the ocean, staring at the roaring surf, working up the courage to throw himself between the waves and the rocks. As he stood there, with the waves pounding and the wind whistling, the angel of the Lord walked up to him and asked, "Can I do something for you?"
>
> Startled, the man replied, "Pardon me?"[47]

The angel could have "pardoned" him, but he didn't really ask.

Jesus's question uses a verb that in various contexts can mean to "seek, search for, look for, try to find (out), investigate, research, desire, wish for, try to obtain, aim for, intend, try to do, request, demand." I recently learned about a new personality test, called the enneagram, that categorizes people into nine types.[48] Each type has, among other things, a set of goals.

1. The *Reformer* wants "To be good, to have integrity, to be balanced."
2. The *Helper* want to "feel loved."
3. The *Achiever* wants to "feel valuable and worthwhile."

---

47. I'm grateful to my colleague David S. Stabnow for alerting me to the profoundness of Jesus's questions and for providing these two illustrations of how we might miss God's offer to do for us more than we expect.

48. See www.enneagraminstitute.com © 2017 The Enneagram Institute. Quoted with permission. I was alerted to this by my counselor friend, Pike Williams.

4. The *Individualist* wants to "find themselves and their significance (to create an identity)"
5. The *Investigator* wants to "be capable and competent."
6. The *Loyalist* wants to "have security and support."
7. The *Enthusiast* wants to "be satisfied and content—to have their needs fulfilled."
8. The *Challenger* wants to "protect themselves (to be in control of their own life and destiny)."
9. The *Peacemaker* wants to "have inner stability, 'peace of mind.'"

One of the keys to good Bible study is to have things in mind that you're looking for—questions to ask. If we're not looking for anything when we read the Bible, we aren't likely to find anything. "Ready, fire, aim!" is not a very effective process. The same might be true of our lives. We often hear that "everybody's looking for something," regardless of whether we realize what it is. It may be something eternally valuable, but it also might be something ultimately useless. The U2 song, "I Still Haven't Found What I'm Looking For," may reflect the thoughts of someone who's been looking for the wrong things in the wrong places. Jesus deals often in this Gospel with people who are hungry or thirsty, two universal symbols of human need. In John 6:27, Jesus said to the crowd he had just miraculously fed, "Don't work for the food that perishes but for the food that lasts for eternal life, which the Son of Man will give you." Craig Koester explains, "Those who make perishable food [or anything else] the ultimate object of their life have set a direction that will end in their own deaths."[49] What are *you* looking for? What do you want Jesus to do for *you*? Make change? Keep you healthy? Financially stable? Or something deeper and lasting?

Jesus's question may also allude to the many references (more than thirty) to "seeking the Lord" in the Old Testament, especially to passages about Israel and even the nations seeking him in the last days (Isa 55:6; Jer 50:4; Hos 3:5; Zech 8:22, etc.). The verb for "seek" is a key word in John, occurring thirty-four times, although it only occurs here in the first chapter.

---

49. Koester, *The Word of Life*, 60. Although there is much of value in Koester's book, he agrees with Bultmann and especially Terrence Forestell that John does not teach substitutionary atonement. Koester makes faith the instrument and mechanism of salvation. The cross, he says, is only the catalyst that inspires faith, because it proves God's love for the world. "By conveying the divine love that evokes faith, the crucifixion gives people eternal life ... And when the love of God calls forth faith, it overcomes the world's hostility by bringing people back into relationship with the One who made them" (p. 45). See Max Turner's response to Bultmann and Forestell in "Atonement and the Death of Jesus in John," 99–122.

The disciples respond to Jesus's question with another question: "Where are you staying?" They had many questions, but what they were looking for was to get to know Jesus, the Lamb of God, and he was glad to oblige. Their addressing him as "Rabbi" also suggests they wanted to become his students, his disciples.[50] His amazing invitation for them to "come and see" (a phrase used again in v. 46) constituted his acceptance of their application and the beginning of a never-ending journey with Jesus. The verb for "stay," *menō*, occurs three times in vv. 38–39; otherwise, its significance might be missed. It was a favorite word of John's, used forty times in the Gospel and twenty-four in 1 John (out of 118 times in the New Testament). John already used it twice of the Spirit "resting" on Jesus in vv. 32–33. It could also mean to "remain, continue, stand firm, wait on, reside." Jesus used the noun form *monē* in 14:2 of the home or "room" he is preparing in order for us to live with him in heaven. Of particular interest is the use of *menō* with the preposition *en*, "in." Christ's word is to reside or remain *in us* (5:38; 15:7; 1 John 2:14, 24), and we are to continue *in his word* (8:31). We are to remain or reside *in Christ* (John 6:56; 1 John 2:6, 27–28; 3:6, 24; 4:13; also *in the Father*—1 John 2:24; 4:15–16), as God the Father resides *in Christ* (14:10) and as Christ (and the Father) remains or resides *in us* (15:4–7; 1 John 3:24; 4:12–13, 15–16).[51] We are also to remain *in Christ's love* (15:9–10), and his love is to remain or reside *in us* (1 John 3:17). The Spirit also remains or resides *in us* (14:17; 1 John 3:24; 4:13). John's concept of the believer's mutual residing with Christ is called "union with Christ" and is most vividly portrayed by John in Jesus's imagery in John 15 of the vine and the branches. John Murray declares that union with Christ is "really the central truth of the whole doctrine of salvation."[52] It may be compared to the apostle Paul's concept of "in Christ" and "Christ in you" (Rom 8:1–2, 39; 2 Cor 5:17; Eph 1:3; Col 1:27, etc.).[53]

---

50. Klink, *John*, 145.

51. As Donald Fairbairn explains, "The loving relationship between Father and Son, the glorious presence of the Father with the Son, is not simply a model that we are to follow. That relationship is the substance of what Jesus says Christians are to possess. Christ is not simply giving us an example; he is offering himself to us as a person, that we might share in his most deeply personal relationship, the relationship he has with God the Father." He also concludes, "Jesus shows us that the key to Christianity as it is meant to be is linking our lives to him, and indeed linking our lives directly to his own relationship with God the Father." See *Life in the Trinity*, 26–27, 28.

52. Murray, *Redemption Accomplished and Applied*, 161.

53. See K. Munzer, "μένω," *NIDNTT*, 3:224–26. Marcus Peter Johnson says that "union with Christ" terminology and imagery is "just as ubiquitous and regnant in the Johannine corpus" as it is in Paul's writings (*One with Christ*, 20).

An essential implication of our mutual residing with Christ, so vivid in the imagery of the vine and the branches and also in Paul's "body of Christ" imagery (Rom 12:5; 1 Cor 12:12–27), is the resultant organic union that exists between believers. Although the verb *menō* does not occur there, the vital, organic union of Father, Son, and believers may be seen in Jesus's prayer in John 17:21–23.

> "May they all be one, as you, Father, are in me and I am in you. May they also be in us, so that the world may believe you sent me. I have given them the glory you have given me, so that they may be one as we are one. I am in them and you are in me, so that they may be made completely one, that the world may know you have sent me and have loved them as you have loved me."

So the disciples' "staying" with Jesus in John 1:38–39 prefigures or gives us a taste of the depth of riches to be uncovered in John's Gospel and to be experienced by the one who believes, receives Christ, and becomes a child of God.[54]

I'll never forget my first trip to the annual meeting of the Society of Biblical Literature, where thousands of Bible scholars meet each year in hotels and convention centers in different major cities of the country. I had recently finished my doctoral dissertation on text-linguistics and the book of Malachi and was excited to attend the session on Hebrew linguistics. In my studies I had discovered with delight the writings of a Dutch scholar named Eep Talstra, and he was presenting a paper at the session! When the session was over, I went up, introduced myself, and asked him a question. He answered me and then asked if I'd like to go sit down and talk! So this superstar and I sat in the hotel bar for about an hour talking about Hebrew linguistics! I was on cloud nine for a very long time after that. So I can almost imagine the disciples' excitement when they got to spend the rest of the day (and likely the night) with Jesus the Messiah! In fact, the Greek preposition meaning "with" here in v. 39 can mean "beside," implying closeness (see Luke 9:47; John 8:38; 14:17, 23, 25; 17:5; 19:25). I can imagine them sitting at a table or on the floor with Jesus for hours, glued to his every word.

We should also note the time reference in v. 39. It was "about four in the afternoon," that is, "about the tenth hour." Contrary to the views of many, who think of John as the "symbolic" and "theological" Gospel, Bauckham makes a compelling case that "John's Gospel is notable for its chronological and geographical precision."[55] How John's "hours" correspond to ours (no

---

54. See Bauckham, *Gospel of Glory*, 149.

55. Bauckham, *Gospel of Glory*, 135. Also see his study of "Historiographical Characteristics of the Gospel of John," in his *Testimony of the Beloved Disciple*, 93–112.

pun intended) is somewhat controversial, depending on whether "hours" began at midnight (in which case the tenth hour would be ten o'clock) or sunrise (in which case it would be four o'clock in the afternoon). But according to the Roman writer Pliny (AD 23–79), "the common people everywhere" counted the hours of the day from sunrise to sunset, and Roman sundials marked noon with a "VI."[56] This seems to be confirmed by Jesus's question, "Aren't there twelve hours in a day?" in John 11:9. So four o'clock is probably correct. The primary significance of this seemingly trivial time reference, however, is that this is "one of [John's] small touches which point to an eyewitness"[57] (see 4:6, 52; 18:28; 19:14; 20:19). Andreas Köstenberger also points out that "since the main meal was usually taken in the late afternoon, 'tenth hour' may also indicate that Jesus extended table fellowship to these two disciples of John the Baptist."[58] Furthermore, if this time is correct, Keener suggests it would have been too late for them to walk home. "Ancient hospitality would have required him to have offered for them to spend the night."[59]

Day Four: Peter Follows Jesus (1:40–42)

> *40 Andrew, Simon Peter's brother, was one of the two who heard John and followed him. 41 He first found his own brother Simon and told him, "We have found the Messiah" (which is translated "the Christ"), 42 and he brought Simon to Jesus.*
>
> *When Jesus saw [or "looked closely, intently, thoughtfully, or directly at"] him, he said, "You are Simon, son of John. You will be called Cephas" (which is translated "Peter").*

Although v. 40 does not begin with "the next day," as we find in vv. 29, 35, and 43, the reference to "that day" in v. 39, as well as the time indication there, which would be late in the afternoon (see comments on v. 39), probably suggests that a new day began in the next verse.[60] If this is the case, then the statement in v. 41 that Andrew "*first* found his own brother Simon" means it was the first thing he did the next day. This was evidently the understanding of at least some in the early church, since two or three Old Latin

---

56. See Finegan, *Handbook of Biblical Chronology*, 7–11; Carson, *Gospel according to John*, 156–57; Morris, *Gospel according to John*, 157–59.
57. Morris, *Gospel according to John*, 158.
58. Köstenberger, *John*, 75–76.
59. Keener, *Gospel of John*, 470.
60. See Carson, *Gospel according to John*, 168.

manuscripts have *manē*, "in the morning."[61] Andrew probably rushed out of the house as soon as he awoke and ran to get his brother to introduce him to Jesus. Some scholars, however, believe that finding Simon was the first thing Andrew did *as soon as he was called*. If so, before following Jesus to where he was staying, Andrew went to get his brother. Verses 40-42 would then be a "footnote" to v. 39.[62] If this is the case, how did Andrew find where Jesus was staying? Perhaps Jesus and the other disciple went with Andrew to get Simon; but the wording of vv. 41-42a makes it seem that Andrew went alone: "He first found his own brother Simon and told him, 'We have found the Messiah' . . . , and he brought Simon to Jesus." The simplest interpretation seems to be that a new day started with v. 41.

We do not know what Andrew and the other disciple discussed with Jesus for several hours the previous day, but it was enough to convince them that they had "found the Messiah." Although the Greek word *christos*, from *chriō*, "to anoint," means "anointed one," the Greek word *messias*, from Hebrew *mashiach*, "anointed one," occurs in the New Testament only here and in John 4:25. Perhaps John used it to stress that Jesus was the fulfillment of Old Testament expectations of a deliverer sent from God, although he makes clear elsewhere that Jewish expectations were often inadequate. Although Jesus's disciples recognized that he fit their expectations of a deliverer, their understanding of who he was had a long way to go. For example, the New Testament presents Jesus as the anointed Prophet, Priest, and King, yet Nathanael's words in v. 49 suggest that they thought of the Messiah primarily as "King of Israel."[63]

Verses 40-41 illustrate the principle of connection that drives the progress of the gospel of Christ. God sent the Baptist, who directed his disciple Andrew to Jesus. Then Andrew found and led his brother and fishing partner, Simon Peter, to Jesus (Keener suggests that the word "first" indicates Andrew went on to lead others to Christ as well[64]), and probably through them Jesus "found Philip," who was from their hometown (1:43-44). Philip

---

61. Most scholars follow the textual reading πρῶτον, an adverb meaning it was the first thing Andrew did. The Latin *mane* could be traced to a Greek reading πρωι, "early in the morning." See Metzger, *Textual Commentary*, 172.

62. This is the view of McHugh, *John 1-4*, 154. He also indicates on p. 113 that he understands vv. 35-42 as occurring on the third day and vv. 43-51 on the fourth. This is confused, however, by his conclusion on p. 154: "Whichever reading be preferred, it is best to treat vv. 41-42 (or 40-42) as a footnote to the preceding scene, describing what Andrew did, *perhaps 'in the morning'*" (my emphasis). If Andrew went to get Peter *in the morning*, then it would be on the next day, and vv. 40/41-42 would not just be a footnote to vv. 35-39.

63. See L. W. Hurtado, "Christ," *DJG*, 114-17.

64. Keener, *Gospel of John*, 475.

brought Nathaniel, echoing Jesus's words to "come and see" (1:45–46). Then they brought others, who brought others, and the word of God spread (Acts 6:7; 13:49) until they had "turned the world upside down" (Acts 17:6) and filled it with followers of Jesus, each one a witness to others, "who [would] believe in [Jesus] through their word" (John 17:20), even though they had not seen for themselves what the first disciples saw (John 20:29). So Andrew "became the first in a long line of successors who have discovered that the most common and effective Christian testimony is the private witness of friend to friend, brother to brother."[65] As Godet says, "One lighted torch serves to light another."[66] We also see here Paul's principle that "what you have heard from me in the presence of many witnesses, commit to faithful men who will be able to teach others also" (2 Tim 2:2). We must not miss the fact, however, that in each case personal faith needs more than the witness of another person. It also requires a personal encounter with Jesus.

Although virtually nothing is known about Andrew (who is mentioned only a few times in the New Testament), he preceded and was used by God to lead his more famous brother to faith. Morris points out that every time Andrew is mentioned in John, "he is bringing someone to Jesus."[67] Did he become jealous of his brother? Or, rather, did he practice the selflessness of his mentor, John the Baptist? We know he was hanging out with his brother, as well as James and John, before Jesus's sermon on the Mount of Olives (Mark 13:3–4). But the only other time we hear from Andrew is when Jesus was about to feed the 5,000 (John 6:5–9). Jesus had "tested" Philip with the question, "Where will we buy bread so that these people can eat?" Philip did not have a clue. But Andrew knew that "there's a boy here who has five barley loaves and two fish." He did not know how that would help, but he thought it was worth mentioning to Jesus. Does that tell us anything about Andrew? He also shows up in John 12:20–22 with Philip bringing some Greeks to Jesus.

In v. 42 Simon ("the most common of all known Jewish male names" according to Bauckham[68]) gets a new name, or a nickname. We all know people who for various reasons have changed their name. I became "Ray" instead of "Ewell Ray" when I moved and entered the fourth grade; Cassius Clay changed his name to Mohammed Ali; Norma Jeane Mortenson changed her name; certainly no one blames Marion Mitchell Morrison for changing

---

65. Carson, *Gospel according to John*, 155. For an example of how powerful a personal testimony can be, see the account of J. I. Packer's conversion in Ryken, *J. I. Packer: An Evangelical Life*, 30–39.

66. Cited in Morris, *Gospel according to John*, 163.

67. Morris, *Gospel according to John*, 160.

68. Bauckham, *Jesus and the Eyewitnesses*, 85.

his name. Woody Allen was born Allan Stewart Konigsberg; Alphonso Joseph D'Abruzzo became Alan Alda. Do you know who Frances Ethel Gumm became? Someone else whose name was changed to "Rock" was Roy Harold Scherer Jr. (Rock Hudson). But having someone else change your name is less common than changing it yourself. Here we learn that the apostle Peter actually had three names: his original name, Simon, then a new Aramaic name given by Jesus, Cephas (or *Kepha'*), and its Greek equivalent, *petros*, Peter (also Mark 3:16). Only in Matt 16:18 are we told that it means "rock, stone," although the meaning would have been assumed here. It is a fitting name for an apostle or for any member of God's household.

> So then you are no longer foreigners and strangers, but fellow citizens with the saints, and members of God's household, built on the foundation of the apostles and prophets, with Christ Jesus himself as the cornerstone. In him the whole building, being put together, grows into a holy temple in the Lord. In him you are also being built together for God's dwelling in the Spirit. (Eph 2:19-22)

Since Adam named the animals in the garden (Gen 2:19-20), the giving of names has indicated possession or authority over something (sometimes a city; Gen 4:17; Num 32:38; Ps 147:4) or someone (Dan 1:7). When God gives a name to someone, however, it is not a humiliation but an exaltation to a new status (Isa 43:1). I will not be lost or forgotten or obscured in the mass of humanity. God has given me a name. A eunuch would have believed his life was meaningless, and he was destined to be forgotten. But Isaiah the prophet said,

> No foreigner who has joined himself to the LORD should say, "The LORD will exclude me from His people"; and the eunuch should not say, "Look, I am a dried-up tree." For the LORD says this: "For the eunuchs who keep my Sabbaths, and choose what pleases me, and hold firmly to my covenant, I will give them, in my house and within my walls, a memorial and a name better than sons and daughters. I will give each of them an everlasting name that will never be cut off." (Isa 56:3-5; see Acts 8:27-39)

A new name may also describe something about that person or thing—what he/she/it *is* (Gen 29:35; 1 Sam 1:20) or will *become* (Gen 17:5, 15; 32:28; Matt 1:21). The prophet Isaiah declared to the people of Israel, "Nations will see your righteousness and all kings, your glory. You will be given a new name that the LORD's mouth will announce" (Isa 62:2; also see Rev 2:17). John Oswalt explains that the Lord's salvation was to bring about a change in Israel's "condition and character as evidenced by a *new name*."[69] So Peter's new name signified Jesus's presence and authority in his life, his new status as a beloved disciple, and the transforming work Jesus would do in Peter's life and through him in the church. In the words of Klink, "The same man, named Simon, yet now different and new, is now also called Peter. Peter is a new man, yet not one thing in him made it so. It was only Jesus and his declaration that changed Peter."[70] The same is true of all who "come and see" and begin to follow Jesus. "He calls his own sheep by name and leads them out" (John 10:3).

Day Five: Philip and Nathanael Follow Jesus (1:43–51)

Jesus Finds Philip (1:43–44)

> 43 The next day Jesus decided to leave for Galilee. He found Philip and told him, "Follow me."
>
> 44 Now Philip was from Bethsaida, the hometown of [lit. "from the town of] Andrew and Peter.

Although Jesus decided on day five to head for Galilee, he had two more disciples to gather before they left. Little is known of Philip. Leon Morris may be reading into the text more than he is exegeting it, but his sanctified imagination is worth considering. He takes Philip as an example of an "ordinary" believer of "limited ability" serving Jesus.

> John brings him before us on a number of occasions. Each time he seems somewhat out of his depth, and it is probable that he was of limited ability. His contribution to feeding the multitude is the information that they could not be fed even with "two hundred shillings' worth of bread" (6:7). When the Greeks came to him asking to see Jesus he did not know what to do. He had to consult with Andrew before the men were brought to Jesus (12:21f.). And it was Philip who requested Jesus in the upper room to show them the Father—that is all they ask! (14:8f.). The fact that on this occasion he did not seek Jesus, but Jesus went to find him may indicate some lack of initiative. If so it is encouraging to reflect that Jesus went out of His way to find this perfectly ordinary Philip and to enlist him in the apostolic band. Some of the apostles were undoubtedly men of great ability, but

---

69. Oswalt, *Isaiah, Chapters 40–66*, 579 (emphasis original).
70. Klink, *John*, 148.

Philip compels us to reflect that others were perfectly ordinary people. Christ had and has use for such followers.[71]

According to Mark 1:21–31 (also Matt 8:14), the house of Peter and Andrew was in Capernaum, where Peter's mother-in-law was, and presumably Peter's wife (1 Cor 9:5). Bethsaida could be called "the town of Andrew and Peter," perhaps, because they grew up there or were living there when Jesus's ministry began. The suggestion may be that Andrew and Peter were somehow involved in connecting Philip and Jesus. Nevertheless, Jesus's direct initiative and action in "finding" and calling Philip is what is explicit. Although his use of witnesses is typical in bringing people to himself, God is perfectly capable of reaching individuals directly with his Word and his Spirit.

Jesus's invitation to Philip to "follow me" could have been an invitation to accompany them to Galilee, but its occurrence so many times in the Gospels on the lips of Jesus makes us think it was surely more than that. Jesus wanted Philip to be his disciple, and these men begin to be referred to as his "disciples" in John 2:2. Can you imagine a famous college professor, having heard about a particular graduating senior, coming to his or her house to invite them to come to his university to study with him? Perhaps a football coach might come to enlist an extraordinary, all-star high school football player, as in the movie *The Blind Side*. But this is Jesus, the Messiah, the King of Israel, the divine Creator. And Philip was an ordinary sinner, not a star football player! What a Savior, who came from heaven to seek and save lost sinners like me, and to invite us to live with and learn from him!

Philip Finds Nathanael (1:45–46)

> 45 Philip found Nathanael and told him, "We have found the one Moses wrote about in the law (and so did the prophets): Jesus the son of Joseph, from Nazareth."
> 46 "Can anything good come out of Nazareth?" Nathanael asked him.
> "Come and see," Philip answered.

Nathanael is not mentioned in the Synoptic Gospels but may be the same as Bartholomew (Matt 10:3), which is not really a name but means "son of Tholomai."[72] He appears only in these verses (1:45–49) and again in 21:2, where he is gathered with six other disciples by the Sea of Tiberius and is referred to as "Nathanael from Cana of Galilee."

---

71. Morris, *Gospel according to John*, 162.
72. See Bruce, *Gospel of John*, 59.

The verb "find" is used five times in vv. 41-45. Andrew "found" Simon, Andrew and his fellow disciple "found" the Messiah, Jesus "found" Philip, Philip "found" Nathanael, and the disciples "found the one Moses wrote about." John liked this verb when talking about Jesus making disciples. But why? As in Jesus's parables of the lost sheep, the lost coin, and the lost son (Luke 15), the emphasis on finding is usually on the joy over what has been found (also Matt 13:44). Does it imply seeking? Latin had two verbs for "find": one meant to find after seeking, and the other was used of a chance discovery. These meanings are combined in the one Greek verb *heuriskō*, from which we get "Eureka!" meaning "I have found it!" As Gärtner points out, however, uses of the verb with accidental finding are in the minority. The precarious human condition of lostness means that we are "so careworn, burdened and longing for rest," that we are always seeking (note the use of the verb for "seek" in v. 38).[73] Finding could also be either literal (as when Joseph's cup was found in Benjamin's sack) or figurative (1 Chr 28:9: "The LORD searches every heart and understands the intention of every thought. If you seek him, he will be found by you"; Isa 55:6: "Seek the Lord while he may be found; call to him while he is near").

The "finding" in all five cases in these verses probably assumes a search of some kind has been made. Andrew and the others were looking and praying for the Messiah. Andrew wanted his brother to meet Jesus and went after him, and Philip wanted to introduce his friend Nathanael to Jesus. This was also likely the case with Jesus, who had probably heard about Philip from Andrew and Peter and wanted Philip to become his disciple. How amazing that the sovereign Creator God should descend his throne to come after his rebellious children with persistent determination! One writer, describing the conversion of St. Francis, wrote, "For years he had been fleeing someone or something, and suddenly that someone had caught up with him and blasted him with all the power of his tenderness."[74] C. S. Lewis described his own experience of God's persistent chasing of him in terms of the Francis Thompson (1859-1907) poem, "The Hound of Heaven" (1893), which begins,

> I fled Him, down the nights and down the days;
> I fled Him, down the arches of the years;
> I fled Him, down the labyrinthine ways
> Of my own mind; and in the mist of tears
> I hid from Him, and under running laughter.
> Up vistaed hopes I sped;

---

73. B. Gärtner, "εὑρίσκω," *NIDNTT* 3:529-30.
74. Quoted by McCullough, *Waking from the American Dream*, 19.

And shot, precipitated,
Adown Titanic glooms of chasmèd fears,
From those strong Feet that followed, followed after.
But with unhurrying chase,
And unperturbèd pace,
Deliberate speed, majestic instancy,
They beat—and a Voice beat
More instant than the Feet—
'All things betray thee, who betrayest Me.'[75]

Another example of God chasing down an individual may be found in a missionary story from Russia.

> In the 1930's Stalin ordered a purge of all Bibles and all believers. In Stavropol, Russia, this order was carried out with vengeance. Thousands of Bibles were confiscated, and multitudes of believers were sent to the gulags—prison camps—where most died, unjustly condemned as "enemies of the state."
>
> [A mission group called] the CoMission once sent a team to Stavropol. The city's history wasn't known at that time. But when the team was having difficulty getting Bibles shipped from Moscow, someone mentioned the existence of a warehouse outside of town where these confiscated Bibles had been stored since Stalin's day.
>
> After much prayer by the team, one member finally got up the courage to go to the warehouse and ask the officials if the Bibles were still there. Sure enough, they were. Then the Co-Missioners asked if the Bibles could be removed and distributed again to the people of Stavropol. The answer was "Yes!"
>
> The next day the CoMission team returned with a truck and several Russian people to help load the Bibles. One helper was a young man—a skeptical, hostile, agnostic collegian who had come only for the day's wages. As they were loading Bibles, one team member noticed that the young man had disappeared. Eventually they found him in a corner of the warehouse, weeping.
>
> He had slipped away, hoping to quietly take a Bible for himself. What he found shook him to the core.
>
> The inside page of the Bible he picked up had the handwritten signature of his own grandmother. It had been her personal Bible. Out of the thousands of Bibles still left in that warehouse,

---

75. See https://www.poemhunter.com/poem/the-hound-of-heaven. See also "The Hound of Heaven: A Modern Adaptation" at https://www.youtube.com/watch?v=RXlgz4aBKt8.

he stole the one belonging to his grandmother—a woman persecuted for her faith all her life.

No wonder he was weeping—God was real. His grandmother had no doubt prayed for him and her city. His discovery of this Bible was only a glimpse into the spiritual realm—and this young man was in the process of being transformed by the very Bible that his grandmother found so dear.[76]

We should also notice that the term "find" is one of several related key words and phrases in 1:37–46, along with "follow," "stay," "come and see," and "look for."[77] The relationship between these terms is a logical one with implications for discipleship and evangelism:

seek → come and see → find → stay/follow

The result of the process seems contradictory at first. How can I both "stay" and "follow"? But, of course, "staying" simply means remaining with Jesus, which means that when he is on the move, so is his disciple. Bauckham points out that the last use of "find" in John's Gospel is in the post-resurrection encounter of Jesus with the seven disciples who have been fishing (21:1–14). As they begin to return from a discouraging night on the water, Jesus calls to them, "Cast the net on the right side of the boat, . . . and you'll find some" (the verb "find" has no object in the Greek text).[78] Other than the "fish" Jesus used to feed the five thousand in John 6:9, 11, all John's references to fish and fishing (eight of them) are in chap. 21, the essential and programmatic epilogue to the Gospel. Unless read in the context of the connection Jesus makes in the other Gospels between fishing and evangelism (Matt 4:19; 13:47–48; Mark 1:17), Jesus's miracle in John 21 seems rather pointless, contrary to John's indication in the first verse that it involved Jesus's self-disclosure (21:14 uses the same verb *phaneroō*, but in the passive, "was revealed/appeared"). Read in the broader context, however, the point of the incident as recounted in John's epilogue (especially just before the reinstatement and commissioning of Peter in 21:15–19) is that Jesus's disciples were assigned the task of fishing for people, and that his continued guidance and provision for this task would be essential and available to them. Jesus did not leave his disciples on their own to wonder what to do with their lives after his crucifixion and resurrection (as perhaps Peter

---

76. Andrea Wolfe, on staff with The CoMission in Raleigh, North Carolina, in one of her Christmas newsletters, cited in Hughes, *1001 Great Stories and Quotes*, 393–94.

77. See the chart in Bauckham, *Gospel of Glory*, 148, although he misses one use of "find" in v. 41.

78. Bauckham, *Gospel of Glory*, 149.

felt with his "I'm going fishing" in v. 3). As Ridderbos puts it, "The story ... symbolizes the effective authorization and promise of the Risen One to fulfill the missionary mandate that he has given to his disciples."[79] Thus, as Bauckham says, "1:41, 45 already prefigures the disciples' post-Easter mission to bring other disciples to Jesus."[80]

"The one Moses wrote about" in v. 45 is equivalent to "the Messiah" in v. 41. "The Law and the Prophets" was a common way of referring to the Hebrew Scriptures we call the Old Testament (Matt 7:12; 22:40; Luke 16:16; Acts 13:15; 28:23; Rom 3:21), although "The Law, the Prophets, and the Psalms" also occurs (Luke 24:44). The most common term the New Testament uses for the Old Testament is "the Scriptures" (twenty times in the New Testament), meaning "the Writings." Luke tells us that after Jesus's resurrection, "beginning with Moses and all the Prophets, [Jesus] interpreted for them the things concerning himself in all the Scriptures" (Luke 24:27). Philip and others considered that the testimony of those books was united and consistent that God would send a deliverer. He would be a descendant of Eve, Abraham, and David, and was called the Lion of Judah, the Commander of the armies of the Lord, Son of God, and Son of Man. He would gather and redeem Israel, subdue all the enemies of God's people, bring justice to the oppressed, remove the wicked from the earth, and rule forever with justice and mercy over all the earth.

I recently wrote the following:

> The TV show *Alfred Hitchcock Presents* aired from 1955 to 1965. It always began with a life-sized line drawing of a man in profile, into which the rotund Alfred Hitchcock walked, to the tune of "Funeral March of a Marionette" by Charles Gounod. The drawing fit him perfectly. The NT writers and (according to them) even Jesus himself declared that Jesus is found in the OT (cf. Luke 24:27; John 1:45; 5:39,46; Acts 3:24; 10:43; 26:22). Christians disagree over how to describe the nature of that discovery and how certain "messianic passages" in the OT are to be interpreted, and the literature on that topic is vast. But Jesus's statement that Moses "wrote about me" (John 5:46; see also Heb 11:26) [suggests] a degree of intentionality and understanding on Moses's part ... No NT writer would be shocked or disappointed to find that a book had been written that laid out the OT teaching about Jesus the Messiah. Paul wrote that "the sacred Scriptures [in the OT] ... are able to give you wisdom for salvation through faith in Christ Jesus" (2 Tim 3:15). Like

---

79. Ridderbos, *Gospel of John*, 660.
80. Bauckham, *Gospel of Glory*, 149.

the line drawing, the OT leaves out a great deal that the NT fills in. Nevertheless, the NT revelation of Jesus fits perfectly the OT composite "line drawing" of him that is derived from so many OT passages (although it could be described as a *dotted* line).[81]

We might be surprised that Philip identified Jesus as "Jesus the son of Joseph, from Nazareth," because that isn't how we refer to people, and we know that Joseph was not Jesus's natural father. But calling someone "____ the son of ____" was like our referring to someone by their full name (see "Simon, son of John" in 1:42; 21:15). Jesus is also referred to as "Son of David, Son of Abraham" in Matt 1:1. The addition of someone's hometown was also a common way of making clear their identity. In the only other place Nathanael is mentioned, he is called "Nathanael from Cana of Galilee" (John 21:2). For thirty years the people in and around Nazareth would have known Jesus as "the son of Joseph, from Nazareth." He probably had a reputation for being hard-working, kind, honest, faithful, etc. Yet, like Clark Kent and Bruce Wayne, no one who knew him would have guessed who he really was. Later Christians, whose theological understanding was more mature, would simply identify him as "Jesus of Nazareth" (Acts 2:22).

Nathanael might have jumped on the unlikelihood of the Messiah being the son of a carpenter; instead, it was Jesus's hometown that bothered him. "From Nazareth" comes first in his comment: "From Nazareth?! What good can come from that podunk town?" It had only a few hundred inhabitants. His disparaging remark about Nazareth may represent only a sense of town rivalry, since he was from nearby Cana, boasting about a thousand residents.[82] Although Galileans were looked down on by people from Judea, we have no evidence of Nazareth having a bad reputation at the time. In fact, the town is not mentioned in the Old Testament or in other contemporary writings, which is probably significant. Nathanael's comment may have expressed only his expectation that the Messiah would come from a well-known and significant place like Jerusalem (or even Bethlehem), instead of from "Nowheresville."[83] Bauckham points to the irony of Nathanael's referring to Jesus as "anything good," whereas Jesus was actually "the supreme Good."[84] Philip's response echoed Jesus's invitation to his first two disciples to "come and see" (v. 39). Presenting evidence and making a case for belief has its place, but faith demands an encounter with Jesus. As Keener says,

---

81. Clendenen, "'Messenger of the Covenant' in Malachi 3:1 Once Again," 81–82.
82. Bauckham, *Gospel of Glory*, 163.
83. Bruner, *Gospel of John*, 109.
84. Bauckham, *Gospel of Glory*, 165.

"An encounter with Jesus becomes the Fourth Gospel's ideal apologetic for those with open hearts."[85]

Jesus and Nathanael (1:47–51)

> 47 Then Jesus saw Nathanael coming toward him and said about him, "Here truly is an Israelite in whom there is no deceit."
> 48 "How do you know me?" Nathanael asked.
> "Before Philip called you, when you were under the fig tree, I saw you," Jesus answered.
> 49 "Rabbi," Nathanael replied, "You are the Son of God; you are the King of Israel!"
> 50 Jesus responded to him, "Do you believe because I told you I saw you under the fig tree? You will see greater things than this."
> 51 Then he said, "Truly I tell you, you will see heaven opened and the angels of God ascending and descending on the Son of Man."

The Messiah is often called "the Coming One" (see Ps 118:26; Matt 11:3; 21:9; 23:39; John 6:14; 11:27; 12:13; Acts 19:4; Heb 10:37; Rev 1:4, 8; 4:8). The verb "come" occurs twelve times in this first chapter of John, mostly of Jesus's coming. Four times Jesus is said to be "coming," using the participle. He "was coming" into the world, he "came" to his own, he "was coming" after John, and in v. 29 John watched as Jesus was "coming toward him." But here Nathanael was "coming toward" Jesus, while Jesus watched. And parallel to John's testimony regarding Jesus—"*Here* is the Lamb of God, who takes away the sin of the world!"—Jesus testifies about Nathanael (so that he can hear), "*Here* truly is an Israelite in whom there is no deceit."

The word for "truly" (*alēthōs*) occurs seven times in John, at least twice as often as in any other New Testament book. After two days with Jesus, the Samaritans declared, "This *really* is the Savior of the world" (4:42). During the annual festival of Shelters, after the people saw Jesus feed the 5,000, they declared, "This *truly* is the Prophet who is to come into the world" (6:14). After seeing Jesus boldly confront the Jewish leaders in the temple without rebuke from them, the people wonder, "Can it be *true* that the authorities know he is the Messiah?" (7:26). Then on the last day of the festival, after Jesus claimed to be the source of "living water," some of the crowd declared, "This *truly* is the Prophet" (7:40). After "many believed in him," Jesus told them, "If you continue in my word, you *really* are my disciples" (8:31). Finally, at the end of his teaching ministry, in Jesus's prayer for his disciples, Jesus declared, "I have given them the words you gave me. They

---

85. Keener, *Gospel of John*, 487. See also p. 485.

have received them and have known *for certain* that I came from you" (17:8; emphasis added in each of these quotations). If we add the occurrences of related words—*alēthinos*, "true, genuine," nine times (see 1:9), *alētheia*, "truth," twenty-five times (see 1:14, 17), and *alēthēs*, "true," fourteen times—we can see that John's Gospel places an overwhelming emphasis (fifty-five times, the same number as in all Paul's letters) on the issue of what is true or genuine. If we include John's letters and the book of Revelation, that's thirty-eight more (totaling ninety-three), out of a total in the New Testament of 183. John and the other New Testament writers consider the issue of what is really true to be of paramount importance.

Why the big deal about what is true? One way to answer that is to recall that the current human situation is the result of Satan's first lie, in which he accused God of lying to Adam and Eve: "No! You will not die" (Gen 3:4, 13). Revelation 12:9 also speaks of the "great dragon," who is "the ancient serpent, who is called the devil and Satan, the one who deceives the whole world." His deceiving will only end when he is bound and thrown into the abyss for a thousand years and then into the lake of fire and sulfur forever (Rev 20:1–3, 10). We exist in a world of deception, uncertainty, misinformation, misdirection, pretense, trickery, posturing, hypocrisy, affectation, and artificiality. We are constantly confronted with counterfeits, hoaxes, imitations, rip-offs, forgeries, simulations, facades, frauds, and illusions. The apostle Paul said that people by nature "suppress the truth" (Rom 1:18). Yet there is no more important question than Where can truth be found? Who or what is true or real? Douglas Groothuis wrote, "Truth is a daunting, difficult thing; it is also the greatest thing in the world."[86]

Pilate mused, "What is truth?" (John 18:38). If Pilate was confused and skeptical, how much more are we today? Linguists tell us that the meanings of words are determined by usage, which changes over time. Is the situation the same with truth? Is it a moving target, or perhaps an illusion? Is it ever possible to assert, "This is the truth"? Or must we be content with "This is how it seems to me"? Can it be that the only question worth answering is What is expedient for me to get what I want? Yet it is difficult to get away from questions like What really happened? And no one likes the experience of being disoriented. We always want to know where we are in relation to what is familiar. We also want to know where we are going, and why. Life without boundaries, foundations, and direction is intolerable. Perhaps God made us this way. Perhaps that is why he asked Adam, "Where are you?" (Gen 3:9). God created mankind to abhor rootlessness. At the beginning of his work on *Metaphysics*, Aristotle wrote, "All men naturally desire

---

86. Groothuis, *Truth Decay*, 9.

knowledge."⁸⁷ Adam had the capacity to know where he was in relation to the foundation of life. John's purpose was that we may have life (20:31), and without being properly related to the One who defines and comprises life, truth, and reality (1:4; 14:6), we have no life and can do nothing (15:5). Only God has all truth, but he has given us access to truth and calls on us to follow it as it leads us to him.

Just as through revelation John knew who Jesus was, Jesus knew who Nathanael was (v. 47). The exchange between Jesus and Nathanael presents us with what we could call the first miracle of the book: Jesus's supernatural knowledge of Nathanael. When we come to Jesus, we find that our lives and our hearts are already known by him. Our "own attitude and life history or life secret" are "an open book to him."⁸⁸ As Jesus said, "I know my own, and my own know me" (John 10:14). In John 2:24–25, John wrote, "Jesus, however, would not entrust himself to them, since he knew them all and because he did not need anyone to testify about man; for he himself knew what was in man." Jesus knew about the life of the Samaritan woman at the well (John 4:16–18, 28–29), but even more amazing, he knew Nathanael's heart. "Jesus knows people's identities, deep down inside, and he wants *them* to know who they are or are going to be, as well, and to know what he thinks of them."⁸⁹

How does such divine knowledge of you make you feel? David begins Psalm 139 by declaring, "LORD, you have searched me and known me." The word "searched" speaks of a thorough investigation, "a diligent probing (cf. Job 28:3) or a cross-examination in a legal case (cf. Prov 18:17),"⁹⁰ resulting in total and intimate knowledge. The Lord's knowledge of him is the kind of exhaustive knowledge one might expect to have after extensive research, "leaving no stone unturned." Of course, with God such effort is not required. It is *as if* he had "searched." We often try to figure out what people are really thinking and feeling and why they are doing or saying what they are. We use behavioral clues, projection of our own imagined feelings under similar circumstances, and perhaps testimony of others involved. The end result is a guess, usually wrong. But God *knows*, just as Jesus knew Nathanael.

How does David feel about being known so well by God? In v. 5 he tells us he feels "encircled." That word almost always was used of laying siege to a city (Deut 20:12; 2 Sam 11:1; 2 Kgs 18:9; Isa 29:3; Dan 1:1), although it could also refer to securing valuables in a bag (Deut 14:25; 2 Kgs

---

87. See http://www.perseus.tufts.edu/hopper/text?doc=Perseus:abo:tlg,0086,025:1.
88. Ridderbos, *Gospel of John*, 89.
89. Bruner, *Gospel of John*, 111 (emphasis original).
90. Estes, *Psalms 73–150*, 552.

5:23; 12:10; Ezek 5:3). Did being known so well by God scare David, or make him feel secure? In the next verse he calls it "wondrous knowledge," or does he? The word translated "wondrous" actually refers to something "extraordinary." It is often used of God's "miracles," but it can also refer to "extraordinary plagues" in Deut 28:59, "your miraculous power against me" in Job 10:16, an "astonishing" downfall in Lam 1:9, and "terrible" and "outrageous" things in Dan 8:24 and 11:36. Or it can mean that something is "difficult" to do or understand (used in Judg 13:18 of the angel's name being "beyond understanding"). Such extraordinary knowledge, David says in v. 6, is "beyond me" (literally "from me"). The phrase "extraordinary from" someone always refers to something too difficult to be done or understood (Gen 18:14; Deut 17:8; 30:11; Job 42:3; Ps 131:1; Prov 30:18; Jer 32:17). The reason such knowledge is too difficult for the psalmist is that it is "lofty," that is, inaccessibly high, like a high wall or a city on a cliff (Deut 2:36; Ps 91:14; Prov 18:10–11; Isa 26:5; 30:13). Then he declares, "I am unable to reach it." But the Hebrew says simply, "I am not able to it." That phrase occurs also in Gen 32:26; Esth 6:13; Ps 129:2; Jer 1:19; 15:20, where it always speaks of the inability to overcome or prevail over someone. So what the psalmist is actually saying is that he is no match for God's knowledge of him. At this point in the psalm, he feels trapped and overpowered. The very next verse (v. 7) confirms this interpretation, where the psalmist asks, "Where can I go to escape your Spirit? Where can I flee from your presence?"

Sometimes, when we feel that we have grasped the nature and character of God by means of all our theological categories (words like *immutability*, *immensity*, *incorporeality*, and don't forget *incomprehensibility*), and we can predict his will and his actions so that we almost feel that *God* is subject to *us*, like the dinosaurs in *Jurassic Park*, God breaks out and turns the tables on us and shows us how ignorant and puny we really are. By the end of his psalm, however, David has come to see not just the futility and foolishness of trying to run from God's knowledge, but the precious blessing such knowledge can be. It entails being led and protected by a wise, powerful, and loving God (v. 10). He has come to "praise" God for creating, knowing, and guiding him (vv. 14–16), for God's "precious" thoughts of him (v. 17), and God's presence with him (v. 18). David swears allegiance to God against all his enemies (vv. 19–22), and pleads for God to "search," "know," "test," and "lead" him.

When Nathanael heard what Jesus said about him in John 1:47, could Psalm 139 have run through his mind? Could Jesus's knowledge of him have scared Nathanael just a little? We don't know, of course. But if so, he moved pretty quickly to the same submissive faith that David experienced.

In both the "Here is" statements by the Baptist (1:29, 36) and by Jesus, there was a contrast. The temple was full of lambs all the time, especially during the festivals (and Passover was near, according to 2:13), but Jesus was the one final and ultimate Lamb to whom they all pointed. Now here Jesus implies a contrast between Nathanael and false "Israelites," who were full of deceit. He said, "Nathanael, you are the real thing."[91] The term "Israelite" is found in the New Testament only nine times: once in the Gospels (here), five times in Acts (always "fellow Israelites," lit. "men, Israelites"), and three times in Paul's letters. Paul gives us the meaning: "I too am an Israelite, a descendant of Abraham" (Rom 11:1; also 2 Cor 11:22). Bauckham points out that, whereas Gentiles referred to them as "Jews," "Israelite" was the term they typically used of one another.[92] The nation of Israel was the covenant people to whom God had entrusted the law, the temple, and the promises (Rom 9:4). But all of Abraham's descendants did not benefit from or enjoy God's gracious promises. Paul wrote, "Not all who are descended from Israel are Israel. Neither are all of Abraham's children his descendants" (Rom 9:6-7). As he explained, "Though the number of Israelites is like the sand of the sea, only the remnant will be saved . . . Israel, pursuing the law of righteousness, has not achieved the righteousness of the law. Why is that? Because they did not pursue it by faith, but as if it were by works" (Rom 9:27, 31-32). The blessings of God's salvation require being connected to his life-giving vine by faith (see John 15:1-8). At first, all the branches of the vine were physical descendants of Israel (Isa 5:1-7). But failure to produce the fruit of justice, honesty, and humility demonstrated the absence of faith and resulted in branches being cut off, leaving only a faithful remnant to enjoy God's blessings, to which would be added new branches exhibiting the faith of Abraham—Gentiles, who would be grafted onto the vine (Rom 11:17-32; Gal 3:7-9).

Although the word "truly" is an adverb rather than an adjective, and some scholars object that "true Israelite" is an incorrect translation,[93] Nathanael seems to represent to Jesus that remnant—a true Israelite.[94] But why did Jesus focus on Nathanael's lack of "deceit"? Perhaps Jesus only meant that Nathanael, like Thomas, was an honest seeker, who spoke his mind ("Can anything good come out of Nazareth?") and was not a phony. The word translated "deceit" and its related words occur about ninety times in the Septuagint (as well as fourteen times in the New Testament), beginning

---

91. Bruner, *Gospel of John*, 111.
92. Bauckham, *Gospel of Glory*, 168.
93. See Ridderbos, *Gospel of John*, 89; Carson, *Gospel according to John*, 160.
94. Keener, *Gospel of John*, 485; Klink, *John*, 151.

with Jacob (Israel) deceiving his father and stealing his brother Esau's blessing (Gen 27:35–36). Then Jacob's sons pretended to be favorable toward their sister's suitor and deceived him (Gen 34:13). The two most common types of deceit found in Scripture are treachery and slander: (1) pretending to be someone's friend in order to get close to them and do them harm (like Judas?), and (2) spreading lies about someone in order to do them harm (bearing false witness). Deceit and violence often go together (Pss 5:6; 10:7; 27:12; Isa 53:9; Mic 6:12; Zeph 1:9). Jesus's enemies practiced both kinds of deceit (Matt 26:4; Mark 14:1). The prophet Jeremiah described the deceitfulness of Israel in his day (9:4, 6, 8):

> Everyone has to be on guard against his friend. Don't trust any brother, for every brother will certainly deceive, and every friend spread slander . . . You live in a world of deception. In their deception they refuse to know me. This is the LORD's declaration . . . Their tongues are deadly arrows—they speak deception. With his mouth one speaks peaceably with his friend, but inwardly he sets up an ambush.

Moses's father-in-law advised him to select leaders under him who were "able men, God-fearing, trustworthy ["men of truth"], and hating dishonest profit" (Exod 18:21). Isaiah 53:9 (quoted in 1 Pet 2:22) describes the Suffering Servant, however, as one in whom there was no deceit: "He was assigned a grave with the wicked, but he was with a rich man at his death, because he had done no violence and had not spoken deceitfully." And according to Zeph 3:13, "The remnant of Israel will no longer do wrong or tell lies; a deceitful tongue will not be found in their mouths. They will pasture and lie down, with nothing to make them afraid." The psalmist declares, "How joyful is a person whom the Lord does not charge with iniquity and in whose spirit is no deceit!" (Ps 32:2). In several New Testament passages deceitfulness is a key characteristic of the lost (Mark 7:22; Acts 13:10 Rom 1:29; 3:13), and its absence is a key characteristic of a child of God (1 Pet 2:1; 3:10; Rev 14:5). Esau makes a pun on Jacob's name when he says, "Isn't he rightly named Jacob? For he has cheated me twice now" (Gen 27:36). But Jacob had a life-transforming encounter with God, who signified what he was going to do in him by changing his name to "Israel," "because you have struggled with God and with men and have prevailed" (Gen 32:28). Keener suggests that "Jesus deliberately contrasts this representative Israelite with his ancestor Jacob."[95] Morris portrays Nathanael as a "God-fearing, trustworthy" man, one of the remnant, "an Israelite in whom there is no Jacob."[96]

95. Keener, *Gospel of John*, 486.
96. Morris, *Gospel according to John*, 166.

But what should we make of Jesus's reference to the fig tree? John does not seem to call attention to it; he only seems to use it to reveal Jesus's divine character. Several Old Testament references to being under a fig tree, however, invite us to look more closely. In 1 Kgs 4:25, for example, Solomon's golden age of peace and safety is pictured as "each person under his own vine and his own fig tree" (see also 2 Kgs 18:31 and the apocryphal 1 Macc 14:12). The coming messianic age is pictured similarly in the Prophets. According to Mic 4:4, in the last days "each person will sit under his grapevine and under his fig tree with no one to frighten him." In Zech 3:8–10, the Lord says that when he brings his servant, "the Branch," and takes away "the iniquity of this land in a single day," then "each of you will invite his neighbor to sit under his vine and fig tree." The situation of peace and security in the messianic age in Mic 4:4 is also expressed by the words, "with no one to frighten him." This translates a common Hebrew expression that can be traced back to the covenant blessings in Leviticus (Lev 26:6) and is also found in other restoration passages in the Prophets (Jer 30:10; 46:27; Ezek 34:28; 39:26; Zeph 3:13). Combined with Jesus's statement about finding "no deceit" in Nathanael, the reference to the fig tree, then, seems to be a thread we might grasp that leads to several Old Testament passages describing the Lord's renewal and blessing of the remnant of Israel in the last days. According to Bauckham, in fact, Zeph 3:12–13 and Mic 4:4 are "crucial for understanding John 1:47–50."[97] The connection can be shown by this chart:

Micah 4:4	under the fig tree	nothing to fear	
Zephaniah 3:13		nothing to fear	no deceit
John 1:47-48	under the fig tree		no deceit

Seen in this context, Jesus clearly considers Nathanael (and the other disciples) to represent the remnant of Israel that he has come to gather, and to whom he will begin to impart the peace and security of the messianic age. The result is pictured in Revelation 14 as 144,000 of the Lord's redeemed standing with the Lamb, singing the "new song," and following the Lamb "wherever he goes." They are the "firstfruits for God and the Lamb," in whose mouths is found "no lie" (Rev 14:1–5).

The parallel we noticed between Jesus's coming toward the Baptist in John 1:29 and Nathanael's coming toward Jesus in 1:47 may suggest something else about Nathanael's lack of deceit. As the Baptist responds with "Here is the Lamb of God," Jesus responds with "Here truly is an Israelite." Both also add a relative clause. Whereas the Baptist adds, "who takes away

---

97. Bauckham, *Gospel of Glory*, 167.

the sin of the world," Jesus adds, "in whom there is no deceit." Why is there no deceit in Nathanael? Is it because he's such a good guy—so much better than deceitful Jacob? More likely, it's because Jesus has begun to take away sin.

The disciples, of course, almost certainly understood none of Jesus's and John's allusions to the Old Testament. What Nathanael made of Jesus's claim that he possessed "no deceit" we do not know. Evidently Nathanael did not balk shamefully at it. He may have barely heard it. He was struck rather by the fact that Jesus knew who he was, so he asked in amazement, "How do you know me?"

Many years ago I took my teenage son to Atlanta to a Braves baseball game. I remember the amazement (and confusion) I felt when approached by a total stranger. While heading down the stands to our seats, a young lady came up to me, pointed to me and said, "I know you." I was puzzled and embarrassed that I had no idea who she was (a bit flattered too). When she kept pointing at my shirt, I finally looked down and realized I was wearing my tee shirt that said, "You Don't Know Me—Witness Protection Program."

Jesus's knowledge of Nathanael, however, was no joke. Jesus's disciples also later told Jesus, "Now we know that you know everything and don't need anyone to question you. By this we believe that you came from God" (John 16:30). As was also the case with the Samaritan woman (4:19, 29), Jesus's statement to Nathanael in v. 48 was enough to convince him of Jesus's identity as "the Son of God" and "the King of Israel." The latter term is used only four times in the Gospels (see Matt 27:42; Mark 15:32; John 12:13) but is essentially equivalent to the more common (especially among Gentiles; see John 18:33, 39; 19:3, 19, 21) "King of the Jews." Ridderbos points out that both "Son of God" and "King of Israel" are messianic titles and have essentially the same meaning.[98]

This is the first of several references in John to Jesus as "King." But aside from the 5,000 people Jesus had fed in 6:15 wanting to "make him king," all the others occur during the last week before his death, and most of them involve Pilate. Nevertheless, the connection between Messiah and King is fairly easy to understand. Where Nathanael derived his understanding of Jesus as Son of God, however, is puzzling. The purpose of John's Gospel was "so that you may believe that Jesus is the Messiah, the Son of God, and that by believing you may have life in his name" (20:31). Without reading John's Gospel, however, and without a "spoiler alert," Nathanael proclaimed Jesus's divine Sonship upon first meeting Jesus!

---

98. Ridderbos, *Gospel of John*, 91. See too Bauckham, *Testimony of the Beloved Disciple*, 229–30.

More, therefore, must be said about Nathanael's use of the title "Son of God." Jesus is called (or disputed to be) "the Son of God" thirty-nine times in the New Testament (nine times by the devil or demons, once by an angel, four times by Jesus himself), but he is identified as God's Son, "the Son," or "my Son" 124 times.[99] As Köstenberger and Swain point out, in John's Gospel, Jesus is referred to as "S/son" forty-five times:[100]

son of Joseph	1:45; 6:42
one and only Son	1:14, 18; 3:16, 18
Son of God	1:49; 3:18; 5:25; 10:36; 11:4, 27; 19:7; 20:31
Son of Man	1:51; 3:13, 14; 5:27; 6:27, 53, 62; 8:28; 9:35; 12:23, 34 (twice); 13:31
the Son	3:16, 17, 35, 36 (twice); 5:19 (twice), 20, 21, 22, 23 (twice), 26; 6:40; 8:36; 14:13; 17:1 (twice)

Along with this "opening salvo" by Nathanael, Jesus is called by various people "the Son of God" eight times in John's Gospel" (besides one reference to Jesus as "the Son of God" by his opponents in 19:7):[101]

Nathanael	1:49
Author	3:18
Jesus	5:25
Jesus	10:36
Jesus	11:4
Martha	11:27
Author	20:31

Although Jesus does not call himself the Son of God in the Synoptic Gospels (he comes close in Matt 26:63; Luke 22:70), he is referred to in that way by demonic or human enemies, an angel, his disciples, and a Roman centurion. According to Bauckham, Nathanael's use of the term alongside "the King of Israel" referred to the Davidic Messiah and was based on Old Testament predictions in 2 Sam 7:14; Ps 2:7; and Ps 89:26–27 that the promised Davidic descendant would be God's Son. "Evidence for the use of this title for the Messiah in late Second Temple Judaism is not plentiful, but it is sufficient

---

99. D. R. Bauer, "Son of God," *DJG*, 769, 774.
100. Köstenberger and Swain, *Father, Son and Spirit*, 76.
101. Köstenberger and Swain, *Father, Son and Spirit*, 79–80.

to indicate that it was sometimes, if not very often, used."[102] Although the title "the Son of God" means much more to John and to us, then, it probably meant simply "Messiah" to Nathanael.[103]

In v. 50 Jesus's question could be interpreted as a criticism of Nathanael for basing his faith on such a little thing as Jesus's knowledge of him. But this, of course, is not his point. Elsewhere, Jesus stresses the *necessity* of faith, not its basis. There is an infinite number of paths to faith in Christ. Some come to him after an exhaustive philosophical or scientific investigation, and others come because of a word spoken, a surprising event, an act of kindness, etc. Someone told me once there is no such thing as "proof"; there are only convincing arguments. Ultimately, it is the Spirit who brings us to faith (John 1:13; 3:6). Jesus's point is that this was just the beginning of even "greater things" Nathanael and his fellow disciples would see that would feed their faith. The statement serves to "tease" us with the expectation of further signs that Jesus would do and John would begin to relate in chapter 2. The phrase "greater than these" occurs twice more in John. In 5:20 Jesus told the Jews he was doing the works that his Father showed him to do and that he would show him things "greater . . . than these," so that they would "be amazed." Then in 14:12, to our (and their?) astonishment, Jesus told his disciples that his going to the Father would result in their doing things "greater . . . than these" that Jesus did. John's account of Jesus's words and work continues to fuel the excitement of our expectation. Things "greater . . . than these" will continue coming.

While Jesus does not explain what greater things he is referring to, in 1:51 he uses an Old Testament allusion to paint a picture of what they would mean and the effect they would have. Those who believed in him would "see heaven opened and the angels of God ascending and descending on the Son of Man," that is, on Jesus. Very few disciples have ever seen heaven opened (Acts 10:11; Rev 4:1; 11:19; 15:5; 19:11), and there is no biblical account of a vision of angels traveling over Jesus. But Jesus's final statement in v. 51 is not to be taken lightly. It begins with his first of twenty-five uses of the emphatic "truly" (KJV "verily"), which in Greek is *amēn,* and in John is always doubled. Rather than being an assurance that Jesus is not lying, it is a way of highlighting a statement as especially important and is probably best rendered something like "I assure you" (HCSB) or "most assuredly I say to you" (NKJV). Jesus is no longer speaking only to Nathanael, however, but to all his followers, indicated by the plural "you" in "I tell *you, you* will see . . ." It could be rendered, "And he said to him, 'I assure y'all, y'all will see . . .'"

---

102. Bauckham, *Gospel of Glory,* 159.
103. Köstenberger and Swain, *Father, Son and Spirit,* 81.

But if Jesus's promise in v. 51 that they would "see heaven opened" was not intended to be taken literally, what did Jesus mean? The expression is used of a revelation from God. But rather than involving certain information, the revelation would be Jesus, in whom they would see God and experience his salvation. Jesus alludes to Jacob's dream at Bethel recounted in Gen 28:12-19. Many Jews in Jesus's day felt as Jacob had at that time—alone in the dark, without a true home, afraid, cast out and abandoned by God, out of his will and his sight. But Jacob learned that he was not alone or abandoned. In his dream, he saw a "stairway" (or ladder) that was "set on the ground [or the "earth"] with its top reaching the sky [or "heaven"], and God's angels [his "messengers"] were going up and down on it." Jacob also saw and heard the Lord either above the stairway or, more likely, beside him (the Hebrew can be translated either "upon it" or "beside him"[104]), reaffirming for Jacob the covenant promises he made to Abraham and Isaac. The Lord assured him of his presence, protection, provision, and the fulfillment of his promise of land and seed and to make him a universal blessing (Gen 28:13-15):

> "I am the LORD, the God of your father Abraham and the God of Isaac. I will give you and your offspring the land on which you are lying. Your offspring will be like the dust of the earth, and you will spread out toward the west, the east, the north, and the south. All the peoples on earth will be blessed through you and your offspring. Look, I am with you and will watch over you wherever you go. I will bring you back to this land, for I will not leave you until I have done what I have promised you."

When Jacob awoke, he said in vv. 16-17,

> "Surely the LORD is in this place, and I did not know it [compare the Baptist's "I didn't know him" in John 1:31] . . . What an awesome [or "fearful"] place this is! This is none other than the house of God. This is the gate of heaven."

Unlike the tower of Babel, Jacob's "stairway" did not represent the possibility of ascent to God. Rather, it signified heaven coming to earth, God's connection to Jacob in spite of his former life of deception and scheming. It represented God's presence and his work in Jacob's life, with angels serving as "ministering spirits" (Heb 1:14). The Greek translators of the Old Testament

---

104. Hamilton, *Genesis, Chapters 18-50*, 241, interprets the verb for "stand" (נִצָּב) plus the preposition (עַל) here as standing beside or over, in the sense of standing "in a position of authority, to preside over."

rendered the word for "stairway" with the Greek word *klimax*, meaning a stair or ladder. And truly this was a "climactic" event in Jacob's life.

What Jesus was describing, however, was a greater "climax," although there is no stairway. Instead, the angels would ascend and descend on Jesus, who is the new "house of God," "the gate of heaven," the mediator, bridge, and meeting house between earth and heaven, God and humanity (1 Tim 2:5). Instead of a dream intended to reassure Jacob and prepare him to experience God's work in his life, Jesus promises his disciples an experience with him that will lead them to faith in him and prepare them to experience God's work in their lives. Whereas Yahweh elaborates on the significance of Jacob's dream in Gen 28:13–15, especially with the assurance that "I am with you," Jesus leaves his disciples with the tantalizing image of the angels and the Son of Man, which awaits later elaboration, especially in Jesus's words in John 14–16. Jesus's promise here is that his disciples would see God at work on their behalf in Jesus.

Bauckham argues that v. 51 also contains Jesus's first reference to his death and exaltation. The word for "stairway" (Hb. *sullam*) occurs only in Gen 28:12 but is related to the root *sll*, which occurs in the verb meaning either "to lift up, raise" (a road or siege ramp; see Job 30:12; Isa 57:14) or "to exalt" (Ps 68:4), and in the noun *mesillah*, "highway." It is used of the raised highway by which God would bring redeemed Israel back to himself and to the land (Isa 11:16; 40:3; 49:11; 57:14; 62:10). Three of Jesus's "Son of Man" passages in John also use a verb (*hupsoō*) meaning "lift up, exalt." All three passages point ahead to Jesus's death and exaltation:

> "Just as Moses lifted up the snake in the wilderness, so the Son of Man must be lifted up." (3:14)

> "When you lift up the Son of Man, then you will know that I am he, and that I do nothing on my own. But just as the Father taught me, I say these things." (8:28)

> "As for me, if I am lifted up from the earth I will draw all people to myself." He said this to indicate what kind of death he was about to die. Then the crowd replied to him, "We have heard from the law that the Messiah will remain forever. So how can you say, 'The Son of Man must be lifted up'? Who is this Son of Man?" (12:32–34)

Bauckham argues, therefore, from Jesus's allusion to Jacob's dream and his use of the term *Son of Man* that he is pointing ahead to his death and exaltation on the cross.[105]

---

105. Bauckham, *Gospel of Glory*, 172–77.

Jesus refers to himself thirteen times in John as the Son of Man (although in 12:34 it is the crowd quoting Jesus). All these references occur in the first half of the Gospel (1:51; 3:13-14; 5:27; 6:27, 53, 62; 8:28; 9:35; 12:23, 34; 13:31) and seem to climax near the beginning of Jesus's passion week in two passages pointing to his glorification through death and resurrection:

> Jesus replied to them [Andrew and Philip], "The hour has come for the Son of Man to be glorified. Truly I tell you, unless a grain of wheat falls to the ground and dies, it remains by itself. But if it dies, it produces much fruit." (12:23-24)

> When he [Judas] had left, Jesus said, "Now the Son of Man is glorified, and God is glorified in him. If God is glorified in him, God will also glorify him in himself and will glorify him at once. Children, I am with you a little while longer. You will look for me, and just as I told the Jews, so now I tell you: 'Where I am going, you cannot come.'" (13:31-33)

The term *Son of Man* derives from Dan 7:13-14 and refers to the Messiah:

> I continued watching in the night visions, and suddenly one like a son of man was coming with the clouds of heaven. He approached the Ancient of Days and was escorted before him. He was given dominion, and glory, and a kingdom; so that those of every people, nation, and language should serve him. His dominion is an everlasting dominion that will not pass away, and his kingdom is one that will not be destroyed.

Scholars have concluded, however, that the phrase "Son of Man" was not a common way of referring to the Messiah among first-century Jews. Although it seems to have been a common way of referring to oneself in Aramaic, Jesus used the phrase as an allusion to the heavenly being in Dan 7:13-14.[106] Scholars sometimes point out that one of the advantages of Jesus

---

106. See the excellent survey of scholarly discussion with careful conclusions in Davies and Allison, *Gospel according to Saint Matthew*, 43-52. One of their conclusions is that "until further evidence is forthcoming, it appears methodologically unsound to approach the synoptic data with the assumption that most first-century Jews, upon hearing the phrase, 'Son of man', would immediately have thought of a transcendent redeemer figure, the judge of the last day. The most one can say is that the phrase, within the appropriate context or with the appropriate markers, could cause one to recall the theophany of Dan 7" (p. 46). Jesus used a common idiom, they say, meaning something like "a human being," to specify a prophetic individual. They compare this to the generic phrase, "the war," in England, which is used to refer to their war with Germany in 1939-45. They also compare it to Jesus's use of the phrase "I am" in the Gospel of John in such a way as to give it "the status of a title" (p. 47). They also conclude, "We are inclined to think that Jesus used the son of man idiom on more than one occasion in a

using this term was that it did not carry a lot of baggage, as terms such as Messiah and King of Israel did.[107] Jesus was more free to fill it with the truth of who he is—our Suffering Servant (also Matt 20:18, 28; 26:2, 24, 45; Mark 8:31; 9:12, 31; 10:33, 45)[108] and Everlasting Lord, who would be "lifted up" on the cross but then raised from the dead (also Matt 17:9, 12, 22) and exalted to heaven, from which he will come to judge (also Matt 13:41; 16:27–28; 24:27–44) and rule the world (also Matt 19:28; 25:31; 26:64), as indicated in John 5:26–27:

> For just as the Father has life in himself, so also he has granted to the Son to have life in himself. And he has granted him the right to pass judgment, because he is the Son of Man.

This is the one John will continue introducing to us in order that we may have life in him.

---

novel or quasi-titular manner with the intent of directing his hearers to Dan 7, and that he saw in Daniel's eschatological figure a prophecy of his own person and fate" (p. 50).

107. See Carson, *Gospel according to John*, 164.

108. Jeremy R. Treat discusses the relationship between the Suffering Servant and the Son of Man in *The Crucified King*, 96–99.

4

Day Seven: Jesus's First Sign (2:1–11)

Setting for the Miracle (2:1–2)

> *1 On the third day a wedding took place in Cana of Galilee. Jesus's mother was there, and 2 Jesus and his disciples were invited to the wedding as well.*

John's account of the final day of Jesus's opening week begins with the oddly surprising notation that this is "the third day." Since we've been counting the days of Jesus's first week, and the last day was the fifth (1:43–51), John's reference here to a "third day" is confusing. But he has not been using our words "day one ... day two," and so forth, or even the Greek word for "day" (*hēmera*). Rather, he's been using simply a sequential word that can mean "tomorrow" or "on the next day" (*epaurion*), generally referring to the next morning (1:29, 35, 43).[1] So his reference to a "third day" here is not a reference back to our day three, nor does it likely refer to the third day of the week, that is, Tuesday. Most scholars reasonably take it as referring to three days after the last event, which happened on day five. If we were playing monopoly with some first-century Jews, however, and one of them rolled a three, they would count the space they were already on as *one*. So, according to inclusive Jewish reckoning, the equivalent of "on the third day" would be our "day after tomorrow" or "two days later." In other words, the

---

1. The word ἐπαύριον (=ἐπί, "upon," + αὔριον, "the following day, tomorrow") occurs in the LXX twenty-three times, sometimes clearly indicating the following morning (Gen 19:34; Exod 18:13; 32:6; Num 11:32; Judg 6:38–40; 9:42; 21:2–4; Jonah 4:7). The seventeen uses in the New Testament follow the same pattern (see Acts 10:23–24; 14:20; 20:7). The word αὔριον is found in the LXX about sixty times, eight of which are in the phrase, "tomorrow at this time" (see Exod 9:18).

wedding took place on day seven of Jesus's opening week, and John skipped a day in his account.

We suppose the missing day (or at least one of the days) was when Jesus and his disciples traveled to Cana, Nathanael's hometown (21:2). Presumably "his disciples" would be those introduced in John 1:37–51 (Andrew, Peter, Philip, Nathanael, and probably John). Although Cana is usually identified with Khirbet-Qanah, about nine miles north of Nazareth,[2] we don't know exactly how long their journey took, since we don't know exactly where they started.[3] But a day or so would have been plenty of time. Bauckham suggests they could have left on day five and may even have arrived on day seven.[4] Since John tells us nothing about what happened on day six, was it a day in Jesus's life, like one of ours, when "nothing happened"? Or was it one of those days John alluded to in 20:30 when "Jesus performed many other signs in the presence of his disciples that are not written in this book"? Probably not, in view of John's telling us in v. 11 that changing water to wine was "the first of his signs." Yet Jesus told his disciples in John 4:34, "My food is to do the will of him who sent me and to finish his work." And in 5:17 Jesus said to the Jewish leaders, "My Father is still working, and I am working also." So even if he performed no miracles on the sixth day, did the incarnate Son of God, who was on the earth in the flesh only slightly more than thirty years, ever spend a day "doing nothing"? Our lack of information does not entail a lack of significance. Significant things happen all the time that we don't know about or recognize, even in our own lives, let alone in the lives of others, and certainly in the life of Jesus. How vast and how deep is our ignorance! Jesus is doing all sorts of things in our lives all the time that we don't see or appreciate. Even when we think *we* are "doing nothing," *he* is at work. What about the day Jesus was in the tomb and God was silent? Even then, if we had been listening very carefully and had "ears to hear" (Mark 4:9), perhaps we could have heard the humming of heavenly machinery at work, preparing for what was going to happen on the third day.

Scholars disagree over whether the reference to "the third day" in 2:1 is an allusion to the resurrection.[5] Although the resurrection is said to have happened on "the third day" in Matthew (16:21; 17:23; 20:19; 27:64) and

---

2. Keener, *Gospel of John*, 495–96.

3. According to R. Riesner, "Archaeology and Geography," *DJG*, 35, "In recent time various more precise attempts to pin down the location [of Bethany across the Jordan] have not succeeded."

4. Bauckham, *Gospel of Glory*, 140.

5. See the arguments against it in Ridderbos, *Gospel of John*, 102; Carson, *Gospel according to John*, 167. On the other side of the issue is Keener, *Gospel of John*, 497–98; Bruner, *Gospel of John*, 127; Bauckham, *Gospel of Glory*, 182.

DAY SEVEN: JESUS'S FIRST SIGN (2:1–11)   103

Luke (9:22; 18:33; 24:7, 21, 46), John uses that phrase only here. But in 2:19 Jesus says, "Destroy this temple, and I will raise it up in three days." Because of other parallels between Jesus's opening week and the week of his passion and exaltation (like the references to Bethany in 1:28 and 12:1, the appearance of Jesus's mother only here and in 19:25–27, and the mention of "six days before the Passover" in 12:1 and "the first day of the week" in 20:1, 19),[6] we may guess that John intends those of us who know what's coming to see here a foreshadowing of a future day of silence followed by a third day of rejoicing.[7] As Frey explains, the phrase "on the third day" here "alerts one to an 'Easter dimension.'"[8]

We can only speculate on the days of the week when Jesus's opening week began and ended. The Mishnah mentions the Jewish custom of a virgin's wedding being held on the fourth day of the week, which would be our Wednesday (*m. Ketubbot* 1:1).[9] If this custom was followed in Cana in the time of Jesus, then Jesus's opening week began on a Thursday, and the third day of that week, when Andrew and John began following Jesus (1:35–39), would have been the Sabbath.

---

6. See Bauckham, *Gospel of Glory*, 134–35.

7. The exact Greek phrase (τῇ ἡμέρᾳ τῇ τρίτῃ), translated here "on the third day," is found twenty-five times in the LXX (although two of these are apocryphal: Add Esth 15:1; 1 Macc 11:18), and John's use of the phrase could allude to one or more of these, such as Exod 19:11, 16; Hos 6:2. On the other hand, the phrase may suggest a turning of events or a momentous or climactic event, such as the day Abraham saw the mountain of sacrifice (Gen 22:4), Simeon and Levi's slaughter of the men of Shechem (Gen 34:25), the day Joseph's dream interpretation was fulfilled (Gen 40:20), Joseph letting his brothers out of jail (Gen 42:18), the day Yahweh descended on Mount Sinai (Exod 19:11, 16), the Israelite defeat of the Benjaminites after two days of defeat (Judg 20:30), David's defeat of the Amelekites after they burned Ziklag (1 Sam 30:1), David receiving news of Saul's death (2 Sam 1:2), Jeroboam receiving the news that led to rebellion against Rehoboam (1 Kgs 12:12; 2 Chr 10:12), Hezekiah is healed and goes to the temple (2 Kgs 20:5, 8), the day of Queen Esther's courageous appearance before the king (Esth 5:1), and Israel's repentance and resurrection, foreshadowing the resurrection of Christ (Hos 6:2; 1 Cor 15:4). It could also be a time of purification (Lev 7:18; 19:6; Num 19:12; 31:19).

8. Frey, *Glory of the Crucified One*, 95.

9. Keener, *Gospel of John*, 496; Bauckham, *Gospel of Glory*, 140.

Day One	Thursday	Baptist and Jewish leaders
Day Two	Friday	Baptist introduces disciples to Jesus
Day Three	Saturday	Andrew and John
Day Four	Sunday	Peter meets Jesus
Day Five	Monday	Philip and Nathanael
Day Six	Tuesday	Travel (which may have begun on day five)
Day Seven	Wednesday	Wedding

That's probably as likely an itinerary as any. However, Jewish weddings comprised the bride being brought to the groom's home on the eve of the wedding, followed by the wedding day, consisting of celebration, a meal, and the consummation at the end of the day. Then the feasting and celebrating normally lasted a week.[10] So the event that "took place" in 2:1 might have been the arrival of Jesus and his disciples at the wedding feast. The feast may have been going on for some time, based on the headwaiter's comment to the groom in 2:10. Some scholars suggest that the day of silence, day six, as with Jesus's final week, was the Sabbath, and the events at Cana parallel Jesus's resurrection on Sunday.[11] But this would mean Jesus and his disciples were traveling on the Sabbath, which is unlikely. On the other hand, if the parallel to the six days of creation is pressed, then the events of 2:1–11 would have occurred on the Sabbath,[12] though this too seems unlikely. We do not really know which days of the week are in view, so we may suppose that John did not consider it very important.

Many other questions arise from these first two verses that John gives us no answer for. What relationship did Mary, Jesus, and his disciples have to the families at the wedding? As a rule, plural subjects in a clause require plural verbs, so in English, "They was invited to the wedding" would be bad grammar. Yet the Greek verb "invited" in v. 2 is singular, although the subject is "Jesus and his disciples." This has suggested to some that Jesus was the one invited, and his disciples just "tagged along," resulting, perhaps, in the crisis of insufficient wine.[13] But Greek grammar does not require this conclusion, and it seems beside the point.[14] The disciples' presence was not

---

10. See D. J. Williams, "Bride, Bridegroom," *DJG*, 87; King and Stager, *Life in Biblical Israel*, 55–56; *DNTB*, 685–86.

11. Köstenberger, *John*, 91.

12. Carson, *Gospel according to John*, 168.

13. Whitacre, *John*, 78.

14. Greek grammar allows this lack of agreement with a compound subject when the first subject ("Jesus" here) is highlighted, as we would expect whenever "Jesus and his disciples" is the subject (as in Matt 9:19; Mark 8:27; John 3:22). See Wallace, *Greek*

unexpected but seems incidental until we get to v. 11—"his disciples believed in him."

Another question is, Did Mary have responsibilities at the wedding feast? Is this why she knew about the lack of wine and sought Jesus out to remedy the situation? Is this the basis on which she gave instructions to the servants in v. 5? Perhaps, although again John does not seem very interested in answering our question. Ridderbos makes a wise observation: "In this fundamentally sober narrative [John] highlights certain details of the historical situation above other details—no less interesting to us—that remain in the shadows or are left unmentioned as apparently irrelevant to the thrust of the narrative."[15]

The reference to "the mother of Jesus" in 2:1, 3 is more interesting. She is explicitly referred to in John only here and in 19:25-26, when Jesus was on the cross (besides an allusion to her in 6:42). So this is another element of Jesus's opening week that foreshadows his final week. She is never called Mary in John, only "Jesus's mother" here and "his mother" in 19:25-26, suggesting that their relationship is what is in view (compare Matt 1:18; 2:11; Acts 1:14).

Mary's Problem (2:3-5)

> 3 When the wine ran out, Jesus's mother told him, "They don't have any wine."
> 4 "What does that have to do with you and me [or "with me"], woman?" Jesus asked. "My hour has not yet come."
> 5 "Do whatever he tells you," his mother told the servants.

Bible teachers often discuss at this point what a serious breach of social etiquette it would have been to run out of wine at a Jewish wedding feast, and we might contrast it to the much less severe situation of running out of wedding cake today or of turkey on Thanksgiving. Lack of sufficient wine would

---

Grammar Beyond the Basics, 401. His translation, "Jesus was invited to the wedding and [so were] his disciples," he thinks, connotes, "Jesus was invited to the wedding and his disciples tagged along." The clause, however, contains two uses of Greek καί, typically "and" or "also." Most translations render the first one "also" (ESV, NIV, NLT) or "as well" (CSB). Two uses of καί together like this, however, can also be rendered "both ... and," as in NKJV, "both Jesus and his disciples," thus losing the connotation favored by Wallace. See Porter, *Idioms of the Greek New Testament*, 75. McHugh, *John 1-4*, 178, also favors this view: "Especially after the verb [ἐκλήθη, "invited"] in the singular, the double καί serves to underline the dual and complementary presence, both of Jesus and of his disciples: he is there to manifest his glory, they are to witness it."

15. Ridderbos, *Gospel of John*, 101-2.

not only be embarrassing but would also bring dishonor and shame on the family.[16] I'm sure John assumes his readers will understand the seriousness of the situation, but he does not explicitly draw attention to it. He could have said, "But in the middle of the feast the wine ran out!" Instead, he only says, "When the wine ran out." Without a knowledge of the culture, we might have supposed that it was an ordinary occurrence for the wine to run out at a wedding. Bruner makes the interesting point that instead of beginning v. 3 with "but," John begins with the Greek word often translated "and" (*kai*; left untranslated here in most Bible versions). Bruner draws out the implication that "it is normal for crises, or emergencies, or at least for problems like this to arise in life and in marriage."[17] Even Mary's words to Jesus just appear matter-of-factly to describe the present circumstance: "They don't have any wine." Was she just passing along some juicy gossip, or did she nudge him and speak in an urgent whisper, with a desperate, pleading look on her face? We may suppose it was the latter, but again John does not choose to tell us.[18] John's word translated "ran out" does imply a sense of need, as when efforts have come short of achieving the goal, like our "running out of gas." It's used, for example, of "fall[ing] short of the glory of God" in Rom 3:23. So there was a need at the wedding, and for whatever reason, Mary was looking to Jesus for help.

The response Mary gets from her son in v. 4 informs us that he saw in his mother's statement of fact an implied request. If I were to tell my wife about a terrible itch in the middle of my back, she would probably receive the message that I needed her help. This is clearly the message Jesus receives. But what exactly was Mary expecting? That her son would turn water into wine? This was the view of some in the early church.[19] But this is not likely. Stories of Jesus as a boy bringing clay birds to life are fictitious.[20] John 2:11 tells us this was "the first of his signs." The eighteenth-century clergyman and Greek scholar Johann Albrecht Bengel supposed that Mary was hinting

---

16. Burge, *John*, 91.

17. Bruner, *Gospel of John*, 128.

18. John's wording in v. 3 might suggest that this was not a casual remark. McHugh calls attention to the "more formal and respectful construction" here, λέγω with πρὸς αὐτόν for "say to him" rather than λέγω with the dative αὐτῷ as in John 1:22, 25, 38, 41, 43, 45, 46, 48, 50, 51; 2:10. The construction here, he says, "underlines the importance of the words that follow" (McHugh, *John 1–4*, 179).

19. McHugh, *John 1–4*, 179–80.

20. The earliest form of it is in the second century Gnostic *Infancy Gospel of Thomas*, II.1–3. See http://gnosis.org/library/inftoma.htm (accessed 7/15/2018). The work also contains stories of Jesus cursing two boys who interfere with him, causing one to wither and the other to die. Also see T. P. Henderson, "Gospels: Apocryphal," *DJG2*, 350–51; Hock, *Infancy Gospels of James and Thomas*.

that Jesus and his friends should leave, in order to spare the poor newlyweds more embarrassment.[21] We generally assume, however, that since Joseph is no longer mentioned after Jesus was twelve years old (Luke 2:41–50), and Jesus entrusted his mother to John at the cross (John 19:27), Mary at some later point became a single mother, coming to depend more and more on her eldest son. She might have expected Jesus and his friends quietly to collect money to give the servants to go out and buy more wine. We don't know. Whatever she expected involved the servants, because of her instructions to them in v. 5 to "do whatever he tells you."

More significant, however, not to mention more puzzling, is the nature and meaning of Jesus's reply to his mother in v. 4, which is not immediately apparent to us. It is, in fact, one of Jesus's most puzzling statements in the Gospels. John's Gospel and certainly this episode contain much to challenge the Bible reader's skills of interpretation. But almost forty years ago I read this statement by the New Testament scholar and churchman B. F. Westcott (1825–1901), and its wisdom has proven true time after time:

> The first steps towards the solution of a difficulty are the recognition of its existence and the determination of its extent. And, unless all past experience is worthless, the difficulties of the Bible are the most fruitful guides to its divine depths. It was said long since that "God was pleased to leave difficulties upon the surface of Scripture, that men might be forced to look below the surface.[22]

That is true here. If we did not have Jesus's enigmatic words to Mary in v. 4, his changing the water to wine would have been what some critics have called a "luxury" miracle.[23] His other miracles involved things like feeding the hungry, healing the sick, and raising the dead. But here all he does is provide the wine for a wedding and save some people from embarrassment. Was that really a worthwhile use of his creative power, worthy of the Son of God and consistent with his mission to save the world? Would such a "sign" have prompted John to select it for recounting out of all those he had to choose from (20:30–31)? I believe that these very words that so perplex us serve as a doorway into the significance of this miracle, which, like all his miracles, is a sign pointing to an aspect of his glory and preparing

---

21. McHugh, *John 1–4*, 180.
22. Westcott, *The Bible in the Church*, x.
23. Macgregor, *Gospel of John*, 48, cited in Little, *Echoes of the Old Testament*, 9. Little surveys some critics of John's account, who would have preferred that Jesus turned wine into water (p. 10).

us to understand, appreciate, and appropriate his redemptive cross and resurrection.[24]

His response has two parts. First, he says, "What does that have to do with you and me, woman?" (v. 4). Probably the most striking thing to our ears here is Jesus addressing his mother as "woman." The Greek word, *gunē*, could have one of three meanings, depending on the context: woman, wife, or bride. The latter two are clearly not appropriate here. The New Living Translation and the first edition of the NIV tried to soften it by rendering it "dear woman," but this is not what the word means, so the latest NIV changed it to "woman," like most other translations. The derogatory connotation in our culture of addressing an adult female as "woman" was not part of the word's usage in Jesus's day. It remains, however, that Jesus did not call her "Mom" or even "Mother," and we know of no other instance in Greek literature where a son uses this term to address his mother.[25] Some have suggested "Lady" or "Madam" or "Ma'am," but each of these has its own problems of usage. Carson, for example, likes the term "Ma'am," but he points out that in the southern United States the term on the lips of a child addressing his mother implies a submissive attitude, the opposite of what Jesus probably intended here.[26] Jesus, rather, seems to be gently suggesting that his relationship of submission to his mother had changed. Jesus addresses several other women in the Gospels using the same polite but somewhat formal term (Matt 15:28; Luke 13:12; John 4:21; 8:10; 20:15). His use of the same form of address on the cross when he entrusts her to the care of his beloved disciple (John 19:26) affirms that, although his affection and some level of responsibility for his mother continued until his death (notice John does call her Jesus's "mother" in 2:1, 3, 5, 12), the beginning of his ministry had changed the nature of their relationship. We might compare the incident in Matt 12:46–50, when Jesus's mother and brothers come to see him while he's speaking to a crowd.

> While he was still speaking with the crowds, his mother and brothers were standing outside wanting to speak to him. Someone told him, "Look, your mother and your brothers are standing outside, wanting to speak to you." He replied to the one who was speaking to him, "Who is my mother and who are my brothers?" Stretching out his hand toward his disciples, he said, "Here are my mother and my brothers! For whoever does the will of my Father in heaven is my brother and sister and mother."

---

24. See Tasker, *St. John*, 55.
25. Köstenberger, *John*, 94.
26. Carson, *Gospel according to John*, 170.

Jesus's mission in life was now strictly to serve the Father who had sent him. The situation was somewhat similar to that of the son who marries and, as a result, "leaves his father and mother and bonds with his wife" (Gen 2:24). At the wedding in Cana, Jesus the son has become Jesus the groom (see the Baptist's remark in 3:29), for whom the church is being prepared as "the bride, the wife [*gunē*] of the Lamb" (Rev 21:9). The disastrous marriage between the first Adam and his wife Eve will be replaced by the perfect marriage between "the seed of the woman," the last Adam, and the redeemed of the ages.

In view of this, it's interesting that after the fifth century Mary, already known by earlier churchmen as "the mother of God," should be so highly exalted as becoming the object of intense devotion and prayer. As one writer says, "She was approached as the most potent of all intercessors; the supreme *saint* who could command the ear of Christ, and thus intercede for the suffering on earth, just as she had once interceded successfully for a poor couple in Cana, and gained for them (and for the world) an abundance of new wine."[27]

So the second council of Nicaea (AD 787) advocated the use of "venerable and holy images" in the churches not only of the Lord Jesus but also of "our undefiled Lady, the holy God-bearer," as well as of angels and saints.[28] The attitude of many was expressed by the fourteenth-century priest and poet Guillaume de Machaut, who wrote,

> "Blessed virgin, mother of Christ, . . .
>   Sweetest one, . . .
>   Purest one.
> Implore thy son, most pious maid,
> That he may drive away the many evils
> And many torments
>   Which we suffer . . .
> Source of grace and virtue,
> Our only hope of safety, have pity on us,
> For we are forsaken,
>   And help us . . .
> Keeper of the court of heaven
> Who lends ear to the sorrowing,
>   Star of the sea,
> Who, as a mother, consoles
> And prays for the fallen,

---

27. McGuckin, *Patristic Theology*, 351.
28. See Bettenson, *Documents of the Christian Church*, 94.

Humbly; . . .[29]

And yet, what seems clear from Jesus's words to Mary is that if he decided to meet the needs of this "poor couple in Cana," it would be for his own reasons, not because his mother had asked him to. Even the Catholic interpreter Raymond Brown admits, "It must be honestly noted that the evangelist does nothing to stress the power of Mary's intercession at Cana. If the miracle is a response to her persistent faith, this motif is not made explicit."[30] Besides, as Keener points out, others in the Gospels ask Jesus for help for servants or family members, and we do not turn them into mediators.[31]

Another problem with Jesus's reply to Mary is his question, which uses a common Hebrew idiom, literally, "What to me and to you?" Raymond Brown claims that it's used in the Old Testament in two senses. First, "When one party is unjustly bothering another, the injured party may say . . . [in effect], What have I done to you that you should do this to me?" (see Judg 11:12; 1 Kgs 17:18; 2 Chr 35:21). The idiom is also used in this sense elsewhere in the New Testament by demons or unclean spirits (Mark 1:24; 5:7), who complain to Jesus with the question, "What to us/me and to you?" (CSB, "What do you have to do with us/me?"), meaning "Why are you interfering with us?" Or "Go away and leave us alone." But Jesus's words to Mary certainly do not seem to have that sense.

The other use Brown finds for the idiom in the Old Testament is "when someone is asked to get involved in a matter which he feels is no business of his, he may say . . . [in effect], That is your business; how am I involved?" (see 2 Kgs 3:13; Hos 14:8). Brown considers Jesus's use of it here to be this one, and he translates it, "What has this concern of yours to do with me?"[32] I would add a slightly different use of the idiom also found in the Old Testament. When one of David's followers, Abishai, wants to execute Shimei, a supporter of Saul, who is uttering curses against David, David uses the idiom to mean "You and I are not thinking alike" (CSB, "Do we agree on anything?"; 2 Sam 16:10; again in 2 Sam 19:22).[33] Based on the second and third uses, Jesus's point would seem to be that he and she are not on the same page, not concerned about the same things, having different agendas.

---

29. See Petry, *Early and Medieval Church*, 435–36.
30. Brown, *John 1–XII*, 103.
31. Keener, *Gospel of John*, 505.
32. Brown, *John I-XII*, 99.
33. A related use, perhaps, occurs in Josh 22:24. When confronted by the other tribes for building an altar east of the Jordan River, the Transjordan tribes explain their fear that future generations might question their relationship with Yahweh, saying (literally), "What to you and to Yahweh, the God of Israel."

Whereas she is concerned about the lack of wine at a wedding and (presumably) the shame this will cause the family, he is concerned about fulfilling the mission that his Father sent him to do.³⁴ I disagree, then, with the CSB translation, "What does that have to do with you and me." The issue is not between Jesus and Mary on the one hand and the wedding party on the other hand. It is between Jesus and his mother.

This is perhaps confirmed by the second half of Jesus's response: "My hour has not yet come."³⁵ The implication seems to be that Mary is asking Jesus to do something that it is not time for him to do. Some have thought that Jesus was referring to the proper time for him to reveal his glory by perhaps performing some sign. The problem with this understanding is that Jesus and John refer many times in the Gospel to Jesus's "hour" and to an "hour" that is either "coming" or, as Jesus enters into the final week of his earthly life, "has come." These references clearly have in view the time determined by the Father for Jesus's crucifixion, in particular, but also his exaltation.

Jörg Frey points out that the signs in John's Gospel are "narrated signs," where "in every individual episode something of the whole of the salvific event is expressed." Readers are "repeatedly compelled, starting from the narrated individual event, from each 'miracle,' to think further and to reflect upon this in light of the passion and Easter event." This first sign is no exception. It "points ahead to the 'hour of Jesus,' to the event of death and resurrection, in which Jesus' mother will be present again. The wine already conveys something of the taste of salvation, which is grounded in that hour, and it is thus much more than a wonderfully made drink for a village wedding."³⁶

By tracing the theme that Jesus introduces here with his reference to "my hour," we find that we are pulling on a thread that begins to unravel and display the skeletal structure of John's Gospel of the cross (emphasis added):

---

34. Jesus's mild rebuke of Mary has been compared to his rebuke of Peter in Matt 16:23: "Get behind me, Satan! You are a hindrance to me because you're not thinking about God's concerns but human concerns." See Köstenberger's citation (*John*, 95) of Maccini, *Her Testimony Is True*, 102-4. This is a quite different matter, however. Peter was trying to obstruct Jesus's path to the cross. Mary is only trying to prevent someone's emotional pain.

35. See McHugh's argument (*John 1-4*, 183-84) for taking the Greek wording here as a question rather than a statement: "Is not my hour already come?" Although he attempts to respond to objections, he fails to vanquish the objection that until John 12:23, all the other references to Jesus's hour in John point to a time to come, not one that is already here (4:21, 23; 5:25, 28; 7:30; 8:20). No wonder, as even McHugh admits, "no modern English version for public use translates the second sentence as a question." I'm not aware of any translation agreeing with his understanding.

36. *Glory of the Crucified One*, 288-89.

"*My hour* has not yet come." (2:4)

Then they tried to seize him. Yet no one laid a hand on him because *his hour* had not yet come. (7:30)

He spoke these words by the treasury, while teaching in the temple. But no one seized him, because *his hour* had not yet come. (8:20)

Jesus replied to them, "*The hour has come* for the Son of Man to be glorified. Truly I tell you, unless a grain of wheat falls to the ground and dies, it remains by itself. But if it dies, it produces much fruit." (12:23–24)

"Now my soul is troubled. What should I say—Father, save me from *this hour*? But that is why I came to *this hour* . . . Now is the judgment of this world. Now the ruler of this world will be cast out. As for me, if I am lifted up from the earth I will draw all people to myself." He said this to indicate what kind of death he was about to die. (12:27, 31–33)

Before the Passover Festival, Jesus knew that *his hour had come* to depart from this world to the Father. Having loved his own who were in the world, he loved them to the end. (13:1)

Jesus spoke these things, looked up to heaven, and said: "Father, *the hour has come*. Glorify your Son so that the Son may glorify you." (17:1)

The "hour" Jesus speaks of to Mary as not having come would be the time of fulfillment of his mission, the time of his sacrificial death as the Lamb of God for the sin of the world. That's the time for which and toward which Jesus was moving and about which he was concerned. Yes, he cares about people's genuine needs and hurts, and we often see him in the Gospels and in our own lives meeting those needs: healing and comforting. But he never loses sight of the goal of redemption and never veers off-course into the weeds of superficiality and face-saving.

We, however, like Mary, are often in those weeds. What are we concerned about? How do those concerns compare with those of Jesus? He instructed us to ask God to provide "our daily bread," that is, our needs at the present time. But my concerns often exceed my current needs. I'm often concerned about pleasing others, being liked, and having a good reputation (see Acts 12:3; 1 Cor 4:3–4; Gal 1:10; 1 Thess 2:4). What will others think of me if I wear sandals to the restaurant, if my car isn't freshly washed, if my jokes aren't funny, if my grammar isn't impeccable, if I cry while talking about an incident that touched my heart, if my children misbehave? I'm also concerned about the future. What if something bad happens? What if I lose my job, my health, or my loved ones? What if a fire or flood destroys all my books, my photos, my battleship Arizona cap? In spite of my preparations, will I have enough money when I retire? What if I die before I get to see Yosemite National Park or the northern lights, or before I finish writing this book? What if my kids and grandkids don't come to see me on my birthday? And then there's the past. How could I have done all the stupid, wicked things I did and disappointed people who were counting on me? Why did God allow all those painful things to happen to me? Why couldn't the Tennessee Titans have won the Super Bowl? And finally there's the present. Why hasn't God heard my prayers and intervened in this horrible situation? Those are the kinds of things that too often concern me. What does God think of my concerns? Do they match his concerns for my life? Am I wasting mental and emotional energy on things only he can control or has already dealt with? I need to ask every day whether my concerns match his, echoing Jesus's question to his first two disciples in John 1:38: "What are you looking for?" Am I looking for Jesus or for something else?

An incident occurred later in Jesus's life when his unbelieving brothers urged him to attend the Festival of Shelters (or Tabernacles) in Jerusalem and to do miraculous works there to impress the crowds (John 7:1–5). They say, in effect, "Now is your chance to show the world what you can do!" Perhaps in view of the recent defection of "many of his [so-called] disciples," who were offended by some of his teachings (6:60–66), the brothers did not want Jesus to miss his chance for fame. They may also have wanted to capitalize on their miracle-working brother and share in his notoriety.[37] The brothers evidently believed Jesus could do wonders, but they had no clue who he really was or how much they needed what he had come to provide. Morris writes that, despite their seeming acceptance and even enthusiasm for Jesus, "there is a deep-seated rejection of all that He really stood for. They were interested not in His purposes but in their own."[38] It's easy to understand Jesus's lack of interest in his brothers' agenda. As Carson explains, "John's readers already know that [the display the brothers want] would pander to corrupt motives (6:14, 15, 26ff.) and in any case would not ensure genuine faith (2:23–25; 4:48)."[39]

---

37. Perhaps they wanted him to be like Simon the sorcerer in Acts, who amazed the Samaritans and tried to buy the ability to impart the Holy Spirit like Peter and John (Acts 8:9–24).

38. Morris, *The Cross in the New Testament*, 169.

39. Carson, *Gospel according to John*, 307. For an alternative interpretation that Jesus's brothers were mocking him, see Klink, *John*, 353–54.

Nothing in 2:1–11 would suggest Mary had such a blundering agenda for Jesus. Yet the issue of motives arises in both incidents. Before his brothers approached Jesus, John told us that Jesus "did not want to travel in Judea because the Jews [that is, the Jewish authorities in Judea] were trying to kill him" (7:1; see 5:18). Jesus's response in vv. 6–8 was to tell his brothers, "Go up to the festival yourselves. I'm not going up to this festival, because my time [*kairos*, not *hora*, "hour" as in 2:4, and so not referring specifically to the cross] has not yet fully come." They could go whenever they liked, he told them, since they were part of the world that hated Jesus and loved darkness, and they had no divine mission to perform. But Jesus was not ready. As at the wedding in Cana, Jesus was following an agenda and schedule determined by his Father (see John 11:1–7). As Bruner says, "Jesus lives by his Father's clock, not the world's. His brothers live by the world's clock, which is always saying *'Carpe diem,' 'Seize the day!' 'Go for it!' Make your move!*"[40]

But then, surprisingly, "after his brothers had gone up to the festival [how long after we don't know], then he also went up, not openly but secretly" (v. 10). A superficial reading of this passage may cause us to think Jesus lied to his brothers or was vacillating. Perhaps because of that, some early Greek manuscripts, followed by some translations (KJV, NKJV, HCSB), changed "I'm not going" to "I'm not *yet* going." But even if Jesus said only "I'm not going," the context indicates he was not "planning to stay in Galilee forever."[41] Bruner points out that Jesus did not say "I *will* not go."[42] He would only stay in Galilee while his "time has not yet fully come." Also, when the Father's schedule did allow Jesus to attend the festival, he went "not openly but secretly." These factors tell us that the issue was not "to go or not to go," but when, how, and why Jesus should attend the festival. The issue with Jesus's mother at Cana was similarly not just whether or not to meet the need for wine, but how and, more especially, why.

So Jesus told his mother that their relationship had changed and that they were not on the same page. But did that amount to "Don't bother me. I don't care about their lack of wine. I've got other things to do; you can just deal with the problem as best as you can"? We know that isn't the case, because he did help. And Mary did not interpret Jesus's answer in that way, because of what she said to the servants. What was her clue that Jesus would help in spite of what he said? Was it the look on his face? The tone of his voice? Was it her knowledge of his loving and generous heart? Again, we don't know, but she read him correctly.

---

40. Bruner, *Gospel of John*, 465.
41. Carson, *Gospel according to John*, 309.
42. Bruner, *Gospel of John*, 471.

We are sometimes in impossible situations where we find it difficult to pray because we can't imagine what God could do to help us. We foolishly feel that we need to give him an agenda or instructions on what to do, but we are stymied. In those cases, all we can do is to cry out like Peter when he was sinking into the sea, "Lord, save me!" (Matt 14:30), or like the Canaanite woman with the demon-possessed daughter who fell at Jesus's feet and cried out, "Lord, help me!" (Matt 15:25). I remember hearing a story long ago that is often attributed to Robert Louis Stevenson.[43] A group of passengers of a small ship being tossed about by a storm are huddled, terrified in the galley. Finally, one of them dares to go up and check on the situation. So he courageously ventures out onto the deck and climbs desperately up to where he can see the pilot. After he manages to return to the others and they plead for information, he responds, "It's going to be all right. I have seen the face of the pilot, and he is smiling." That was Mary's situation, and that is sometimes ours. We can be comforted because we know the Pilot, we know he loves and cares about us, and we know he has things well in hand.[44]

In light of what Jesus said to Mary, then, the question is *Why* did he help? This is a stumper. Before answering that question, largely on the basis of Jesus's words to her, we need to consider the rest of the story.

Before we move on, however, we must ask whether anything should be made of Mary's surprising words to the servants in v. 5: "Do whatever he tells you." That is, "Listen to my son, Jesus. He's going to give you instructions." That word "whatever" suggests limitless applications.[45] An interesting parallel may be found in Gen 41:55: "When the whole land of Egypt was stricken with famine, the people cried out to Pharaoh for food. Pharaoh told all Egypt, 'Go to Joseph and do whatever he tells you.'"

There may be wisdom in Bruce's words: "The recorded words of Mary are few; these particular words have an application beyond the immediate

---

43. Many versions of the alleged story, often called, "The Pilot," may be found on the Internet.

44. Bruner, *Gospel of John*, 138, quotes from Luther's sermon on this incident. He considered Mary's instructions to the servants as the key sentence of the story because it exemplified the nature of faith, which, contrary to the evidence, "adheres firmly to the conviction that he is kind, refusing to give up this opinion because of the thrust she received and unwilling to dishonor him in her heart by thinking him to be otherwise than kind and gracious."

45. The word "whatever" is almost ubiquitous in current English as an exclamation expressing "indifference, skepticism, or exasperation" (*New Oxford American Dictionary*). Here it translates the Gk. phrase ὅ τι ἂν, found elsewhere only in Luke 10:35; John 14:13; 15:16. It is synonymous with ὃ ἐάν, found fifteen times in the New Testament, including only 15:7 in John's Gospel.

occasion which called them forth."[46] Most of us have had the experience sometime of trying to comprehend and follow instructions that turned out to be frustrating, incomprehensible, or just wrong. Then there are those people (men?) who refuse to read directions and prefer to figure out things for themselves. But the importance of waiting on and listening to the Lord's instructions, being poised to act quickly in accordance with them, is a theme that runs through Scripture. The angel of the Lord's words to Joseph to stay in Egypt "until I tell you" in Matt 2:13 share some elements with Mary's words to the servants.

The Old Testament certainly places great emphasis on doing whatever God commands. Doing "everything [that] the LORD [has] commanded"[47] could be a source of great blessing to God's people (Deut 12:28; Josh 1:7-8; 1 Kgs 9:4-5; 11:38). Even the troublesome prophet Balaam knew that "whatever the LORD says, I must do" (Num 23:26). God assured Israel through Moses in Deut 4:1-14 that his instructions would be a source of life and blessing, resulting in God's glory—in which they would share—if they were careful to listen, learn, remember, and follow exactly his instructions. As Josh 11:15 says, "Just as the LORD had commanded his servant Moses, Moses commanded Joshua. That is what Joshua did, leaving nothing undone of all that the LORD had commanded Moses." The Lord would leave out nothing they needed to know (Deut 1:18), and they were not to forget or neglect anything he told them to do. Failure to follow his instructions would be disastrous (Deut 28:15; 2 Kgs 18:9-12; Jer 11:6-8). Sometimes God told his people to do some pretty crazy things, as when God told Noah to build a ship in the desert (Gen 6:14), when he led Israel to a dead end by the sea (Exod 14:1-14), or when he told Moses to make a bronze image of a snake and to mount it on a pole (Num 21:4-9), or when he told Joshua to have Israel march around Jericho blowing trumpets for seven days (Josh 6:1-5). Then there are the really weird things God had some of the prophets do, like marrying a prostitute, going about naked and barefoot for three years, burying their underwear in the desert, or lying on their side for 390 days next to the model of a city (see Hos 1:2; Isa 20:1-4; Jer 13:1-11; 16:1-9; Ezekiel 4-5, 12). How thankful I am not to be a prophet! But every time God's instructions were carried out, they accomplished his purposes. The same would occur in this case, as the perplexed servants did what Jesus told them to do. I doubt that the lesson was lost on the Gospel writer.

---

46. Bruce, *Gospel of John*, 70.

47. The Hebrew phrase כָּל־אֲשֶׁר צִוָּה יְהוָה is found sixteen times in the Old Testament, mostly in Exodus and Numbers. Many additional references to *doing everything* the Lord *commands* also occur.

Jesus's Solution (2:6–8)

> 6 Now six stone water jars had been set there for Jewish purification. Each contained twenty or thirty gallons.
> 7 "Fill the jars with water," Jesus told them. So they filled them to the brim. 8 Then he said to them, "Now draw some out and take it to the headwaiter." And they did.

These verses begin with some helpful background information, signaled by the word "now," as in 1:44 ("Now Philip was from Bethsaida"). Those of us who are cinematically inclined might imagine at this point the camera panning from Jesus and Mary to a wall in the back, along which six large stone jars are lined up (or possibly, as McHugh suggests, embedded in the ground[48]). We might wonder what they contain and what is their purpose. Do they hold some wine that's been forgotten about, the answer to Mary's dilemma? We might even see beyond them some servants racing about with anxious expressions, wondering who's going to tell the headwaiter or the groom about the problem they've recently discovered. No one is paying any attention to the jars, which are certainly large ones. If they all contained wine, there should be more than enough—120 to 180 gallons of it. One website I consulted (www.evite.com) recommended that for a modern party of two hundred moderate wine drinkers, drinking nothing but wine for eight hours, seventy-two gallons of wine should be plenty. If there were five hundred drinkers at the party, 180 gallons would be about right. In Jesus's time and place, however, wine was almost always mixed by two to four parts water with one part wine.[49] These jars, then, could have supplied a superabundance of wine for many days! Unfortunately, as the camera swings to a vantage point above the jars, giving us a look inside, our hearts sink as we see nothing but a little water.

Some of John's modern readers might be confused by the word "contained" in v. 6: "Each [water jar] contained twenty or thirty gallons." Were they already full of water? But the word for "contained" just means that they would "hold" that much liquid (see the ESV, NIV, NLT). We know they are either empty or contain just a little water because in v. 7 Jesus tells the servants to "fill the jars with water," and they fill them "to the brim." This last phrase shows the servants' strict and zealous obedience,[50] and perhaps

---

48. McHugh, *John 1–4*, 184.
49. Keener, *Gospel of John*, 500.
50. Bruner, *Gospel of John*, 131, makes an interesting point that some Bible readers focus too much on trying to imitate the faith or obedience we find in various characters in such a story. We must have the faith of Mary and the obedience of the servants if we want God's abundant blessings. "Sometimes expositors turn gracious stories about

that the jars contained "nothing but water,"[51] or possibly symbolized that "the appointed time for the ceremonial observances of the Jewish law had run its full course"[52] or come to fulfillment.[53] More likely it stresses the superabundance that Jesus was about to supply.[54]

Something else about John's account here that we may wonder about is when and how Jesus performed the miracle of turning water into wine. Did the water become wine as the servants poured each bucket into the jars? Or did it happen after each jar or all the jars were full? Or was it not until a servant would draw some out (Tasker and McHugh; but Morris notes that the size of the jars would then be irrelevant)?[55] We would like a "Shazam! All the water became wine!" But John's account is so subtle that all he tells us is in v. 9, where we learn only that it had happened by the time the headwaiter tasted it: "after it had become wine." It reminds me of an element in the otherwise spectacular creation account of Genesis 1, which is full of "Let there be . . ." and "So God made . . . ." For about ten years while my son Jon was growing up, we'd go camping and fishing in the mountains of Colorado every summer. The night before we headed home, we'd always lie on the picnic table, gazing in awe at the stars, and talking—a priceless experience. What a God we have! But many in the ancient world were under the deceptive spell of astrology, believing that the stars were divinities that somehow controlled human destiny. Probably for that reason, Moses downplays their importance. After telling us how God created the sun and moon as "signs for seasons and for days and years," to light the earth and rule the day and night, he tells us with just two words in Hebrew about God creating the stars: literally, "and the stars." That's all he says about God's creation of the planets and stars and nebulas and galaxies and comets, and more! And here in John 2, all the inspired writer tells us about Jesus turning water into wine

---

Jesus into burdensome requirements for heroic believers and so make the wrong persons the stories' heroes and thus ruin the gospel inside the Gospel . . . The story honors a divine miracle, not a human achievement."

51. Morris, *Gospel according to John*, 183.
52. Bruce, *Gospel of John*, 71.
53. Klink, *John*, 166–67.
54. According to Ridderbos, *Gospel of John*, 107, "If there is a clear hint anywhere for the understanding of the meaning of a miracle, then surely it is here, in the manner in which the Evangelist quantifies the capacity of the 'vessels of the law' in order to enable the reader to measure by that standard the abundance of what Jesus Christ provided." After the miracle, "there is wine as plentiful as water, indeed as plentiful as all the water of purification, which has flowed continually but cannot take away the sin of the world."
55. See Tasker, *St. John*, 55; McHugh, *John 1–4*, 186; Morris, *Gospel according to John*, 184.

without the benefit of grapes or sugar or yeast or fermentation time is "after [the water] had become wine."

Probably the reason he did not make more of the miraculous nature of what happened is that this was a "sign" (2:11). As Köstenberger explains, "This oblique way of referring to the actual turning of the water into wine further underscores the way in which John downplays the miraculous in favor of the 'sign-ificance' of the feat performed by Jesus."[56] Very seldom do we stand and marvel at a sign. Its function is to point elsewhere. Before the days of President Eisenhower's interstate highway system, my family traveled in Texas at fifty-five miles per hour on two-lane highways lined with barbed-wire fences. On the fenceposts were often relatively small signs. One clever manufacturer of shaving cream put small signs at intervals of about a quarter of a mile, each containing part of their message. One series of signs read "Henry VIII . . . Did he have trouble! . . . Short-term wives . . . and long-term stubble . . . BURMA SHAVE." Each sign was like a clue in a treasure hunt, pointing to the next one, until the final sign pointed you to the store to buy Burma Shave. Even now many tourist attractions all over the country are announced by a dozen or so signs along the highway, leading climactically (or in some cases anticlimactically) to a place that must not be missed. Like John the Baptist, whose purpose and importance was to point to Jesus, the role of the miraculous events recounted in John's Gospel is to point to Jesus "so that you may believe that Jesus is the Messiah, the Son of God, and that by believing you may have life in his name" (John 20:31). Like the Baptist and like us (Acts 1:8), they are witnesses to Jesus's identity and character and to what he came to do for us. As Jesus says in John 5:36, "These very works I am doing testify about me that the Father has sent me" (also 10:25). Focusing too much on the sign, however, rather than on the one to which it pointed, led to false, nonsaving faith (2:23–25; 6:26–66). In Calvin's comments on v. 6 he criticized those "scoundrels" in his day who claimed to have relics of these water jars, which people could pay to see and have their time in purgatory reduced![57]

The narrator does not allow us all this time for questions, however. He quickly informs us of the purpose of the jars. They are there "for Jewish purification," which is why they were made of stone rather than clay, which was more susceptible to defilement.[58] As people would come to the house in preparation for the wedding feast, the servants would administer this water for washing hands before and after meals (see Mark 7:1–5) and for washing

---

56. Köstenberger, *Theology*, 192.
57. Calvin, *St. John 1–11*, comment on John 2:6.
58. See Keener, *Gospel of John*, 509; Klink, *John*, 166.

the dishes used in the feast (Matt 23:25–26).[59] Many scholars of the ancient[60] as well as modern church believe the mention of the jars' purpose is the key or "clue" to interpreting Jesus's miracle. According to Tasker, Jesus turned this symbol of the "inadequacy of Judaism as a religion of salvation" into "a fitting symbol of the new spiritual power made available for mankind by the shedding of the blood of Jesus."[61] Similarly, Bruce says the water "stands for the whole ancient order of Jewish ceremonial, which Christ was to replace by something better."[62] Jesus took the means of "Jewish purification" or "cleansing" (Gk. *katharismos*) and turned it into wine, symbolizing abundant blessing and joy, as when "your vats will overflow with new wine" (Prov 3:10; also Gen 27:28; Judg 9:13; Pss 4:7; 104:15; Eccl 9:7).[63] Jesus spoke of his coming as involving a break from Jewish practices that were incompatible with the gospel, for "no one puts new wine into old wineskins. Otherwise, the skins burst, the wine spills out, and the skins are ruined. No, they put new wine into fresh wineskins, and both are preserved" (Matt 9:17). Jewish teachers in Jesus's day were famous for focusing on superficial minutiae and externals such as hand washing (see Mark 7:1–4), while neglecting the importance of heart change that God required and that Jesus came to provide (see Matt 12:34–37; 23:1–28). Morris observes that some have seen symbolism in the number of water jars, six representing incompleteness or imperfection. But he also observes that there is nothing in the text supporting this. "Jesus does not create or produce a seventh pot." Not everything in John is symbolic. Sometimes a tree is just a tree.

Morris does think, however, that a negative view of Jewish purification is taken here: "It is precisely Judaism that is transformed by the power of God in Christ."[64] The issue of Jewish purity laws is dealt with in Mark 7, culminating in Jesus's statement that what goes into a person does not defile him; rather, we are defiled by what comes out of our hearts. At this point the inspired Gospel writer explains, "Thus he declared all foods clean" (Mark 7:19). According to Stephen Westerholm, "For Mark's Gentile readers Jewish purity concerns are foreign (7:3–4) and irrelevant, representing in part

---

59. See the discussion of ritual purity in the Gospels by S. Westerholm in "Clean and Unclean," *DJG*, 128–29.
60. See Bruner, *Gospel of John*, 134.
61. Tasker, *St. John*, 55.
62. Bruce, *Gospel of John*, 71; also Burge, *John*, 92.
63. See also Little, *Echoes of the Old Testament*, 19–26.
64. Morris, *Gospel according to John*, 183. Likewise, Marianne Meye Thompson states, "Jesus is seen transforming the water set aside for the Jewish rites of purification into the wine symbolic of the presence of the messianic age" ("John, Gospel of," *DJG*, 373).

a human tradition which has come to displace fundamental aspects of the divine will, and in part divine commands belonging to an old order now set aside with the dawning of the new age." Also in the account of the wedding at Cana, "Doubtless John sees the changing of water (set aside for rites of purification) into wine by Jesus as symbolic of the transition from the old age to the new (2:1–11)."[65] Keener agrees: "In John's symbolic world, even his language here will suggest replacement of some sort." Using these jars to hold wine, he says, meant that they could no longer be used for purification. "Wine is specifically mentioned as a substance that must not be mixed with the water if it is to be valid for purifications ... Strict Pharisees would have regarded transforming the content of waterpots set aside for ritual purposes (2:6) as disrespect toward the tradition of ritual purity, as casting off the law."[66] Köstenberger, too, thinks that the jars being "at least partially empty" may contain John's "subliminal message regarding contemporary Judaism."[67]

Rather than focusing only on the empty water jars as a critique of Judaism, we might turn our attention back to the lack of wine. Absence of

---

65. Westerholm, "Clean and Unclean," *DJG*, 129–30.

66. Keener, *Gospel of John*, 509–10.

67. Köstenberger, *John*, 97. Whereas most scholars think some sort of "replacement" is in view, there seems to be a lack of precision in what exactly is being replaced. Köstenberger, for example, speaks of "the mention of Jewish purification (required by the law)" as perhaps "subtly reinforc[ing] the contrast drawn by the evangelist between the law given through Moses (1:17) and the new messianic provision by Jesus." But then he suggests that the message involved "contemporary Judaism" (Köstenberger, *John*, 97). In *Theology*, 163, he speaks of "the barrenness of contemporary Judaism." Is it the Mosaic law that is being superseded, or is it later Judaism? The Old Testament never speaks of stone water jars to be used for "purification." The term καθαρισμός, "cleansing, purification," is used only eighteen times in the LXX, and seven of those are in books not found in the Hebrew Bible. Only in Lev 15:13 is water specifically to be used for "cleansing." This is for the man who has a "discharge." If he touches anyone without first rinsing his hands, the other person becomes unclean. After he is "cured," he is to wait seven days, then wash his clothes, bathe, and "he will be clean." However, after this he is to bring an offering of turtledoves or pigeons to the sanctuary where the priest is to "make atonement for him before the LORD because of his discharge" (v. 15). Therefore, water alone is insufficient. The emphasis on ritual washing of hands seems to have gained prominence in Judaism after the close of the Old Testament period. Therefore, while there may be implied here a critique of later "Judaism" or "Pharisaism," it may be reading too much into this passage to say that Jesus or John is implying an end to "the poverty of the old dispensation with its merely ceremonial cleansing" (Barrett, *Gospel according to John*, 192), "the whole ancient order of Jewish ceremonial" (Bruce, *Gospel of John*, 71), "the old age" (Westerholm, "Clean and Unclean," *DJG*, 130), or "the water/vessels of the law" (Ridderbos, *Gospel of John*, 107). Such language is at least unclear. I'm not saying that a case cannot be made for "the poverty of the old dispensation" elsewhere. I only want to caution against drawing more from this passage than is here, and to urge greater clarity.

wine in the Old Testament could represent the covenant curses on Israel for their disobedience (Deut 28:39; Hos 2:8; 9:2; Joel 1:10). So God's salvation is often symbolized by abundance of wine. The prophesied lion of Judah is described with wine imagery in Gen 49:10–12.

> The scepter will not depart from Judah or the staff from between his feet until he whose right it is comes and the obedience of the peoples belongs to him. He ties his donkey to a vine, and the colt of his donkey to the choice vine. He washes his clothes in wine and his robes in the blood of grapes. His eyes are darker than wine, and his teeth are whiter than milk.

Jeremiah prophesied that the regathering and restoration of God's repentant remnant who have been ransomed and redeemed would bring unrestrained celebration (Jer 31:12):

> They will come and shout for joy on the heights of Zion; they will be radiant with joy because of the LORD's goodness, because of the grain, the new wine, the fresh oil, and because of the young of the flocks and herds. Their life will be like an irrigated garden, and they will no longer grow weak from hunger.

The coming Messianic age is described as a time when "the mountains will drip with sweet wine, and all the hills will flow with it" (Amos 9:13) and "the vats will overflow with new wine and fresh oil" (Joel 2:24; also Isa 25:6; Hos 14:7; Joel 3:8).

Carson, for example, puts less emphasis than some on the water jars. He believes that this Old Testament imagery of an abundance of wine symbolizing the messianic age leads Jesus to use this situation to say that "the hour of great wine, the hour of his glorification, has not yet come." At Cana, he says, Jesus makes a connection between the wedding and his own role as messianic bridegroom, who "will supply all the 'wine' that is needed for the messianic banquet." Jesus "graciously makes good the deficiencies of the unknown bridegroom of John 2, in anticipation of the perfect way he himself will fill the role of the messianic bridegroom."[68] Jesus compared his first coming to the groom's arrival at his wedding feast (see Matt 9:14–15). Then at Jesus's last supper with his disciples, he spoke of his departure but also his return for them in terms of a messianic banquet: "I will not drink from this

---

68. Carson, *Gospel according to John*, 173. Little, *Echoes of the Old Testament*, 47–48, also notes the Johannine irony that "the true Bridegroom of Israel should manifest his glory as a guest at a wedding in Cana ... The steward therefore makes his remarks about the quality of the wine to the 'official' bridegroom of the story, unnamed and hitherto unremarked (John 2:10). The reader recognizes Jesus, the unknown provider of the wine, as the real but hidden bridegroom of the story."

fruit of the vine from now on until that day when I drink it new with you in my Father's kingdom" (Matt 26:29).

Köstenberger offers a helpful summary of what we have learned so far in answer to our question of why Jesus provided wine for the wedding:

> In conjunction with Jesus' messianic ministry, his miracle performed at a Jewish wedding signifies that Jesus is the messianic bridegroom, with John the Baptist serving as the "friend of the bridegroom" (John 3:29). John's evaluation of the state of first-century Judaism (note the empty stone jars used by the Jews for ceremonial washing mentioned in John 2:6) is contrasted with the fullness and abundance of life and joy brought by Jesus the Messiah (cf. John 10:10). This is further underscored by both the quantity (John 2:6) and the quality (John 2:10) of the wine provided by Jesus.[69]

Like signs on the highway for traveling tourists, Jesus's miracle pointed ahead to what he had come to do, and John used the account to begin building his case that "Jesus is the Messiah, the Son of God" so that "by believing you may have life in his name" (20:31). There is more, however, that John has to teach us, even in these verses. Edmund Little rightly questions whether messianic joy is the end of this story.[70]

The Headwaiter's Discovery (2:9–10)

> 9 When the headwaiter tasted the water (after it had become wine), he did not know where it came from—though the servants who had drawn the water knew. He called the groom 10 and told him, "Everyone sets out the fine wine first, then, after people are drunk, the inferior. But you have kept the fine wine until now."

The term translated "headwaiter" occurs only here, so we know little about who this person was. The Greek *architriklinos* is constructed from a word that means "first, head" (*archos*) and another word (*triklinos*) that means "dining room" (or according to its etymology, "with three couches"). He was the boss of the dining room. It is often translated something like "master of the feast/banquet" or "head steward," and sometimes "master of ceremonies." Köstenberger describes him as "master of the banquet," a position of honor, one of whose primary duties was to regulate distribution of wine. He was a kind of "headwaiter in charge of catering," who "supervised the

---

69. Andreas Köstenberger, "Wine," *DJG2*, 995.
70. Little, *Echoes of the Old Testament*, 61.

serving of food and drink, with several servants under him."⁷¹ Although he was responsible for serving the wine, however, evidently the groom was responsible for providing it. What the groom knew about the lack of wine or about the sudden appearance of vast quantities of it John does not tell us. Since he tells us only that "the servants who had drawn the water knew," and since we suppose that as the groom he would have had other things on his mind, we are probably to assume that he was totally in the dark and walked away from his encounter with the banquet master scratching his head. We might guess that he went to the servants and asked them what was going on and why the wine was suddenly so superb.

Ridderbos makes the reasonable point that "the entire description is intended to render unquestionable the genuineness of the miracle." Also, because the steward does not know where the wine came from, "he is also unsuspecting and hence the most objective judge and witness" to the quality of the wine⁷² And he is not a novice; he has attended many weddings and perhaps served as banquet master at many of them. We may surmise this from his statement that "everyone sets out the fine wine first, then, after people are drunk, the inferior." The word "everyone" is emphatic: "every man/person" (*pas anthrōpos*). He is saying in effect, "I have attended lots of weddings. And at every one of them before today the best wine is served first." There's no suggestion that he's criticizing the wine served previously. Before he tasted the new wine, he probably thought the other wine was fine. He is only praising the higher quality of Jesus's wine. Some say Ethel Waters originated the statement often found on tee shirts and bumper stickers: "God doesn't make junk!" My wife Gigi has taught me a great deal about God's incredibly amazing creatures: sloths (her favorite), thousands of species of beautiful moths and butterflies, and especially creatures in the ocean, like seahorses, sea dragons, and narwhals. There is certainly no end to God's creativity. So it is no surprise that if Jesus is going to make wine, it will be the finest ever. God's provisions are not only abundant, like food (John 6:12, 13, 26), joy (3:29; 15:11; 16:24; 17:13), and grace and truth (1:14, 16);⁷³ his provisions are also perfect.

But the quality of Jesus's wine in and of itself is not the point. The point, in fact, is what it points to. On the one hand, the wine points back to the inadequacy or inferiority of what it was replacing. As Gary Burge writes, "The Messiah . . . has come to fulfill and indeed upend what he finds there."⁷⁴

---

71. Köstenberger, *John*, 98.
72. Ridderbos, *Gospel of John*, 107–8.
73. See Keener, *Gospel of John*, 513.
74. Burge, *John*, 99.

Jesus made the vessels of purification "obsolete for purification."[75] Not only was he supplanting Jewish purification rituals, however, but in some sense he was surpassing even the goodness of the law of Moses (see 1:17). Scholars often like to speak of John's delight in "dualisms." That is, he (as well as Jesus) likes to highlight the nature and work of God in terms of contrasts like heaven and earth, God and the world, spirit and flesh, life and death, light and darkness, good and evil, truth and lies, God and the devil, faith and unbelief/disobedience, freedom and slavery, salvation and judgment, love and hate, joy and pain.[76]

Richard Bauckham has listed and categorized many of these. One of his categories comprises contrasts between what he calls "provisional good and eschatological good." Provisional good refers to things that God had done in the past for and through Israel, such as the law of Moses, worship at the temple in Jerusalem, manna in the wilderness, and Israel the vine that God had planted (Isaiah 5). Eschatological good refers to things God has done, is doing, and will do through Christ.[77] The inferior wine symbolizes those things that were provisionally good. The wine that Jesus created out of the waters of purification points back to the inferiority not only of Jewish ritual, but also of all those things that were only provisionally good. It does this by pointing ahead to the glorious nature of the messianic age Jesus came to bring. Most mornings about 5:30 I take my coffee up to my study on the east side of our house and sit at my desk by the window for prayer and Bible study. It's still dark then, so I have to turn on all my lights. But by the time I go down to eat breakfast, the lights are superfluous. They've been far surpassed by the light of the sun streaming through the window—so much so that I often forget to turn off my lights. What the banquet master is saying, without knowing it, is "We thought we had it good! God had given us blessings upon blessings, which we didn't deserve, so that our cup was overflowing. But look at what he has done now! He has reserved the best for last! He has given us Jesus! In him we will have grace upon grace! And we will worship the Father in Spirit and in truth!"

A word in verses 8–9 has given scholars trouble through the years. When Jesus tells the servants in verse 8 to (literally) "draw now and take" (there is no object in Greek), he is evidently referring to the liquid they have just put into the jars. Then verse 9 refers back to the servants as having "drawn the water." In both verses John uses the verb *antleō* that usually refers to drawing water from a well. Some have argued, therefore, that the

---

75. Burge, *John*, 103.
76. See the study of Johannine dualism in Frey, *Glory of the Crucified One*, 101–67.
77. Bauckham, *Gospel of Glory*, 121–22.

water/wine brought to the banquet master did not come from the water jars but from a well. Morris correctly points out that if this were true, there would have been "no reason at all for mentioning the waterpots or for the command to fill them up."[78] As Keener says, "Context takes precedence over usual word usage. The source of water for 2:8 is the pots of 2:7."[79] But Klink makes an even more significant point. We could say that the waters of purification were labeled "for external use only." They were not to be drunk but were only for washing. John's use of a verb normally referring to drawing drinking water from a well serves to emphasize that the waters of purification have "now" become "*something to drink*. The implication is far reaching: true purification is no longer in reference to external things (e.g., hands and pots) but is entirely internal."[80] Its source is not "the will of the flesh" or "the will of man, but of God" (John 1:13). Jesus himself is "the life" (1:4), and he provides the water of life (4:14: "whoever drinks from the water that I will give him will never get thirsty again. In fact, the water I will give him will become a well of water springing up in him for eternal life"). He is also the "bread of life" (6:51: "I am the living bread that came down from heaven. If anyone eats of this bread he will live forever. The bread that I will give for the life of the world is my flesh"). Therefore, Jesus says in John 6:53–57,

> "Truly I tell you, unless you eat the flesh of the Son of Man and drink his blood, you do not have life in yourselves. The one who eats my flesh and drinks my blood has eternal life, and I will raise him up on the last day, because my flesh is true food and my blood is true drink. The one who eats my flesh and drinks my blood remains in me, and I in him. Just as the living Father sent me and I live because of the Father, so the one who feeds on me will live because of me."

Many in Jesus's audience found these shocking words to be too big a pill to swallow (pun intended). But this is one of the most wonderful truths John has to teach us. As we observed in John 1:4, not only does eternal life consist in knowing God (John 17:3), but it consists of being so united with Christ that we may be said to be *in him* and he may be said to be *in us* (John 15:4–5). To eat and drink Jesus by faith is, in fact, the only way to have real life at all. As John wrote in his first letter (1 John 5:11–12), "And this is the testimony: God has given us eternal life, and this life is *in his Son*. The one who *has the Son has life*. The one who does not have the Son of God does not have life" (emphasis added; also see John 5:24). What countless numbers of

---

78. Morris, *Gospel according to John*, 183.
79. Keener, *Gospel of John*, 511.
80. See Klink, *John*, 167 (emphasis original).

new Christians have received the peace of assurance of salvation from these marvelous words! And for the one who has walked with Jesus for many decades, the Christian life consists of eating and drinking Jesus until at the great marriage banquet we see him face to face (see Ps 11:7; Rev 22:4).

The author of Hebrews refers colorfully to the same concept in 13:10: "We have an altar from which those who worship at the tabernacle do not have a right to eat." As Westcott says,

> "Primarily there is but one sacrifice for the Christian and one means of support, the sacrifice of Christ upon the Cross and the participating in Him . . . The only earthly 'altar' is the Cross on which Christ offered Himself: Christ is the offering: He is Himself the feast of the believer . . . Christ Himself, Christ crucified, is necessarily regarded as 'the altar' from which we draw our sustenance, and on (in) which (to go on to a later idea) we offer ourselves."[81]

Philip Hughes quotes from the eighteenth-century Scottish theologian John Brown's 1862 exposition on Hebrews:

> We are permitted to feast on the whole sacrifice of Jesus Christ. We not only eat his flesh, but we do what none of the priests durst do with regard to any of the sacrifices, we drink his blood. We enjoy the full measure of benefit which his sacrifice was designed to secure. We are allowed to feed freely upon the highest and holiest of all sacrifices. Our reconciliation with God is complete, our fellowship with him intimate and delightful.[82]

Brown's words take on added significance when we consider that at the Passover feast the lamb served two functions: its blood marked the door, providing deliverance from death, and its flesh was eaten in its entirety—nothing was to be left over for later, providing nourishment to sustain life (Exod 12:4). When Passover was over, the lamb was gone. It was wholly consumed as a substitutionary sacrifice.[83] And when Jesus celebrated the

---

81. Westcott, *Hebrews*, 438.

82. Hughes, *Hebrews*, 576. Against Catholic scholars who have connected the altar in this verse with the Lord's table, Hughes states, "The term 'altar' is nowhere in the New Testament associated with the institution or the observance of the Lord's Supper, nor is it found as a synonym for the eucharistic table—indeed, it is perfectly plain that no altar was present when Christ inaugurated this sacrament in the upper room. And it is evident throughout this epistle that the author is not concerned to speak about the eucharist, though he might effectively have done so, had he so wished" (p. 577). Hughes also explains that the use of "altar" for the Lord's table began with Cyprian in the third century. Aquinas identified it either with the cross or with Christ himself (p. 578).

83. This is highlighted in Jeffery, et al., *Pierced for Our Transgressions*, 37.

Passover with his disciples, he referred to the bread and the wine, but he never mentioned the lamb on the table, "since the [true] Lamb is sitting at the table with them."[84]

Now before we move on to John's concluding verse summarizing the significance of this account, we must take another look at Jesus's statement, "My hour has not yet come." In trying to answer the question of why Jesus turned the water into wine, we've considered and celebrated the way the miracle of the wine announces an end to Pharisaical self-righteousness and externalism and also how it announces the transition from the old age of things that were "provisionally good" to the new messianic age of unimaginable "eschatological good." But we haven't considered yet how the miracle relates to Jesus's mission as the Lamb of God, who takes away the world's sin, brings light into the darkness, defeats evil and the slavery of sin, and brings eternal life and joy to the perishing, providing for those who believe an eternal home in the Father's presence. Nor have we discussed the mechanism by which Jesus would accomplish this. Perhaps he reserved these aspects of his mission for later elaboration. On the other hand, maybe a hint is given in his words to Mary. He had told her, "You and I are not concerned about the same things. You are concerned about satisfying social expectations and saving face. I have no interest in that. I came to meet real human needs, preeminently people's ultimate and eternal need for redemption, and I am driving toward that goal, which lies ahead. I'm not there yet, but everything I do must be consistent with that."

An interesting parallel to Jesus's conversation with Mary might be found in his conversation with Peter after his confession at Caesarea Philippi, "You are the Messiah, the Son of the living God" (Matt 16:13–20; cf. Mark 8:27–30). The writer then tells us (Matt 16:21),

> From then on Jesus began to point out to his disciples that it was necessary for him to go to Jerusalem and suffer many things from the elders, chief priests, and scribes, be killed, and be raised the third day.

This scenario was the farthest thing from Peter's agenda for the Messiah. So, probably on the first occasion that Jesus spoke to them of this, Peter became so agitated that he "began to rebuke" his Master (the One who had "*rebuked* the winds and the sea" in Matt 8:26 and would "*rebuke*" the demon in 17:18)! Jesus had surely been too long in the sun or was suffering from an ailment that affected his thinking, or perhaps he was just feeling discouraged! Peter was not a "yes-man" and would not allow his Master to persist in

---

84. Jeffrey, et al., *Pierced for Our Transgressions*, 39.

faulty thinking. So he said to him, "Oh no, Lord! This will never happen to you!" (Matt 16:22). Peter quickly learned that in trying to correct "the Son of the living God," he was on thin ice. Jesus's response in the next verse was immediate and strong:

> Jesus turned and told Peter, "Get behind me, Satan! You are a hindrance to me because you're not thinking about God's concerns but human concerns."

The phrase "God's concerns" is literally "the things of God," and "human concerns" is literally "the things of men." Peter's views were not the same as God's, since he did not get them from God. Rather, they were derived from faulty premises, faulty human understanding, and faulty reasoning—not a good place to get our ideas. Peter had some faulty assumptions about why Jesus had come and what he was planning to do—just like Mary. The rock over which Peter, the rock, had stumbled was the cross, which the apostle Paul tells us was always "a stumbling block [Gk. *skandalon*] to the Jews" (1 Cor 1:23; also Gal 5:11).

But, to a degree, this was also Mary's problem. She was not thinking about the things of God; she was thinking about the things of men. Jesus's rebuke of her was not nearly as strong as his later rebuke of Peter, but any attempt to divert Jesus from his mission as the Lamb of God was of the devil. We've already seen in our comments on John 2:4 that Jesus's reference to "my hour" in the context of John's Gospel can be nothing else but a reference to his death on the cross. Looking again at John 12:27, 31–33, as he begins the last week of his earthly life Jesus prays,

> "Now my soul is troubled. What should I say—Father, save me from *this hour*? But that is why I came to *this hour* . . . Now is the judgment of this world. Now the ruler of this world will be cast out. As for me, if I am lifted up from the earth I will draw all people to myself." He said this to indicate what kind of death he was about to die. (Emphasis added)

When Jesus spoke to Mary and later to Peter and the other disciples, he knew this was where he was headed, and he knew that he faced Satanic opposition. The word Jesus used that is translated "hindrance" in Matt 16:23 (*skandalon*) is the same word for "stumbling block" in 1 Cor 1:23. Danker's Greek lexicon gives the meaning as either a "trap" or "an action or circumstance that leads one to act contrary to a proper course of action or set of beliefs," that is, "temptation to sin, enticement."[85] Peter was inadvertently trying to get Jesus to "act contrary" to his "proper course of action." My wife

---

85. BDAG, 926.

Gigi and I recently read together John Bunyan's *Pilgrim's Progress*, in which Christian and his companion Hopeful face many obstacles, temptations, diversions, and detours on their way to the Celestial City. Even Jesus had to fight against these—things that could divert his focus from his mission as the Lamb of God. Everything he did, in fact, had to contribute to the accomplishment of his purpose—even providing wine at a wedding. Jesus was not *only* showing kindness and mercy. As if for a treasure hunt, Jesus was planting clues for his disciples and for us that pointed to why he had come.[86]

This miracle was a clue or signpost pointing ahead to the cross. When Jesus told Mary that his purposes were different from hers, he followed his statement with a reference to the cross that contained an implied "but." He had other concerns of an eternal nature that he would eventually satisfy, *but* the time for him to satisfy them had not yet come. In conversations we never say everything we're thinking. We make assumptions about what the other person should know and what they should be able to figure out about what we're saying. The father who asks his son if he wants to go fishing and receives as a reply, "Is the Pope Catholic?" or "Do whales swim in the sea?" can easily infer the correct meaning. We can also usually pick up on irony and sarcasm. If the son had said, "No, Dad, I'd rather stay home and clean out the gutters," again, the father would certainly be able to supply the real answer. My point is that when Jesus was speaking to his mother, he left some stuff out that he expects us to be able to supply. Notice, I did not say he expected *Mary* to supply. Some might object to my explanation of Jesus's words that Mary would not have understood what he meant, and this is exactly right. I think it likely that when Mary heard Jesus's reply to her, she looked at him for a few seconds with a blank expression on her face like a deer in the headlights before she finally told the servants to do whatever he said. It was not that she had finally comprehended Jesus as saying he would supply the wine. Rather, she just set his words aside to be pondered later and supplied her own answer to her request, probably based solely on her knowledge of Jesus. Carson comments that several of John's characters "cannot possibly understand what they rightly confess."[87]

Is it hard for us to imagine Jesus saying something that would be not only difficult to understand but initially incomprehensible to his immediate audience? Is it hard for us to imagine Yo-Yo Ma playing the cello? Not at all. We might say, "That's what he does." A quick look at amazon.com turned up sixteen books currently available *in English* on the *Hard/Difficult Sayings*

---

86. The idea that the Johannine signs were like clues in a treasure hunt comes from Wright, *John for Everyone*, 20–21.

87. Carson, *Gospel according to John*, 57.

of Jesus. There was a lot of head scratching whenever Jesus was around. He often spoke to his audience, including his disciples, with puzzling yet tantalizing statements that challenged them to continue watching, listening, asking questions, and patiently investigating to better understand who he was and what he was about. The Gospel of John, in fact, is famous for them.[88] For example, after a few days in Cana, Jesus was in Jerusalem at the Passover and said to his Jewish audience, "Destroy this temple, and I will raise it up in three days." They did not know that he was talking about "the temple of his body" (John 2:19-21). Then, when a Pharisee named Nicodemus came to see him one night, Jesus told him, "Unless someone is born again, he cannot see the kingdom of God" (John 3:3). And if that was not confounding enough, Jesus then said to him, "Just as Moses lifted up the snake in the wilderness, so the Son of Man must be lifted up, so that everyone who believes in him may have eternal life" (3:14-15). The image of the Son of Man being "lifted up" on a pole like a bronze snake must have sounded ridiculous to Nicodemus. In the next chapter, Jesus offered the Samaritan woman at Jacob's well "living water" that would "become a well of water springing up in [her] for eternal life" (4:10, 14). That sounded pretty cool, but she had no idea what it meant. But perhaps most puzzling of all were Jesus's statements about his own death, such as in John 12:23-24 (as well as vv. 31-33 already quoted):

> "The hour has come for the Son of Man to be glorified. Truly I tell you, unless a grain of wheat falls to the ground and dies, it remains by itself. But if it dies, it produces much fruit.

The Son of Man would be "glorified" like a grain of wheat planted in the ground? No living person would understand these statements until after Jesus's death and resurrection, his "glorification" (see John 12:16).

So we should not be surprised if Jesus makes an enigmatic remark to Mary about his coming death. The question is, Why does he say it here? In other words, how might the need for wine and Jesus's satisfying that need be connected to his death on the cross? We must return to the suggestion that Jesus left some stuff out. I am convinced Jesus was making a connection between the wine and the blood that he would shed on the cross. I agree

---

88. See Carson, "Understanding Misunderstandings in the Fourth Gospel," 59-91; Köstenberger, *Theology*, 141-45. Köstenberger explains, "In terms of their effect on the reader, the misunderstandings keep readers' interest by presenting them with riddles they must solve in order to progress to a fuller spiritual understanding of various aspects of Jesus' mission. The misunderstandings thus serve as devices aiming to engage the reader and to convey spiritual truth, especially with regard to Jesus' death and resurrection" (p. 143).

with Tasker: The lack of wine at the wedding "suggested to Jesus" the deeper human need he had come to meet. People "had no inherent strength to save themselves from the dire predicament in which they stood as sinners." Tasker points to the imagery in Isa 63:1–3 of the Messiah treading the winepress alone. Jesus came to "pour out the wine of His own most precious blood . . . The real significance of Jesus' action in turning water into wine at Cana," he says, "must always be hidden from those whose faith is not centred upon Christ crucified."[89] Jesus was saying that he did not come to supply wine but salvation through his blood, although the time for that sacrifice had not yet arrived. Nevertheless, as a *sign* pointing to his eventual satisfaction of our need for forgiveness in his blood, Jesus supplied the wine they needed at the wedding—but not just any wine. It was the finest wine that pointed ahead to the ultimate purification. Daily external cleansing would be replaced by once-and-for-all forgiveness and cleansing of the heart.

Some people object that *blood* is not an appropriate topic of conversation in church: it's nasty and connotes violence. We especially need to keep our kids away from such topics. They see enough violence on TV and in video games. So even talk of the blood of Christ is forbidden in some quarters. I know a lady who taught a Sunday school class for children at a mainline denominational church. When some adults heard she had been talking about the blood of Christ, tempers flared, and she received a visit from the pastor instructing her to keep that topic to herself. Children can be told about Jesus's love, but not about the blood he shed for us at the cross because of that love.

Several years ago, I was asked to teach a topic of my choice in a large Sunday school class in the Baptist church I attended. I had been studying the book of Leviticus and finding a great deal of wonderful truth there regarding the work of Christ. So I decided to survey the first seven chapters of Leviticus and what the offerings could teach us about the cross. After class I learned that the wife of a colleague of mine who was there objected strongly to my description of the nature of the Levitical sacrifices. It grieved me to think that a careful study of seven chapters of the Bible was not appropriate for a Sunday school class in a Bible-believing church. After all, according to my count, blood is mentioned in the Old Testament 362 times (most often in Leviticus, Ezekiel, Exodus, Deuteronomy, and Isaiah, in descending order of frequency), and in the New Testament 97 times (mostly in Hebrews, Revelation, Matthew, Acts, Luke, and John). How can you teach the Bible without talking about blood, especially since "without the shedding of blood there is no forgiveness" (Heb 9:22)?

---

89. Tasker, *St. John*, 56–57.

But is it reasonable to suppose that Jesus might make this connection between wine and blood? The most obvious place to look for such a connection is at Jesus's last supper with his disciples, where he makes it explicit:

> Then he took a cup, and after giving thanks, he gave it to them, and they all drank from it. He said to them, "This is my blood of the covenant, which is poured out for many. Truly I tell you, I will no longer drink of the fruit of the vine until that day when I drink it new in the kingdom of God." (Mark 14:23-25; similarly Matt 26:27-29)

> In the same way he also took the cup after supper and said, "This cup is the new covenant in my blood, which is poured out for you." (Luke 22:20)

The apostle Paul also echoes this connection:

> The cup of blessing that we bless, is it not a sharing in the blood of Christ? The bread that we break, is it not a sharing in the body of Christ? (1 Cor 10:16)

> In the same way also he took the cup, after supper, and said, "This cup is the new covenant in my blood. Do this, as often as you drink it, in remembrance of me." For as often as you eat this bread and drink the cup, you proclaim the Lord's death until he comes. (1 Cor 11:25-26)

As Barry Joslin points out from Heb 9:15, the making of a new covenant required the shedding of blood.[90]

Someone might ask, If John wanted us to connect the felt need for wine at the wedding with the real, universal need for Jesus's sacrificial blood, why didn't he include these words of Jesus at the Last Supper in his account of the upper room in John 13-17? This is a reasonable question. But to repeat something said in the introduction, John almost certainly knew that other Gospels were available and that his readers were aware of Jesus's institution of the Lord's Supper. As Bauckham says, "John presupposes that his readers know Mark's Gospel and deliberately does not repeat what could be read in Mark unless he has a specific reason for doing so."[91] Carson believes the evidence indicates that John had read Mark, probably Luke, and

---

90. "Since Christ is mediator ($\mu\epsilon\sigma\acute{\iota}\tau\eta\varsigma$) of the New Covenant (9:15; cf. 7:22; 8:6; 12:24), there must be blood, since even the Sinai covenant was marked by blood (9:18-22). The New Covenant has a new foundation (the blood of Christ), and is therefore a decidedly new work" (Joslin, "Christ Bore the Sins of Many," 87).

91. Bauckham, *Gospel of Glory*, 104.

possibly Matthew.[92] Some scholars have suggested that John could have left out Jesus's institution of the Lord's Supper to "play down a growing sacramentalism accompanying a growing institutionalization of the church at the end of the first century."[93] According to Carson, "It is even possible that the view of the Lord's supper popular in John's day had become magical . . . Far better then to detach eucharistic allusions from the Lord's supper (which in any case would surely have been widely known) and emphasize instead that to which such allusions point—Jesus himself."[94] Besides, it's *Jesus's* purpose in his words to Mary that is most important. And there is plenty of reason to believe that Jesus may have been associating the wine with his blood, that is, with the cross.[95]

Jesus certainly did not invent the connection between wine and blood at his last Passover in the upstairs room. At least two passages in the Old Testament had already done this. In the key messianic prophecy in Gen 49:8–12, Jacob describes Judah's descendant as a great warrior and ruler who would defeat God's enemies and then rule not only God's people but also the other peoples of the earth—"the obedience of the peoples belongs to him." He would also usher in a time of superabundant prosperity. These would not just be the actions of a tribe, but a person, one who would come, "whose right it is" (vv. 10–12):

> The scepter will not depart from Judah or the staff from between his feet until he whose right it is comes and the obedience of the peoples belongs to him. He ties his donkey to a vine, and the colt of his donkey to the choice vine. He washes his clothes in wine and his robes in the blood of grapes. His eyes are darker than wine, and his teeth are whiter than milk.

King David was clearly the preliminary fulfillment of these verses, but they point beyond him to the coming messianic King.[96] In the context of Genesis, these verses describe the one who would strike the head of the serpent (Gen 3:15) and who would bless "all the peoples on earth" (Gen 12:3). Jumping ahead to the prophet Zechariah and picking up again the reference to "his

---

92. Carson, *Gospel according to John*, 51.
93. Blomberg, *Historical Reliability of the New Testament*, 216.
94. Carson, *Gospel according to John*, 458.
95. Not that I'm suggesting Jesus and John had different purposes (thanks to Craig Blomberg for cautioning me here). Part of my point is to call attention to parallels between Jesus's first week and his last week, opening the way for John to see this first miracle as in some sense a foreshadowing of the cross.
96. See the helpful study of Genesis 49 in the context of the Bible's messianic focus in Beale, *A New Testament Biblical Theology*, 92–99.

donkey" and "the colt of his donkey," this would be "your King [who] is coming to you," who is "righteous and victorious, humble and riding on a donkey, on a colt, the foal of a donkey" (Zech 9:9).[97] He would come to "destroy the pride of the Philistines" (that is, the nations of the earth) and make them "a remnant for our God" (Zech 9:6–7). He would also save "the flock of his people," and they would become "like jewels in a crown, sparkling over his land" (Zech 9:16).

As Iain Duguid suggests, however, the images in Gen 49:11–12 may speak of more than extravagant prosperity. "Clothing stained red with the blood of grapes is evocative of an altogether different kind of activity, of outright warfare."[98] The other Old Testament passage that explicitly connects wine and blood is Isa 49:26:

> I will make your oppressors eat their own flesh,
> and they will be drunk with their own blood
> as with sweet wine.
> Then all people will know
> that I, the LORD, am your Savior,
> and your Redeemer, the Mighty One of Jacob.

This passage makes a striking contrast to Jesus's words in John 6:53–56 where he says that true life can only be gained by eating *his* flesh and drinking *his* blood. We might say that either we eat Jesus's flesh and drink his blood by faith or we will eat and drink our own (see Rev 16:6).

Another Old Testament passage where we find a connection between wine and blood is in Ps 16:4–5, which Jesus might even have had in mind in John 6:53–56. After referring to pagan rituals of pouring out "drink offerings of blood" in Ps 16:4, the psalmist prays in v. 5, "LORD, you are my portion and my cup of blessing; you hold my future." As the *Dictionary of Biblical Imagery* points out, in biblical usage, a cup could contain a life-sustaining blessing or a life-draining curse, sometimes specified as drunkenness, representing God's wrath against sin (see Ps 11:7). "Since a cup can convey love, comfort, strength and fellowship [see 2 Sam 11:1–4], biblical writers sometimes use [the word] cup as a symbol for all the benefits God provides,"

---

97. A good study of these verses may be found in Bateman, et al., *Jesus the Messiah*, 43–52, and in Petterson, *Behold Your King*, 129–48. Petterson, *Haggai, Zechariah and Malachi*, 221–22, argues that the verb form rendered "victorious" here (*niphal* from ישׁע), means "saved" (it is also passive in its only two other occurrences, in Deut 33:29 and Ps 33:16) and alludes to the "suffering David tradition seen in the Psalms and developed in Isaiah's servant songs." During David's exile, he rode on a donkey (2 Sam 16:2) and "was humiliated and nearly defeated by his enemies, before God saved him. The picture of David as he returns to Jerusalem is one of distress and suffering."

98. Duguid, "Messianic Themes in Zechariah 9–14," 268.

as in Ps 16:5 and 23:5 ("my cup overflows").[99] Jesus himself is that "cup of blessing" in his blood (1 Cor 10:16) because he drank the cup of the Father's wrath in our place (Mark 14:36; John 18:11).

So wine speaks not only of the extravagant abundance the messianic King will bring, but also of judgment. Duguid points out that "images of harvest and judgement, of winepress and blood, are completely merged in Revelation 14:20,"[100] where the Son of Man has a sharp sickle in his hand. Wine and God's wrath are associated several times there (vv. 8, 10, 19) and judgment is described as a "sharp sickle" gathering "the cluster of grapes from the vineyard of the earth, because its grapes have ripened" and then throwing them "into the great winepress of God's wrath. Then the press was trampled outside the city, and blood flowed out of the press up to the horses' bridles for about 180 miles" (Rev 14:18–20). According to Dennis Johnson, the chapter describes the ruin of Babylon, "barmaid to the world," who has intoxicated the nations "with her mixed brew of rage [against the saints] and sexual license." Her customers, who are drunk on her adulteries, will be gathered to drain God's goblet of wrath and be crushed in his winepress.[101] Then in Revelation 19 the rider "called Faithful and True" appears, not humbly on a donkey, but on a white horse, his eyes blazing, wearing "many crowns," a sharp sword coming from his mouth, and wearing "a robe dipped in blood, and his name is called the Word of God."[102] Christ will come to "trample the winepress of the fierce anger of God, the Almighty. And he has a name written on his robe and on his thigh: KING OF KINGS AND LORD OF LORDS" (see 19:11–16).

Is it possible to fit both these images—God's Lamb who takes away the world's sin and God's Warrior who executes his wrath—on the same canvas without producing a surreal work worthy of a Picasso? Evidently it is, because the Lord's enemies in Rev 6:16 try to hide from "the face of the one seated on the throne and from the wrath of the Lamb." And in Rev 14:10 the worshiper of the beast "will be tormented with fire and sulfur in the sight of the holy angels and in the sight of the Lamb." Then in 17:14, kings who follow the beast "will make war against the Lamb, but the Lamb will conquer them because he is Lord of lords and King of kings." The same Lamb who washes the redeemed in his blood will shed the blood of those who refuse his redemption, who rebel against him, and who oppress and persecute the

---

99. *DBI*, 186.
100. Duguid, "Messianic Themes in Zechariah 9–14," 268.
101. Johnson, *Triumph of the Lamb*, 201, 206.
102. See the study of these verses in Beale, *Revelation*, 958.

redeemed.[103] The judgment described in Revelation also involves the rescue and vindication of God's people. Revelation 19 alludes to Isa 63:1–6, which, like Isa 49:26 (quoted above), combine judgment with vindication.

> 1 Who is this coming from Edom
> in crimson-stained garments from Bozrah—
> this one who is splendid in his apparel,
> striding in his formidable might?
> It is I, proclaiming vindication,
> powerful to save.
> 2 Why are your clothes red,
> and your garments like one who treads a winepress?
> I trampled the winepress alone,
> and no one from the nations was with me.
> 3 I trampled them in my anger
> and ground them underfoot in my fury;
> their blood spattered my garments,
> and all my clothes were stained.
> 4 For I planned the day of vengeance,
> and the year of my redemption came.
> 5 I looked, but there was no one to help,
> and I was amazed that no one assisted;
> so my arm accomplished victory for me,
> and my wrath assisted me.
> 6 I crushed nations in my anger;
> I made them drunk with my wrath
> and poured out their blood on the ground.

Verse 4 places God's vengeance and God's redemption on two sides of the same coin. Dennis Johnson draws from the reflections of Miroslav Volf on the suffering of his own Croatian people at the hands of the Serbians. He concludes, "Only the biblical confidence that God will bring the unjust to justice at history's end can enable victims to respond to their attackers with nonviolent grace in the present. Volf's thesis is that "the practice of nonviolence requires a belief in divine vengeance."[104]

Our main point here, however, is that wine, blood, and divine wrath appear together on the stage of Scripture many times. They speak of judgment, but also of salvation. And both of those forces converge on the cross, where God's judgment against human sin is poured out on God's unique Son, the slaughtered Lamb, whose blood washes away the sins of all who will look to him in faith. As Bruce Waltke states, "Christ's vicarious death

---

103. Beale, *Revelation*, 951.
104. Johnson, *Triumph of the Lamb*, 271, citing Volf, *Exclusion and Embrace*, 302.

and cleansing blood satisfied God, enabling him to uphold his justice while extending mercy and forgiveness"[105] (see Rom 3:25–26) to all who will join themselves to the Savior by faith. Either Christ must pay for our sins with his life given for us, or we must pay for them ourselves with our own lives poured out for nothing.

At the end of the 1959 movie *Ben-Hur,* a Hollywood adaptation of Lew Wallace's novel, when Christ is hanging on the cross, the rain washes Jesus's blood down the cross, onto the ground, and then in rivulets down the hill. Judah Ben-Hur's mother and sister are suddenly healed of their leprosy. The message could be that there is life and healing in the actual blood of Christ, as many have believed. As several scholars have demonstrated, however, blood in the Bible does not have healing properties. It is rather a symbol that a life has been taken. According to the *Dictionary of Biblical Imagery,* blood was "a powerful and ominous symbol of violence and wrong, guilt and coming punishment. Only in the framework of sacrifice could blood portend good news."[106] In his monumental study of *The Apostolic Preaching of the Cross,* Leon Morris concluded that "the association most likely to be conjured up when the Hebrews heard the word 'blood' was that of violent death."[107]

There is another set of Old Testament passages dealing with blood that offers additional background for Jesus's miracle at Cana. These passages describe another miraculous divine transformation of water—this time into *blood!* As in other passages we've examined, the blood here represents divine judgment.

> Moses and Aaron did just as the LORD had commanded; in the sight of Pharaoh and his officials, he raised the staff and struck the water in the Nile, and all the water in the Nile was turned to blood. The fish in the Nile died, and the river smelled so bad the Egyptians could not drink water from it. There was blood throughout the land of Egypt. (Exod 7:20–21; see also Exod 4:9; 7:17, 19; Ps 105:29)

The same miracle will occur again, when God's agents of judgment turn water into blood, bringing death and destruction to the earth (Rev 8:8; 11:6; 16:3–4).

The association of water and blood is also found in other Old Testament passages, where they are the main agents of ritual purification. In ancient Israel they were the primary means of ending a state of uncleanness,

---

105. Waltke, *Old Testament Theology,* 441.
106. *DBI,* 99.
107. Morris, *Apostolic Preaching of the Cross,* 112–14 (esp. p. 114).

DAY SEVEN: JESUS'S FIRST SIGN (2:1–11)   139

that is, of alienation, rejection, and exclusion from worship and from the life of the community of God's people. They are first found together in Leviticus 14, which prescribes the priestly handling of someone whom God has healed from a defiling skin disease. In order for the person to be reintroduced into the life of God's people, two wild birds would be brought to the priest outside the camp. One bird would be killed over a clay pot containing fresh spring water (literally "living water"), thus mixing some of its blood with the water. Then the other bird would be dipped in the blood and released (like the so-called scapegoat of Lev 16:8, 10, 26), while the rest of the blood (and presumably the water) was sprinkled over the healed person. The person might then reenter the camp after bathing, shaving, and washing his clothes (Lev 14:1–9, 48–53). As Jay Sklar explains, "What the Lord does here by providing *ritual* cleansing serves as a picture of what he does by providing *moral* cleansing (cf. Ps. 51:2), a cleansing ultimately accomplished by the most precious sacrificial blood of all—that of Jesus Christ (Heb. 9:13–14; 1 John 1:9)."[108]

I read a story long ago of two sentries standing guard at different stations at the Rock of Gibraltar. I don't know how accurate the story is, especially since I've seen different versions of it, but I suspect there is a germ of truth in it somewhere. The way I heard it, these two soldiers were each alone at their different stations. One was agonizing over his poor choices in life, his sins, and his failures. He was asking whatever God he believed in whether there was anything he could do, anywhere he could turn, to make amends and find forgiveness and healing for his past sins. The other soldier, stationed alone elsewhere at the rock, had only recently found Christ and was still euphoric as he thought about God's forgiveness he had received through the precious blood of Christ. Suddenly, he was approached by someone and dutifully shouted a challenge, to which the approaching person was to give the password. But rather than the appropriate challenge, he blurted out, *"The Precious Blood of Christ!"* As I heard the story, there are many passageways through the Rock of Gibraltar, and his words carried to the ears of the one for whom God intended them—the young soldier agonizing over his sins, who found in them the answer he'd been seeking. I've always loved the story and recall it anytime I hear that wonderful phrase, "the precious blood of Christ." It may be that it happened exactly as I described it. I hope so.[109]

---

108. Sklar, *Leviticus*, 195.

109. Another version may be found at https://bibletruthpublishers.com/what-the-sentry-said/echoes-of-grace-1932-1933/la125729 (accessed 8/30/2018).

Yet another group of Old Testament passages connecting blood and water forbid the drinking of sacrificial blood. These verses explain why the Jews were so shocked and repulsed by Jesus's words about drinking his blood.

> But whenever you want, you may slaughter and eat meat within any of your city gates, according to the blessing the LORD your God has given you. Those who are clean or unclean may eat it, as they would a gazelle or deer, but you must not eat the blood; pour it on the ground like water ... But don't eat the blood, since the blood is the life, and you must not eat the life with the meat. Do not eat blood; pour it on the ground like water. (Deut 12:15–16, 23–24)

> Eat it within your city gates; both the unclean person and the clean may eat it, as though it were a gazelle or deer. But you must not eat its blood; pour it on the ground like water. (Deut 15:22–23)

These passages echo and reinforce the earlier Levitical prohibition about drinking blood.

> Wherever you live, you must not eat the blood of any bird or animal. Whoever eats any blood is to be cut off from his people. (Lev 7:26–27)

> Anyone from the house of Israel or from the aliens who reside among them who eats any blood, I will turn against that person who eats blood and cut him off from his people. For the life of a creature is in the blood, and I have appointed it to you to make atonement on the altar for your lives, since it is the lifeblood that makes atonement. Therefore I say to the Israelites: None of you and no alien who resides among you may eat blood. (Lev 17:10–12)

These verses associate life with blood because of the role of blood in making atonement. However, the fact that a sufficient loss of blood results in death suggested to many ancient and modern peoples that the power of life, in some literal sense, resided in the blood, the effects of which could be experienced by drinking it (see Gen 9:4–5; Lev 17:14; 19:26–28). But as Sklar points out, the blood of a sacrificial animal brought life only in that it was a symbol of God's offer of atonement through a substitutionary sacrifice. "In short, the animal's lifeblood was accepted as the ransom payment in place of the offeror's: it served as a mitigated penalty on the offeror's behalf, graciously accepted by the Lord (the offended party), in this way rescuing the offeror (the offending party) from due punishment and restoring peace to the relationship between the sinner and the Lord."[110] So, as the Jewish scholar Baruch Levine states, "Basic to the theory of sacrifice in ancient Israel, as in many other ancient societies, was the notion of substitution ... God accepts the blood of the sacrifices in lieu of human blood."[111]

The principle of atonement—being released from God's wrath and cleansed from sin through substitutionary sacrifice, symbolized by blood—is taught throughout Scripture.[112] It received prominence at the beginning of Israel's history on the night of the first Passover (Exodus 12), when the Passover lamb was sacrificed in the place of the firstborn, and Israel was redeemed from slavery. Then the message of substitutionary atonement was to be reiterated every year at the Passover festival in the month of Nisan. The sacrificed lamb provided deliverance from divine judgment, assuming that each family put its blood on the door of their house. The family was also to eat the entire lamb for dinner. The Passover lamb received the divine judgment of death deserved by the people of Israel for their sins of idolatry during their exile in Egypt (see Ezek 20:6–9).[113] T. D. Alexander explains, "Obviously the blood of the sacrifice played a significant part in preventing the death of the male firstborn. Implicit in this is the idea that the Israelites were inherently no different from the male firstborn of the Egyptians. Without the atoning blood of the sacrifice they too would have been struck dead by the 'destroyer.'"[114]

All these concepts symbolized by blood—violent death, divine wrath, rescue from slavery and oppression, substitutionary atonement, and cleansing from sin—meet in and are embodied by Jesus's sacrificial death on the cross. As J. Behm stated, the New Testament is not interested in the "material blood" of Christ, but in "its shedding in violent death."[115] The theme of the cross runs throughout the Gospel of John, beginning with the Baptist's

---

110. Sklar, *Leviticus*, 221.

111. Levine, *Leviticus*, 115.

112. See Jay Sklar's helpful argument that atonement (Hb. כָּפַר, "make atonement") includes both ransom and purification. Both sin and impurity, he shows, have the dual effect of endangering (requiring ransom) and polluting (requiring purification). Ransom rescued the sinner and restored peace with the Lord. Christ's atonement, of course, no longer involves "guilty sinners presenting an atoning sacrifice to ransom themselves, but the offended King who has himself provided the atoning sacrifice to ransom guilty sinners, all because of his love for them" (p. 54). See *Leviticus*, 50–54.

113. See the helpful study of penal substitution in the Passover in Jeffery, et al., *Pierced for Our Transgressions*, 34–42.

114. T. D. Alexander, "The Passover Sacrifice," in Beckwith and Selman, *Sacrifice in the Bible*, 17.

115. J. Behm, "*haîma* [blood]," *TDNT*, 26.

introduction of him as "the Lamb of God, who takes away the sin of the world" (John 1:29).[116] It extends all the way to the soldier's piercing of Jesus's side so that "at once blood and water came out" (19:34). This happened, John explains, because Jesus was already dead when they came to break his legs on the cross (John 19:31–33), which God orchestrated "so that the Scripture would be fulfilled" (19:36) that prohibited breaking even one of the bones of the Passover lamb (Exod 12:46).[117] Referring to John 12:1 ("six days before the Passover"), Jeffery, Ovey, and Sach suggest that "the Gospel of John presents us with a countdown to the Passover as Jesus' death approaches." They cite John 12:7; 13:1–2; 18:28, 39; and 19:14, 31, 42, leading up to 19:35–36.[118]

Between Jesus the Lamb of God in John 1 and the beginning of this "countdown" leading to the flow of blood and water from his side in John 19,[119] Jesus's words about the necessity of ingesting his flesh and blood in 6:53–56 are placed in the context of Jesus's second Passover by the reference in 6:4: "Now the Passover, a Jewish festival, was near." As Carson explains, "This aside is not so much chronological as theological."[120] As we read the rest of the chapter, we are to have the Passover in mind. The reference to it in 6:4 leads to the miracle of the feeding of the 5,000, which leads to the bread of life discourse, where "Jesus identifies his flesh as the true bread that must be given for the life of the world (6:33, 51), the bread that must be eaten if people are to have eternal life."[121] Without the sacrificial death of Christ, there would be nothing but death for all. Carson elaborates the complex connections: "The sacrifice of the lamb anticipates Jesus' death, the Old Testament manna is superseded by the real bread of life, the exodus typologically sets forth the eternal life that delivers us from sin and destruction, the Passover feast is taken over by the eucharist (both of which point

---

116. See Frey's argument that Jesus's death on the cross is *"the inner goal of the Johannine story of Jesus"* (author's emphasis). Part of his argument is from John's five uses of the verb τελειόω. From the beginning, Jesus spoke of his mission to "finish/accomplish/complete" the "work" the Father had given him to do (4:34; 5:36; 17:4). It is this work that Jesus "fulfilled" on the cross (John 19:28). See *Glory of the Crucified One*, 172. It is actually the slightly different verb τελέω, however, occurring only in John 19:28, 30, that is translated in v. 30, "It is finished."

117. On the use of Exod 12:46 in John 19:36, see Beale and Gladd, *Hidden But Now Revealed*, 354–60.

118. Jeffrey, et al., *Pierced for Our Transgressions*, 40.

119. As Augustus Toplady wrote, "Let the water and the blood, / From Thy riven side which flowed, / Be of sin the double cure, / Cleanse me from its guilt and power." See https://en.wikipedia.org/wiki/Rock_of_Ages_(Christian_hymn). Accessed 1/2/2019.

120. Carson, *Gospel according to John*, 268.

121. Carson, *Gospel according to John*, 268.

to Jesus and his redemptive cross-work)."[122] He also cites the words of the late Anglican theologian E. C. Hoskyns, who proposed that these connections are "almost unintelligible" unless the reference to the Passover in John 6:4 picks up the identification of Jesus as the Lamb of God in 1:29, 36 and anticipates his Passover lamb fulfillment in 19:36.[123]

With all this in mind, it is striking that John's first mention of the Passover, which would have been Jesus's first Passover as "the Lamb of God," comes just two verses after the account of the wedding in Cana, in 2:13: "The Jewish Passover was near, and so Jesus went up to Jerusalem." We might even use the words of Hoskyns and say that Jesus's words to Mary, and especially his reference to the "hour" of his death, are "almost unintelligible" unless he was associating the need for wine with the need for his own sacrificial blood to be shed at the cross in order for us to receive the eternal life he came to provide. Jesus makes explicit the relationship between this first Passover and the cross by his statement, "Destroy this temple, and I will raise it up in three days," by which "he was speaking about the temple of his body" (John 2:19, 21).

Leon Morris calls our attention to the fact that "one of the great themes of the fourth Gospel is that of life, divine life, divine life made available for men. And everywhere that life is associated with Christ. John knows nothing of any life worthy of the name which is not a life in Christ and with Christ and from Christ."[124] As Morris notes, we get life by coming to Christ and fail to find it if we refuse to come to him (John 5:40; 6:35). Seeing him and hearing him are also "linked with life." Jesus's teaching on eating his flesh and drinking his blood tells us that "men must be in right relationship to Christ if they are to be the recipients of the life of which He speaks." Because of the cross, Jesus could give the believer the Spirit as "a well of water springing up in him for eternal life" (John 4:14). Marianne Meye Thompson agrees that "it would not be amiss to summarize the Son's mission and the theme of the Gospel of John in terms of 'eternal life.'" But what is "eternal life"? She points out that the Greek phrase for it, *zōē aiōnios*, means literally, "life of the age," that is, "life of the age to come," that which the righteous will inherit in the future.[125]

Jesus's promise is not that my life will extend forever, as many misunderstand the term "eternal/everlasting life." It is rather that because of

---

122. Carson, *Gospel according to John*, 268.

123. Carson, *Gospel according to John*, 269.

124. Morris, *The Cross in the New Testament*, 160–61.

125. Marianne Meye Thompson, "John, Gospel of," *DJG*, 380. Leon Morris also explains "eternal life" as meaning life "pertaining to the age to come" (*Cross in the New Testament*, 165).

Christ's death and resurrection, the reborn child of God will receive a new kind of life—"God's own kind of life, divine life." It's not the kind of life we know in this world, which will end; it's the kind of life God has and we will have fully in the next world, which is eternal. That's why Jesus can characterize it as life "in abundance" (John 10:10). The term "abundance" is a gross understatement. Jesus said, "The Father has life in himself" and has granted that the Son might be a dispenser of that life (John 5:26). Jesus himself is "the eternal life that was with the Father and was revealed to us" (1 John 1:2).

But believers do not just receive that life at the resurrection or when we die. The life of the coming age has invaded the present age.[126] According to 1 John 2:8, "The darkness [of this present evil age] is passing away and the true light [of heaven in Jesus Christ] is already shining." John is clear that eternal life is a present possession of God's child (emphasis added): "Anyone who hears my word and believes him who sent me *has* eternal life and will not come under judgment but *has passed from death to life*" (John 5:24); Jesus says, "The one who eats my flesh and drinks my blood *has* [now in the present] eternal life, and I will raise him up on the last day" (John 6:54); "God *has given* us eternal life, and this life is in his Son. The one who has the Son *has life*" (1 John 5:11-12). Thompson explains, "Eternal life is ... the appropriation by faith of unseen yet present realities that shape one's life in this world and become more fully realized in the next."[127]

On Saturday, June 23, 2018 the twelve members of the soccer team called Moo Pa, meaning "Wild Boars," finished practice and decided to explore a nearby cave in northern Thailand with their coach. The boys ranged in age from eleven to sixteen, and their coach was twenty-five. After about an hour in the cave, they decided to turn back. But they found that the monsoon rains had flooded the stream that ran near the entrance and flooded the cave, trapping them in. The waters kept rising, causing them to move further and further into the cave. They ended up on a rise about two and a half miles from the entrance. When they did not come home, the parents alerted the police, and a search began about midnight. Eventually their bicycles were located, and it was determined they were trapped in the cave. As the rains continued and the water kept rising, hope for their survival kept dwindling. The rescuers tried pumping water out of the cave, and some Thai Navy SEALS were called in to try diving into the cave. Three British cave divers also came to help, and the rescue team became international. The boys were hanging on without food or blankets, and the only drinking

---

126. See Schreiner, *New Testament Theology*, 84–90.
127. Thompson, "John, Gospel of," *DJG*, 381.

water was what dripped down from stalactites in the cave. Finally, the rains stopped briefly and the water in the cave stopped rising. The rescuers were able to pump about 40% of the water out of the first few chambers and began making their way to the boys. Then, after spending ten days alone in the total darkness, on July 2 the boys heard the sound of English, as two British divers appeared with light, supplies, and hope. The journey there and back for the divers took eleven hours. In the efforts to reach the boys, one diver, a retired Thai Navy SEAL and triathlete named Saman Kunan, ran out of air and died on the trip on July 6 as he was trying to deliver oxygen tanks to the boys. His death demonstrated further how difficult the rescue attempt would be, and changes were made to the strategy; but mission impossible had become mission possible. When the boys were found, parents were called, and hope was restored. Nevertheless, getting the boys out was not going to be easy. They had to be taught to breathe underwater using the Scuba gear. Meanwhile, divers, including a doctor, were sent in to stay with the boys for more than a week, caring for them, encouraging them, and getting them ready for the long journey out. Two divers would have to accompany each boy: one in front carrying his oxygen tank, and one behind. Some of the underwater passages were extremely narrow. The three would be tethered together, since the waters through which they swam were so murky, like swimming through coffee. Finally, on July 8, the first four boys were brought out and rushed to the hospital. Four more exited the following day, and the rest on July 10—eighteen days after they became trapped.[128]

The boys had been in a desperate situation that required outside help if they were to survive. Not only did they have to be *taken out* of the cave to the surface, but all they needed to survive until then had to be *brought in*—food, blankets, water, medical supplies, medical assistance, light, and oxygen tanks for the journey out. All those things had to come from the surface. Their life below, as well as their rescue, depended on the world above. And their rescue resulted in the death of one of the divers committed to helping them. I was amazed when I realized how much their experience paralleled that of all who are rescued out of the darkness by Christ. The life of the next world, which is eternal, has been brought down and provided for us through the death and resurrection of Christ, who not only *came* but is *coming back* to get us to live forever with him (John 14:1–3).

It's impossible to overemphasize the importance of the blood of Christ in the Gospel of John, in the New Testament, and in the thought and life of a Christian. Jesus also speaks in 10:11, 15 of his sacrificial death as a good

---

128. Many news stories recount this incident. For example, see https://abcnews.go.com/International/young-soccer-players-rescued-thai-cave-world-teaching/story?id=57331218 (accessed 1/28/2019).

shepherd laying down his life for his sheep. And John quotes and explains the ironic "prophecy" of the high priest Caiphas in 11:50–52:

> "It is to your advantage that one man should die for the people rather than the whole nation perish." He did not say this on his own, but being high priest that year he prophesied that Jesus was going to die for the nation, and not for the nation only, but also to unite the scattered children of God.

In John's first letter, he informs us of our daily dependence on Jesus's blood by using a present tense verb: "The blood of Jesus his Son *cleanses* us from all sin" (1 John 1:7; emphasis added). Also in his visionary book of Revelation he tells us how much we owe to Jesus's blood: "Jesus Christ . . . has set us free from our sins by his blood" (1:5). A new song is sung to the Lamb, declaring, "You were slaughtered, and you purchased people for God by your blood from every tribe and language and people and nation" (5:9). Those coming out of the great tribulation "washed their robes and made them white in the blood of the Lamb" (7:14). Even the dragon, Satan, and his angels are conquered by Christ's followers "by the blood of the Lamb and by the word of their testimony" (12:11).

Jesus's blood could almost be described as a main character in the book of Hebrews. Blood is mentioned twenty-two times, more than in any other book of the New Testament, and the blood of Christ is referred to explicitly thirteen times and implicitly many more times in contrast to the blood of animal sacrifices. Most references to Jesus's blood occur in Hebrews 9–10, where the author contrasts Jesus's once-for-all sacrifice with the innumerable old covenant sacrifices. But he alludes to the contrast in the previous chapters, where he describes Christ's superior priesthood. Even in his first paragraph he speaks of the Son of God making "purification for sins" and then sitting down "at the right hand of the Majesty on high" (Heb 1:3). Then in Hebrews 3–4 he speaks of God's rest, a concept that has intrigued me since writing my seminary thesis on "Yahweh's Rest in Psalm 95."

I've always believed it somehow designated a place where God's people find rejuvenation; freedom from conflict, grief, pain, and fear; and divine provision. But the Hebrew term, occurring almost thirty times (*menuchah*), translated either "rest" or "resting place," is often referred to as *God's* resting place. According to the messianic prophecy in Isaiah 11, when the Messiah comes, "the root of Jesse will stand as a banner for the peoples. The nations will look to him for guidance, and his resting place will be glorious" (11:10). In the ancient world a temple was built as a resting place for a god, where he might be served, and in return, from which he might protect and bless his servants. But we cannot benefit God by our labor, nor can we confine him and cajole him to do our bidding. God says in Isa 66:1, quoted by Stephen in Acts 7:49–50 before being murdered by his Jewish friends and neighbors, "Heaven is my throne, and earth is my footstool. Where could you possibly build a house for me? And where would my resting place be?" But God can build a resting place for us and invite us into it. The "quiet waters" of Ps 23:2 are literally "waters of rest." They belong to our divine Shepherd, and he brings us there to experience freedom from want and fear because he is there.

The tabernacle and later the temple could be referred to as God's "resting place" or "dwelling" (for example, Ps 132:5, 7–8, 14) only provisionally, with the caveat that it was only his "footstool" and was temporary. As Dan Estes explains in comments on Psalm 132, the term *menuchah* used there of the Lord's sanctuary (also 1 Chr 28:2; 2 Chr 6:41) "is vitally connected to God's promise of rest for his redeemed (cf. Ps 95:11) and is a door into an important theme that runs from Genesis to Revelation. Divine and human kingdom-rest in the garden of Eden was disrupted by human sin, but the prospect of its restoration through divine redemption was symbolized by God's rest in the tabernacle and then the temple."[129] The temple was conceived of as a place of divine rest because it symbolized an invitation into a relationship with God. According to Hebrews 4, that invitation is still available because "we have a great high priest who has passed through the heavens—Jesus the Son of God" (Heb 4:14). Because of him, we can "approach the throne of grace with boldness so that we may receive mercy and find grace to help us in time of need" (4:16). What has most recently impressed me about God's rest is that it promises blessings of rejuvenation, freedom, and provision because it promises the presence of God. Like the "eternal life" that Jesus possesses and offers us (John 1:4), the blessings of rest are only to be found *in him*. They can only be experienced by eating and drinking and immersing ourselves in Jesus.

Our divine high priest not only serves but dwells in "the sanctuary and the true tabernacle that was set up by the Lord and not man" (Heb 8:2). There he is seated "at the right hand of the throne of the Majesty in the heavens." The author is speaking of a "heavenly" sanctuary, which served as the "pattern" for the earthly sanctuaries, which were only "a copy and a shadow" (8:5; see Exod 25:40). The heavenly sanctuary is "the true tabernacle" in that it is both the original and also the permanent dwelling place of God. Earthly structures were only cardboard models. That the heavenly sanctuary is said to have been "set up by the Lord and not man"

---

129. Estes, *Psalms 89–150*, 507–8. Also see Beale, *The Temple and the Church's Mission*, especially 60–63.

might suggest we are to imagine a literal structure in heaven. The verb for "set up" is used several times in the Greek Old Testament for pitching a tent (Gen 26:25). A literal tabernacle in heaven, however, is not likely what the author is describing. This is almost certainly figurative language. The point is that God "does not live in shrines made by hands" (Acts 17:24). As Tom Schreiner explains, "The true tabernacle, then, designates the presence of God, the place where God reigns and rules. Jesus is the greatest priest since he dwells in God's presence and ministers in the heavenly realm where God dwells."[130] Schreiner says even more boldly, "Strictly speaking there isn't a tabernacle at all in the heavenly realm. The heavenly tabernacle becomes a vehicle for describing the indescribable, for depicting the presence of God."[131] Barry Joslin is correct that the holy place is synonymous with the right hand of God (mentioned in Heb 1:3, 13; 8:1; 10:12; 12:2).[132] What would be the point of having a sanctuary in heaven? A sanctuary is where, in theory, we can meet God. But if God is in a heavenly sanctuary, he is separated from his heavenly worshipers just as he was before Jesus died. As Gareth Cockerill points out, in Hebrews "the sanctuary" Christ entered is heaven itself (9:24), which is portrayed as "the most holy place" (9:12). "[T]his Temple, in which God truly dwells, is 'heaven itself' and consists of naught but a Most Holy Place."[133] The old covenant, he says, "was a religion of the [anterior] Holy Place confined to its boundaries and excluded from the Most Holy Place. In the New [Covenant] there is no need for a heavenly 'Holy Place' since Christ brings his people into the very presence of God." A literal heavenly sanctuary would be "nothing more than a vestigial remnant" of the old Mosaic order.[134]

Even with the tabernacle and then the temple inviting people into a relationship with God under the old covenant, it was not an easy matter for sinful people to approach a holy God. At Sinai God had told Moses that not even an animal was even to touch the base of the mountain of God's presence, on penalty of death (Exod 19:12–13, quoted in Heb 12:20):

---

130. Schreiner, *Commentary on Hebrews*, 243.

131. Schreiner, *Commentary on Hebrews*, 267. The same is true of the altar mentioned in Heb 13:10, "from which those who worship at the tabernacle do not have a right to eat." Schreiner states, "Clearly the author isn't thinking of a literal altar. The altar where sacrifices were offered points to a better altar where Christ was sacrificed to atone for sins." By the better altar the author refers to Christ's sacrifice on the cross. Our "eating" from it "is a colorful way of describing the grace believers enjoy through the sacrifice of Christ" (p. 420).

132. Joslin, "Christ Bore the Sins of Many," 85.

133. Cockerill, *Hebrews*, 355.

134. Cockerill, *Hebrews*, 391.

> Put boundaries for the people all around the mountain and say:
> Be careful that you don't go up on the mountain or touch its
> base. Anyone who touches the mountain must be put to death.
> No hand may touch him; instead he will be stoned or shot with
> arrows and not live, whether animal or human.

There was a divinely determined protocol involving washings and other procedures; there were temple personnel to deal with, and most especially, there was blood required. And even then, the average faithful Israelite could only get so far. Only the holiest Israelite man of all, the high priest, could get past all the walls and through the doors and the smoke into the inner chamber of the sanctuary, the holiest place. And even the high priest could only go in once a year, on the day set by God, the Day of Atonement. And even he could not go in without blood—for his own sins as well as for those of the people (Heb 9:7). Through all these regulations and requirements, the author of Hebrews tells us, "the Holy Spirit was making it clear that the way into the most holy place had not yet been disclosed while the first tabernacle was still standing" (9:8). That is, as long as the Mosaic sacrificial system was still in effect, and only temporary, external cleansing was possible (9:13–14), "access to God's presence was not yet freely available."[135] The problem was that "it is impossible for the blood of bulls and goats to take away sins" (Heb 10:4). Schreiner suggests a reason for this: "Animals could scarcely provide atonement. They didn't realize why they were slain and had no consciousness of the significance of their death. They certainly didn't give their life voluntarily for the sake of sinners but were coerced to die against their will."[136] He is not arguing that "the death of animals was a mistake from the beginning or contrary to the will of God." Rather, "the blood of animals functioned typologically and symbolically, pointing forward to the blood of Christ, which truly cleanses from sins.[137]

We might see a parallel here between the animal sacrifices and Jesus turning the water of Jewish purification into the wine that pointed ahead to his sacrificial blood shed on the cross for us. The sacrificial death of Jesus, the Lamb of God, is what changed everything. As the author of Hebrews puts it in 9:11b–12,

> In the greater and more perfect tabernacle not made with hands
> (that is, not of this creation), he entered the most holy place
> once for all time, not by the blood of goats and calves, but by his
> own blood, having obtained eternal redemption.

---

135. Schreiner, *Commentary on Hebrews*, 262.
136. Schreiner, *Commentary on Hebrews*, 292.
137. Schreiner, *Commentary on Hebrews*, 293.

There is a striking contrast here between the "once" of Jesus's action and the "eternal" of the divine result. It was possible only because he is the sinless Son of God (see Heb 4:15; 7:27; 9:14).[138] The phrases "by the blood" and "by his own blood" use a Greek preposition (*dia*) that indicates instrumentality. There is no suggestion here that Jesus brought his literal blood into the sanctuary.[139] What it says is that Jesus's dying a sacrificial death on the cross was the means by which he was able to provide us with complete, once-for-all cleansing of sin from our hearts and lives, as well as imparting to us eternal redemption and bringing us into God's very presence. Because Jesus paved the way for us, we can boldly enter the sanctuary of God's presence by means of his blood (Heb 10:19)—something no ordinary Old Testament believer would ever dare to hope for! Barry Joslin makes an important point that Christ's work did not involve two steps as did the high priest's on the Day of Atonement: sacrificing the animal and then taking the blood into the holiest place. Christ's work was completed at the cross. He points out that according to Heb 9:12, Christ had already "obtained eternal redemption" when he entered the most holy place.[140] He also points out the significance of the last clause of 9:14: "so that we can serve the living God." The new covenant involved God writing his laws on our minds and hearts (Heb 8:10).[141] Jesus did not die just to take away sin. The eternal, redeemed life he provides involves the ultimate life fulfillment of serving our great God and Savior Jesus Christ (see Eph 2:10; Titus 2:11–14). As Sklar explains, "Atonement is the means by which sin and impurity are removed, so that fellowship with the Lord can continue and his people can engage fully in his purposes for them."[142]

Returning briefly to the statement in Heb 10:4 that "it is impossible for the blood of bulls and goats to take away sins," someone reading the book of Leviticus (yes, a few people do make it through Leviticus, though some of those are overcome by the book of Numbers), having read Hebrews, may be struck by the repeated assurance given to someone who has just brought an animal sacrifice, "They/he will be forgiven" (4:20, 26, 31, 35; 5:10, 13, 16, 18; 6:7; 19:22). How is this possible? Jay Sklar offers a suggested explanation:

---

138. As Frank Thielman argues, "It is difficult to see why the author [of Hebrews] would place such stress on Jesus' sinlessness precisely in speaking of his sacrificial death, unless this sacrifice contained a substitutionary element" ("The Atonement," 120).

139. Schreiner, *Commentary on Hebrews*, 268. Also see Mark Seifrid, "The Death of Christ," DLNT, 274.

140. Joslin, "Christ Bore the Sins of Many," 82.

141. Joslin, "Christ Bore the Sins of Many," 85. See also his stress on the practical results of atonement on p. 86.

142. Sklar, *Leviticus*, 55.

> Atoning sacrifice in the Old Testament may be compared to writing a cheque ... The purpose of the cheque was to cover the debt of sin. The form of the cheque was an animal sacrifice, whose lifeblood was given in place of the sinner's ... The Lord in his grace received the cheque and declared the debt paid, graciously assuring forgiveness to the offeror. But he did not cash it. In the grand scheme of things, it is not possible for the lifeblood of an animal to fully ransom the lifeblood of a human. To return to the analogy, the cheque would have bounced. So why did the Lord receive it as payment at the time? Because he knew that there would one day be money in the account to cover the debt: namely, when Jesus gave his lifeblood as the perfect and final ransom for the lifeblood of sinners (Heb 10:10, 12–14).[143]

Joslin argues from Heb 9:15 (Christ "is the mediator of a new covenant, so that those who are called might receive the promise of the eternal inheritance, because a death has taken place for redemption from the transgressions committed under the first covenant") that Christ's death covers both Old and New Testament believers: "The sins of the true people of God (those called and marked by faith), in both Old and New Covenant, are forgiven in the atonement of Christ. The person and work of Christ consummated the old order and inaugurated the new."[144]

There are also other important verses dealing explicitly with the blood of Christ that have not been considered. They too are certainly worthy of study. I will list some of them here without discussion for the sake of anyone wanting to dig further into this critical teaching on what Christ has done for us.

> Be on guard for yourselves and for all the flock of which the Holy Spirit has appointed you as overseers, to shepherd the church of God, which he purchased with his own blood. (Acts 20:28)

> God presented him as an atoning sacrifice in his blood, received through faith, to demonstrate his righteousness, because in his restraint God passed over the sins previously committed. (Rom 3:25)

> How much more then, since we have now been declared righteous by his blood, will we be saved through him from wrath. (Rom 5:9)

---

143. Sklar, *Leviticus*, 72. He indicates that he is borrowing this comparison from Williams, *Far as the Curse Is Found*, 216.

144. Joslin, "Christ Bore the Sins of Many," 87.

> In him we have redemption through his blood, the forgiveness of our trespasses, according to the riches of his grace. (Eph 1:7)
>
> But now in Christ Jesus, you who were far away have been brought near by the blood of Christ. (Eph 2:13)
>
> For God was pleased to have all his fullness dwell in him, and through him to reconcile everything to himself, whether things on earth or things in heaven, by making peace through his blood, shed on the cross. (Col 1:19–20)
>
> To those chosen . . . according to the foreknowledge of God the Father, through the sanctifying work of the Spirit, to be obedient and to be sprinkled with the blood of Jesus Christ. (1 Pet 1:1–2)
>
> For you know that you were redeemed from your empty way of life inherited from your fathers, not with perishable things like silver or gold, but with the precious blood of Christ, like that of an unblemished and spotless lamb. He was foreknown before the foundation of the world but was revealed in these last times for you. (1 Pet 1:18–20)

Those of us who have been around for several decades often marvel at the amazing changes that have taken place in our world and in our lives. We often point to technological changes and laugh at young people who don't know how to use a rotary phone. Another change I've seen since my childhood is in the area of specialization. If a man (yes, almost always) said he was a doctor, that meant he could take care of most any physical issues. He was a general practitioner. That's no longer the case. The same is true of auto mechanics. I recently took my car to a large auto garage and asked them to find out why my "check engine" light was on. I was told the guy (female mechanics don't seem to be too plentiful yet) who could do that didn't come in until eleven o'clock! Of course, we have always had specialization. I was once a young outboard motor mechanic. One time I couldn't figure out how to loosen a particular bolt that was cleverly tucked away deep inside an engine. When I asked a more seasoned mechanic for help, he produced a uniquely bent wrench he had designed exactly for that purpose. It worked beautifully. I apologize for the mundane examples, but not long ago the words of the nineteenth-century hymn, "Nothing but the Blood of Jesus," came to mind (written by Rev. Robert Lowry; 1826–1899, Baptist pastor and hymnologist, who also gave us "Shall We Gather at the River?" "I Need Thee Every Hour," "All the Way My Saviour Leads Me," "We're Marching to Zion," "Low in the Grave He Lay," etc.):[145]

---

145. Lyrics may be found at https://library.timelesstruths.org/music/Nothing_but_the_Blood/ (accessed 8/24/2018). I found this interesting paragraph in an article on

What can wash away my sin?
Nothing but the blood of Jesus;
What can make me whole again?
Nothing but the blood of Jesus.

> Refrain:
> Oh! precious is the flow
> That makes me white as snow;
> No other fount I know,
> Nothing but the blood of Jesus.

For my pardon, this I see,
Nothing but the blood of Jesus;
For my cleansing this my plea,
Nothing but the blood of Jesus.

Nothing can for sin atone,
Nothing but the blood of Jesus;
Naught of good that I have done,
Nothing but the blood of Jesus.

This is all my hope and peace,
Nothing but the blood of Jesus;
This is all my righteousness,
Nothing but the blood of Jesus.

Now by this I'll overcome—
Nothing but the blood of Jesus;
Now by this I'll reach my home—
Nothing but the blood of Jesus.

Glory! Glory! This I sing—
Nothing but the blood of Jesus,
All my praise for this I bring—
Nothing but the blood of Jesus.

Of course, only the first verse came to mind. But it was enough for a thought to suddenly sweep over me with considerable emotion: That's really true! There is nothing except the blood of Jesus that could have washed away *my*

---

this hymn on a United Methodist Church website (Discipleship Ministries, "History of Hymns: 'Nothing but the Blood'" by C. Michael Hawn): "The Rev. Carlton R. Young, editor of *The United Methodist Hymnal,* noted that 'Nothing but the Blood' 'was near the top of the list . . . on the most popular religious songs found in the five widely used hymnals and songbooks other than the 1957 Evangelical United Brethren and 1966 Methodist hymnals.' For many, however, this hymn is anathema, especially for those who loathe 'blood' hymns." https://www.umcdiscipleship.org/resources/history-of-hymns-nothing-but-the-blood (accessed 8/24/2018).

sin! Wow! Thank you, Lord! That thought and that image have entered my mind many times since then. Only his blood could have washed away my sin and guilt and shame and made me acceptable to him and fit for his presence. I recently thought of another mundane example. When my daughter Ann was just a girl (What an odd phrase—"just a girl"! She was and still is an amazing delight!), she had a pair of patent leather shoes—white I think. I remember her bringing them to me to see if I could get the scuff marks off (I specialized in fixing things like that). I tried water, soap and water, even turpentine or paint thinner. Nothing touched those scuff marks. There was no Google at that time. I was on my own. Then I remembered my days in the boat business. We used something called acetone as a thinner and cleaner for fiberglass resin. It did a great job and was the only thing for that purpose. Then I remembered that nail polish remover was just acetone. So I found some, put it on a napkin, and rubbed the scuff marks. They vanished like magic! I was a hero. Unfortunately, the spiritual application occurred to me only recently. Jesus's blood is just like that. Nothing but his bloody death on the cross could wipe sin and all its effects from my life. What a wonderful Savior we have! What a wonderful salvation we have! What a wonderful, gracious, merciful, patient, forgiving God we have!

Conclusion (2:11)

> 11 Jesus did this, the first of his signs, in Cana of Galilee. He revealed his glory, and his disciples believed in him.

If this verse were not tucked away in the middle of only the second chapter of John's Gospel, we might almost think this is the end. In the miracle at Cana, Jesus revealed his glory, and the disciples believed in him. The end. But there is that pesky word "first," which suggests there might be more to come. So we keep reading and finding more signs, like the old BURMA SHAVE signs on the highway in Texas. The Greek word translated "sign," *sēmeion*, occurs seventeen times in John's Gospel, indicating that one sign was not enough. According to Barrett, "This is one of the most characteristic and important words of the Gospel."[146] Jesus did unspecified signs at his first Passover festival (2:23). Then he healed a royal official's son at Capernaum, which John calls "the second sign" after returning to Galilee (4:54), but John offers no further help in counting the signs. At another Jerusalem festival, Jesus healed a disabled man (5:1–16; see 6:2), which is often taken as the third sign. The fourth sign was supposedly the feeding of the 5,000 in

---

146. Barrett, *Gospel according to John*, 75.

Galilee (6:14). Jesus's walking on the water could be considered the fifth sign (6:16–22), although John doesn't call it a sign.[147] The fifth sign is usually regarded as the restoring of sight to the man born blind (9:1–41), though it is only obliquely referred to as a sign in 9:16. The raising of Lazarus is usually regarded as the sixth sign (11:1–57; called a "sign" in 12:18). John's reference to "many other signs" in 20:30 is taken by many scholars to include Jesus's cross and resurrection, considered "the greatest sign of them all."[148] Other scholars, however, argue that the latter was not a sign but rather the reality to which the signs pointed.[149] Whatever we decide about how to count the signs, the miracle in Cana was just the start.

But what is a "sign"? The Hebrew equivalent of *sēmeion* is *'ôt*. The latter occurs seventy-eight times in the Old Testament, and seventy-five of those are translated in the Septuagint by *sēmeion*. The Hebrew term designated an object, action, or event that represented or pointed to something else, such as a signal conveying information (1 Sam 14:10), a mark of identification (Exod 12:13; Num 2:2), an indicator or reminder of an agreement (Gen 9:12–13; Exod 13:9; Josh 2:12; 4:6), or the evidence or proof that something is true (Exod 4:8). Although its purpose could be to communicate, it most often was intended to demonstrate, to remind, or to convince in order to arouse faith and motivate a response, especially to recognize the work of God and to hear his voice (Num 14:11; 17:10; Deut 11:1–7).[150] Parallel to John's usage, Moses performed signs in order to demonstrate his identity as God's servant and messenger and to move the people of Israel to trust and follow him (Exodus 3–4). According to Num 14:22, the signs God performed in Egypt and in the wilderness also revealed his "glory." The only other passage in the Old Testament joining "sign" and "glory" is Isa 66:19: "I will establish a sign among them, and I will send survivors from them to the nations—to Tarshish, Put, Lud (who are archers), Tubal, Javan, and the coasts and islands far away—who have not heard about me or seen my glory. And they will proclaim my glory among the nations." The nature of the sign is unspecified, but it could be one or more events that display God's presence and power, demonstrating who he really is. The result will be that

---

147. It also fails Köstenberger's criterion of the signs being "public," that is, works Jesus did in the presence of unbelievers (*Theology of John's Gospel*, 326–27).

148. Carson, *Gospel according to John*, 661.

149. See Köstenberger, *Theology of John's Gospel*, 330–33. See Klink's argument, however, for Jesus's death and resurrection being the seventh sign in *John*, 825–27. Against Köstenberger, he argues that in John 2:18–19, Jesus himself identifies his forthcoming death and resurrection as the seventh "sign" (pp. 181–82, 826).

150. F. J. Helfmeyer, "אוֹת *'ôt*," *TDOT*, 1:167–71.

"the message of God's glory will reach everywhere, even to places that have never heard of Israel's God."[151]

The Greek word *sēmeion* occurs seventy-seven times in the New Testament, with seventeen of those in John's Gospel, more than any other book (seven more are in Revelation). Its use is essentially the same as in the Old Testament, including a signal or mark of identification (Matt 26:48; Luke 2:12), a portent of the end of history (Luke 21:7, 11, 25), or a miraculous event of authentication or confirmation (Acts 2:22, 43). In John's Gospel, which has the least number of miracles, the "signs" are events that are rich in meaning and that point to Jesus as "God's authentic representative."[152] Graham Twelftree explains that in John, "Jesus is in such communion with and so identified with God that he is first and foremost the author of the most stupendous wonders, signs of his unmistakable identity, origin and destiny, seen preeminently in the sign of his death and resurrection."[153]

This first sign, according to 2:11, had a two-stage result: Jesus "revealed his glory, and his disciples believed in him." We also find other instances of Jesus being "revealed" (Gk. *phaneroō*) by what he does. In John 1:31 his baptism by the Baptist reveals him to Israel. Then in 9:3 Jesus explains that he healed the man born blind "so that God's works might be displayed [also *phaneroō*] in him." When Jesus prays in the upper room right before he is arrested and crucified, he says that he has "revealed" God's name (17:6), implying that he has been doing this for three years, ever since his first miracle. After his resurrection, we are told that "Jesus revealed himself again to his disciples by the Sea of Tiberias. He revealed himself in this way" (21:1). This statement is followed by the account of the miracle of the 153 fish, and then by John's concluding statement that "this was now the third time Jesus appeared [or "was revealed"] to the disciples after he was raised from the dead" (21:14; John is probably alluding to the first time in 20:19–23 and the second in 20:26–29). Clearly then, Jesus's revealing of his glory at Cana was not a complete, final, and definitive act. It was simply a step in Jesus's revealing his glory—along the way to John's "so that you may believe" in 20:31. Each of the signs and each of Jesus's revelatory actions is like taking a snapshot at an event. Comprehension requires a composite of all the snapshots. As we read of each of Jesus's actions, we must keep the whole of the Christ event in mind. As Frey points out, only from a post-Easter perspective "can

---

151. Oswalt, *Isaiah, Chapters 40–66*, 689. Motyer, *Prophecy of Isaiah*, 541, proposes, "Knowing as we do that this passage refers to the interim between the comings of the Lord Jesus, the 'sign' can only be his cross."

152. Köstenberger, *Theology of John's Gospel*, 328.

153. Graham H. Twelftree, "Miracles and Miracle Stories," in *DJG2*, 602–3.

Jesus' deeds be narrated and understood as a revelation of his δόξα [glory]."[154] Frey also explains that "in every individual episode something of the whole of the salvific event is expressed. The wine miracle of Cana (2.1–11) points ahead to the 'hour of Jesus,' to the event of death and resurrection, in which Jesus' mother will be present again."[155]

Cana also provided a step along the way for the disciples' belief, which, as the other Gospels show perhaps more clearly, grew in stages. In John as well, we find that Jesus's shocking words at his second Passover caused many people to turn away. But Peter, having been following Jesus for a year, said, "We have come to believe and know that you are the Holy One of God" (6:69). This seems to suggest that the disciples' faith grew gradually until at some point they reached this conviction. Then after another year, when the disciples learned that their friend Lazarus had died, Jesus said, "I'm glad for you that I wasn't there so that you may believe" (11:15). Evidently, their faith still had some growing to do. A few days later, after washing his disciples' feet, Jesus tells them about one who would betray him. Then he says, "I am telling you now before it happens, so that when it does happen you will believe that I am he" (13:19). He even repeats this a short while later, after telling them again of his upcoming departure (14:29). Between these two predictions, Jesus even urges them four times to believe in him (14:1, 10–12).

All this raises the question whether there is such a thing as saving faith. Perhaps Christians, that is, followers of Christ, just grow in faith until they die. Then, if they have mustered up enough faith, they go to heaven. One of many arguments against this is found in 16:27. While they were all still in the upper room, Jesus told his disciples, "For the Father himself loves you, because you have loved me and have believed that I came from God." Jesus uses two perfect tense verbs here: "have loved" and "have believed." A perfect tense verb means that something has happened in the past with continuing results in the present. If someone invites me to dinner at 7 p.m., and I ate at 6 p.m., I could say, "I ate at 6" (using a simple past tense), or I could stress the fact that I am no longer hungry by saying simply, "I've eaten." If the scenario of simply growing in faith until we die were correct, then Jesus's statement to them would only make sense if they were all dead, which is clearly not the case. So apparently we can gradually grow into a conviction that can be referred to as "saving faith," and then we can (and generally do) increase in faith still more.

---

154. See Frey, *Glory of the Crucified One*, 255. He is responding to his question (p. 238), "How can the not-yet-glorified Jesus (7:39) already reveal 'his' δόξα [in 2:11]?"

155. Frey, *Glory of the Crucified One*, 289.

This sounds a bit too tidy, however. Reality is usually much messier than this, as most of us know. After Jesus's statement in 16:27, the disciples say confidently, "By this we believe that you came from God" (v. 30). But Jesus does not let them rest in their self-confidence. He responds, "Do you now believe?" Then he tells them of an "hour" coming when they will turn away from him and go home (also Matt 26:31; Mark 14:27). He does not tell them this to scare or discourage them. Rather, he tells them so that, when it happens, "in me you may have peace. You will have suffering in this world. Be courageous! I have conquered the world" (16:33). Life can throw us curves, and our faith can falter. We can neglect to watch where we're going, or forget where we're going, or take a detour that looks inviting and get lost. Brennan Manning says he was often asked how he could become an alcoholic after he was saved. He would answer,

> "It is possible because I got battered and bruised by loneliness and failure; because I got discouraged, uncertain, guilt-ridden, and took my eyes off Jesus. Because the Christ-encounter did not transfigure me into an angel. Because justification by grace through faith means I have been set in right relationship with God, not made the equivalent of a patient etherized on a table."[156]

We can become disappointed in where life has taken us or how many times we've failed. We can get discouraged, feel hopeless or angry with ourselves, or even with God. Fear can paralyze us. What can we do? The Christian drama team known as "the Skit Guys" has a sketch they call "God's Chisel." Eddie, playing God with a chisel, is trying to hammer away at Tommy and make him more like Jesus. Tommy isn't enjoying the experience and at one point he is wallowing in fear and self-pity and says, "God, I've let you down so many times." To this God replies, "No. You were never holding *me* up. I hold *you* up with my victorious, righteous right hand, and don't you forget that. In this relationship, I hold *you* up."[157] Jesus warns his disciples about times of disappointment, discouragement, and failure "so that *in me* you may have peace." *In me*—not in ourselves. Only in him. That means that when we are down (for whatever reason), we look to him and let him pick us up and show us the next step, which we take by faith. The disciples got scared, discouraged, and hopeless after the confusing experience of seeing Jesus arrested, tried, and crucified. They abandoned and rejected him, lied, and ran away to save their own skins. Yet, after giving his life for them and suffering God's wrath for their sin, he went and found them, comforted them, picked them up, and used them to carry the gospel and change the

---

156. Manning, *Ragamuffin Gospel*, 30–31.
157. See https://www.youtube.com/watch?v=AhfUzodLRvk.

world. He can do the same with you and me. We can be courageous because he has conquered the world, the devil, and our own sinful flesh.

The miracle at Cana was part of the process of pointing the disciples to who Jesus is and what he was going to do for them. That is what John means by Jesus's "glory." His first reference to Christ's "glory" is in 1:14, where he speaks of the disciples' overall experience with Christ: "The Word became flesh and dwelt among us. We observed his glory, the glory as the one and only Son from the Father, full of grace and truth." In our comments on that verse we noted that the verb "observed" means that the disciples watched Jesus closely as a scientist observes the behavior of a creature she is studying, until she feels she has come to an understanding of it. Jesus, however, is not a creature; he is our divine creator. Scientific diligence cannot uncover his nature. We learn in 2:11 and elsewhere that he can only be known insofar as he "reveals" himself, which is what he was doing at Cana.

As we noticed at 1:14, Richard Bauckham explains God's glory as "the visible revelation of God's character, what one would see if one could see the very face of God."[158] Finite creatures will never experience or comprehend God in the totality of his divine being. When we are "glorified," we will experience him in a way never before possible or imaginable. But the child of God by faith can come to know him now and can know about him insofar as he reveals himself to us. Following the Lord for a lifetime can help us know him better. The disciples had known Jesus for only about a week, so they had just begun the journey of a lifetime. Observing his first miracle apparently brought them a quantum leap ahead on that trip. Moses had asked to see God's glory in Exod 33:18 and was taught about God's goodness, grace, and compassion, and then he was allowed a glimpse of God's back, his "afterglow." He and the people of Israel had witnessed God's miracles in Egypt, culminating in the Passover and the parting of the sea. They would see much more during the life of Moses, Joshua, the judges, Samuel, David, Solomon, Elijah, and Elisha. But, like a candle held up to the sun, all that paled in comparison to the glory they were beginning to see in Jesus, the Son of God, who is "the radiance of God's glory and the exact expression of his nature, sustaining all things by his powerful word," who "after making purification for sins, . . . sat down at the right hand of the Majesty on high" (Heb 1:3). That same Jesus will someday soon come "on the clouds of heaven with power and great glory" (Matt 24:30). "The glory of the LORD will appear, and all humanity together will see it, for the mouth of the LORD has spoken" (Isa 40:5). Then "the earth will be filled with the knowledge of the LORD's glory, as the water covers the sea" (Hab 2:14). And "all nations

---

158. Bauckham, *Gospel of Glory*, 72–73.

and languages ... will come and see my glory" (Isa 66:18). As the author of Hebrews reminds us, "Christ, having been offered once to bear the sins of many, will appear a second time, not to bear sin, but to bring salvation to those who are waiting for him" (9:28).

5

Conclusion

WHAT DOES JOHN OFFER us here in these opening sections of his Gospel that can help us live more satisfying and effective lives? We are reminded that finding meaning, purpose, and satisfaction is not something we can do on our own. It must come from the God who created us for his purposes. And he has not left us alone in the silent darkness. God is not just watching, as Bette Midler sang, "from a distance." John reminds us that, as Francis Schaeffer wrote in 1973, [God] is there, and he is not silent.[1] He is the Word. He speaks. He acts. In the Old Testament he spoke to us with a whisper, but in Jesus he sings to us loudly and jubilantly (Zeph 3:17: "He will delight in you with singing"). As Michael Reeves wrote,

> It is of the very nature of this God to have a Word to speak. God cannot be Word-less, for the Word is God. Here then is a God who could never be anything but communicative, expansive, outgoing. Since God cannot be without this Word, he simply could not ever be reclusive. For eternity this Word sounds out, telling us of an uncontainable God of exuberance and abundance, an overflowing God of surplus, a glorious God of grace.[2]

God in Jesus Christ is also light. When we feel we are in the dark, it is only because our eyes of faith are closed. His light is shining in the darkness, and it is not in danger of going out. It is also not a train coming to smash us to pieces; it is the true light coming to bring us the light of life. And it is not coming to bring light to those deserving of it; it's coming to rebellious

---

1. Schaeffer, *He Is There, and He Is Not Silent*. I would have preferred the title, *He Is Here, and He Is Not Silent*, but that would not have echoed his earlier book.
2. Reeves, *Rejoicing in Christ*, 17.

sinners deserving of God's wrath—it's coming to me. The Word, my Creator, whom I had rejected and neglected, the light of life, has come to me. He has come to make me his child—not by physical birth or a human action of any kind—only by his will acting in love and grace and mercy. He is a person, and in Jesus Christ he is a person with flesh and very precious blood.

Paul Harvey was an American radio broadcaster whose program aired from 1952 to 2008, reaching as many as twenty-four million people a week (according to Wikipedia). He is most famous for the segments of his program he called "The Rest of the Story." Perhaps his most famous story is one heard by many people still at Christmas. It's called "The Man and the Birds." A kind but unbelieving man decides to stay home on Christmas Eve while his wife is at church. A heavy snow comes, and he is attracted to go outside by the sound of birds hitting his window. He finds a flock on the ground that has been caught by the storm. His many attempts to lure them into his warm barn fail. Realizing they are afraid of him, he thinks, "If only I could be a bird and mingle with them and speak their language. Then I could show them the way to the safe, warm barn. But I would have to be one of them, wouldn't I? So they could see and hear and understand." Suddenly the man hears the bells of the nearby church, and he sinks to his knees in the snow. Suddenly the gospel makes sense to him.[3]

Jesus came into a cold, dark world to provide for us a place of rest, not just in a warm barn, but around his table. There we sit by faith with our Savior, God's unique Son, who is "full of grace and truth." There we receive "grace upon grace from his fullness" (see comments on John 1:16), that is, from the infinitely vast reservoir of his glorious grace, just as one might take bucket after bucket of water from the ocean "without ever diminishing its content." In Jesus Christ we lie on the soft sand in the sunlight of his love letting wave after wave of his grace wash over us, bringing cleansing from our sins, healing from our hurts, and refreshment to our souls.

As part of my concluding remarks, I must revisit and expand on the comments on 1:12, that believing in/receiving Jesus makes us "children of God." The believer has become God's child by being joined to Christ. As Jesus says in 14:20, "I am in my Father, you are in me, and I am in you." Christ became identified with me so that I might be identified with him. I died and rose in him. As the apostle Paul put it, "Through faith you are all sons of God in Christ Jesus. For those of you who were baptized into Christ have been clothed with Christ" (Gal 3:26–27). Michael Reeves explains, "The Son shares with us *his own sonship*."[4] To repeat the words of Marcus

---

3. See https://www.youtube.com/watch?v=ddai8rkXWRs.
4. Reeves, *Rejoicing in Christ*, 71.

Johnson (see our comments on John 1:12–13), "The relationship of love we have with Jesus includes a sharing in the love the Father has for his Son, so much so that the Father and the Son dwell within us." Jesus prays in John 17:23 (emphasis added), "You have sent me and have loved them *as you have loved me*." As we quoted D. A. Carson, the believer in Jesus is "loved by the Almighty himself . . . with the very same love he reserves for his Son," which is, as he says, "breathtakingly extravagant."

The reason these comments must be repeated is that our culture is full of self-hatred. In fact, as Brennan Manning declared, "One of the most shocking contradictions in the American church is the intense dislike many disciples of Jesus have for themselves. They are more displeased with their own shortcomings than they would ever dream of being with someone else's. They are sick of their own mediocrity and disgusted by their own inconsistency."[5]

My generation (and many since) learned in childhood from the bunny, Thumper, in the 1942 Walt Disney movie, *Bambi*, "If you can't say somethin' nice, don't say nothin' at all." Yet things we might never dream of saying to another person because they would be painful, insulting, discouraging, and crippling, we tell ourselves all the time—things like, "I'm stupid, ugly, and useless. No wonder no one likes me!" Part of making peace with who we are is to stop the negative self-talk and learn to be gentle with ourselves "by experiencing the intimate, heartfelt compassion of Jesus,"[6] and by becoming convinced with all our hearts that we are the beloved of God.[7] Because of our union with Christ, when the voice from heaven said at Jesus's baptism, "This is my beloved Son, with whom I am well-pleased" (Matt 3:17), the Father was not just thinking of Jesus. He was thinking of me.[8] To drive home our identification with Christ, John Calvin borrowed an illustration from

---

5. Manning, *Abba's Child*, 23.

6. Manning, *Abba's Child*, 24.

7. Manning, *Abba's Child*, 24, quotes Henri Nouwen (*Life of the Beloved*, 21): "*Self-rejection is the greatest enemy of the spiritual life* because it contradicts the sacred voice that calls us the 'Beloved.' Being the Beloved constitutes the core truth of our existence" (Manning's emphasis).

8. See Manning's account (*Abba's Child*, 51) of John Eagan, an "unheralded high school teacher" who "spent thirty years ministering with youth" in Milwaukee. He was "an ordinary man whose soul was seduced and ravished by Jesus Christ." His posthumously published journal recounts his thoughts during a "silent eight-day directed retreat": "The basis of my personal worth is not my possessions, my talents, not esteem of others, reputation . . . not kudos of appreciation from parents and kids, not applause, and everyone telling you how important you are to the place . . . I stand anchored now in God before whom I stand naked, this God who tells me 'You are my son, my beloved one.'" See Eagan, *A Traveler Toward the Dawn*, 150–51. Thanks to pastor Julie Vega, I found this interpretation also in Ellen G. White, *The Desire of Ages*, 113.

Bishop Ambrose. Jacob achieved the rights of the firstborn (Gen 27:1–40), which he did not inherently deserve, by concealing himself in Esau's clothes, "which gave out an agreeable odor." As Jacob "ingratiated himself with his father" in this way, "we in like manner hide under the precious purity of our first-born brother, Christ . . . In order that we may appear before God's face unto salvation we must smell sweetly with his odor, and our vices must be covered and buried by his perfection."[9] That describes every believer. Clothed in Christ, we smell like him—not because we are good or obedient or devoted or diligent or prayerful or know our Bibles, but because he has come to dwell in us and we in him by pure grace. When we come to our heavenly Father in prayer, he smells Jesus and pulls us close. That is why we pray "in Jesus's name." And with our vices covered by his blood and "buried by his perfection," we may spread "the aroma of the knowledge of him in every place" (2 Cor 2:14).

It's not that *we* must hide our vices, weaknesses, faults, and failures. Many Christian writers have pointed out that the power of a Christian's message of redemption is often in those things from which Christ has redeemed us and even in the areas of our lives where Satan continues to attack us. Brennan Manning, for example, says,

> In a futile attempt to erase our past, we deprive the community of our healing gift. If we conceal our wounds out of fear and shame, our inner darkness can neither be illuminated nor become a light for others . . . [G]race and healing are communicated through the vulnerability of men and women who have been fractured and heartbroken by life . . . The decision to come out of hiding is our initiation rite into the healing ministry of Jesus Christ.[10]

Manning tells about a man named John Eagan, who spent thirty years ministering to youth in Milwaukee and died in 1987. He "never wrote a book, appeared on television, converted the masses, or gathered a reputation for holiness." But he kept a journal that was published after his death. In it is found "an ordinary man whose soul was seduced and ravished by Jesus Christ." In the introduction, the editor tries to capture Eagan's message: "We judge ourselves unworthy servants, and that judgment becomes a self-fulfilling prophecy. We deem ourselves too inconsiderable to be used even by a God capable of miracles with no more than mud and spit [or six waterpots full of water!]. And thus our false humility shackles an otherwise omnipotent God." Manning adds that Eagan had learned that "we must

---

9. Calvin, *Institutes*, 3.11.23.
10. Manning, *Abba's Child*, 29–30.

forgive ourselves for being unlovable, inconsistent, incompetent, irritable, and potbellied, and he knew that his sins could not keep him from God. They had all been redeemed by the blood of Christ . . . [He] dared to live as a forgiven man." For any, in fact, who judge themselves to be unworthy to serve Jesus, the Lamb of God, Manning quotes Thomas Merton, who urges us to forget our unworthiness and that of others and "to advance in the love which has redeemed and renewed us all in God's likeness. And to laugh, after all, at the preposterous ideas of 'worthiness.'"[11]

"What are you looking for?" Jesus asked. Compared to Jesus, the unique Son of God, the Lamb of God who takes away the sin of the world, what else is there? What could be as satisfying and fulfilling? David's words in Ps 23:1 could be accurately rendered, "The LORD is my Shepherd. What more could I want?" Peter asked Jesus in John 6:68, "Lord, to whom will we go? You have the words of eternal life." And the apostle Paul said in Phil 3:8, "I also consider everything to be a loss in view of the surpassing value of knowing Christ Jesus my Lord. Because of him I have suffered the loss of all things and consider them as dung, so that I may gain Christ." He obviously knew Jesus's words in Mark 8:36: "For what does it benefit someone to gain the whole world and yet lose his life?" And yet we so often exhaust ourselves searching for the wrong things, in the wrong places, in the wrong way, or for the wrong reasons, like the drunk looking for his keys under the lamp post only because the light was better there. We "look and look, but never perceive" (Matt 13:14). We might ask ourselves the question the two angels asked the women at Jesus's tomb: "Why are you looking for the living among the dead?" (Luke 24:5). One of Jesus's disciples, who had spent three years following Jesus, said to him on the way out of Jerusalem that last week (Mark 13:1–2), "Teacher, look! What massive stones! What impressive buildings!" Jesus replied, "Do you see these great buildings? Not one stone will be left upon another—all will be thrown down." We are so easily impressed.

One of the most profound statements of one famous for profound statements, C. S. Lewis, was made in a sermon preached in 1941,

> If we consider the unblushing promises of reward and the staggering nature of the rewards promised in the Gospels, it would seem that Our Lord finds our desires not too strong, but too weak. We are half-hearted creatures, fooling about with drink and sex and ambition when infinite joy is offered us, like an ignorant child who wants to go on making mud pies in a slum

---

11. Manning, *Abba's Child*, 50.

because he cannot imagine what is meant by the offer of a holiday at the sea. We are far too easily pleased.[12]

The message of this book is that whether we are looking for ourselves, or for infinite joy, or godliness, or the glory of God, or any other worthwhile personal destination, the only way to arrive is to focus on Christ. All these things and more can be found only in him, and as Michael Reeves explains, "It matters where we *look*. Before anything else it matters what fills our vision. For whatever it is that occupies our attention ... will steer and shape our every thought, motive and action. *You are what you see.*"[13] Against the background of Moses's experience with God's glory, the apostle Paul wrote these profound words in 2 Cor 3:18: "We all, with unveiled faces, are looking as in a mirror at the glory of the Lord and are being transformed into the same image from glory to glory; this is from the Lord who is the Spirit." Reeves explains,

> We become like him *through the very looking*. The very sight of him is a transforming thing ... So potent is his glory that when we clap eyes upon him physically at his second coming, then "we shall be like him, *for we shall see him as he is*" (1 John 3:2) ... The sight of him now by the Spirit makes us more like him spiritually; the sight of him then, face to face, will finally make us—body and soul—as he is. Contemplating Christ now is thus rather like seeing the morning star at the break of day: both enchanting and full of hope. It is light for now with the promise of so much more to come. It is a taste of heaven.[14]

As we keep our eyes on Jesus, "the source and perfecter of our faith" (Heb 12:2), he not only reveals our imperfections, but he also overcomes and heals them and trains us in godliness as we follow him, "so that what is lame may not be dislocated but healed instead" (Heb 12:13). As healing could be found by the rebellious in the wilderness only by looking at the bronze snake on the pole (Num 21:4–9), so healing now can only come to the one who looks to Calvary (John 3:14–15). And how can we forgive, as Jesus tells us we must, those who have neglected us, lied to us, stolen from us, treated us or our loved ones with cruelty? Manning tells us:

> The demands of forgiveness are so daunting that they seem humanly impossible. The exigencies of forgiveness are simply beyond the capacity of ungraced human will. Only reckless

---

12. Lewis, "The Weight of Glory," 26.
13. Reeves, *Rejoicing in Christ*, 101 (emphasis original).
14. Reeves, *Rejoicing in Christ*, 102 (emphasis original).

> confidence in a Source greater than ourselves can empower us to forgive the wounds inflicted by others. In boundary moments such as these there is only one place to go—Calvary ... On that lonely hill outside the city wall of old Jerusalem, you will experience the healing power of the dying Lord.

The healing, Manning cautions us, seldom comes suddenly or instantly. "More often it is a gentle growing into oneness with the Crucified who has achieved our peace through His blood on the cross. This may take considerable time because the memories are still so vivid and the hurt is still so deep. But it *will* happen."[15]

Reeves points us to a powerful illustration from Charles Spurgeon, "the prince of preachers," who was preaching on 2 Cor 5:17 ("Therefore, if anyone is in Christ, he is a new creation; the old has passed away, and see, the new has come!"). Attempting to explain how the old passes away, he said,

> I cannot liken it to anything that I know of better than the snow which melts in the sun. You wake up one morning and all the trees are festooned with snowy wreaths, while down below upon the ground the snow lies in a white sheet over everything. Lo, the sun has risen, its beams shed genial warmth, and in a few hours, where is the snow? It has passed away! Had you hired a thousand carts and horses and machines to sweep it away it could not have been more effectually removed. It has passed away. That is what the Lord does in the new creation—His love shines on the soul, His grace renews us and the old things pass away as a matter of course ... Where are those old pleasures which you took so much delight in? Where are those old engrossing pursuits? Had you a hard tug to get away from these bonds? Where are those old joys, those old hopes, those old trusts, those old confidences? Was it difficult to shake them off? Ah, no! Beneath the power of the Holy Spirit they have passed away! ... Our Lord Jesus Christ causes all this! Where His blessed face beams with grace and truth, as the sun with warmth and light, He dissolves the bands of sin's long frost and brings on the spring of grace with newness of buds and flowers.[16]

Meanwhile, the light of his transforming glory not only shines *on* us, but it also shines *through* us. Paul writes in 2 Cor 4:7–10,

---

15. Manning, *Abba's Child*, 68.
16. Spurgeon, "Christ the Maker of All Things New."

> Now we have this treasure in clay jars, so that this extraordinary power may be from God and not from us. We are afflicted in every way but not crushed; we are perplexed but not in despair; we are persecuted but not abandoned; we are struck down but not destroyed. We always carry the death of Jesus in our body, so that the life of Jesus may also be displayed in our body.

Tasker explains, "The treasure of the gospel has been entrusted to men subject to the infirmities and limitations, the instability and insecurity of their finite condition. It is as though a most costly jewel were encased in an earthenware jar!"[17]

Reverend Robert Lowry, author of "Nothing But the Blood," is also responsible for a less familiar hymn called "The Mistakes of My Life" (1871),[18] which I find it easy to identify with. It begins,

> The mistakes of my life have been many,
> The sins of my heart have been more,
> And I scarce can see for weeping,
> But I'll knock at the open door.
>
> Refrain:
> I know I am weak and sinful,
> It comes to me more and more;
> But when the dear Saviour shall bid me come in,
> I'll enter the open door.

Brennan Manning provided an afterword, titled "The Scandal of Grace," for the revised edition of his most famous book, *The Ragamuffin Gospel*. These words from that final chapter provide a fitting conclusion to my book:

> Is Jesus enough? Is His love mediated through spouse, children, and friends enough? Must I grasp for something else? . . . Having been given a seat at the wedding feast, the thought of ever going back into the misery and filth—the cold and the darkness of the highways and hedges, the streets and the alleys of a self-centered life—fills me with holy dread.[19]

---

17. Tasker, *Second Corinthians*, 72.

18. See https://hymnary.org/text/the_mistakes_of_my_life_have_been_many (accessed 8/27/2018).

19. Manning, *Ragamuffin Gospel*, 219.

Bibliography

Augustine. *Confessions.* Translated by Henry Chadwick. Oxford: Oxford University Press, 1991.

Balz, Horst, and Gerhard Schneider, eds. *Exegetical Dictionary of the New Testament.* 3 vols. Grand Rapids: Eerdmans, 1990–93.

Barrett, C. K. *The Gospel according to John: An Introduction with Commentary and Notes on the Greek Text.* 2nd ed. Philadelphia: Westminster, 1978.

Bateman, Herbert W., IV, et al. *Jesus the Messiah: Tracing the Promises, Expectations, and Coming of Israel's King.* Grand Rapids: Kregel, 2012.

Bauckham, Richard. *Gospel of Glory: Major Themes in Johannine Theology.* Grand Rapids: Baker, 2015.

———. *Jesus and the Eyewitnesses: The Gospels as Eyewitness Testimony.* Grand Rapids: Eerdmans, 2006.

———. *The Testimony of the Beloved Disciple: Narrative, History, and Theology in the Gospel of John.* Grand Rapids: Baker Academic, 2007.

Beale, G. K. *The Book of Revelation.* The New International Greek Testament Commentary. Grand Rapids: Eerdmans, 1999.

———. *A New Testament Biblical Theology: The Unfolding of the Old Testament in the New.* Grand Rapids: Baker, 2011.

———. *The Temple and the Church's Mission: A Biblical Theology of the Dwelling Place of God.* New Studies in Biblical Theology. Downers Grove, IL: InterVarsity, 2004.

Beale, G. K., and Benjamin L. Gladd. *Hidden But Now Revealed: A Biblical Theology of Mystery.* Downers Grove, IL: IVP Academic, 2014.

Beckwith, Roger T., and Martin J. Selman, eds. *Sacrifice in the Bible.* Eugene, OR: Wipf & Stock, 1995.

Bettenson, Henry, ed. *Documents of the Christian Church.* 2nd ed. London: Oxford University Press, 1963.

Blomberg, Craig L. *The Historical Reliability of John's Gospel: Issues and Commentary.* Downers Grove, IL: InterVarsity, 2001.

———. *The Historical Reliability of the New Testament: Countering the Challenges to Evangelical Christian Beliefs.* Nashville: B&H, 2016.

———. *Jesus and the Gospels: An Introduction and Survey.* 2nd ed. Nashville: B&H, 2009.

Bock, Darrell L. "Precision and Accuracy: Making Distinctions in the Cultural Context that Give Us Pause in Pitting the Gospels against Each Other." In *Do Historical Matters Matter to Faith? A Critical Appraisal of Modern and Postmodern*

Approaches to Scripture, edited by James K. Hoffmeier and Dennis R. Magary, 367–81. Wheaton, IL: Crossway, 2012.

Boda, Mark J. *The Heartbeat of Old Testament Theology: Three Creedal Expressions.* Grand Rapids: Baker Academic, 2017.

Botterweck, G. Johannes, and Helmer Ringgren, eds. *Theological Dictionary of the Old Testament.* Translated by John T. Willis and David E. Green. 15 vols. Grand Rapids: Eerdmans, 1974–2006.

Brown, Colin, ed. *New International Dictionary of New Testament Theology,* 3 vols. Grand Rapids: Zondervan, 1986.

Brown, Raymond E. *The Gospel according to John I–XII.* The Anchor Bible. Garden City, NY: Doubleday & Company, Inc., 1966.

Bruce, F. F. *The Gospel of John.* Grand Rapids: Eerdmans, 1983.

Bruner, Frederick Dale. *The Gospel of John: A Commentary.* Grand Rapids: Eerdmans, 2012.

Burge, Gary M. *John.* The NIV Application Commentary. Grand Rapids: Zondervan, 2000.

Buth, Randall. "Οὖν, Δέ, Καί, and Asyndeton in John's Gospel." In *Linguistics and New Testament Interpretation: Essays on Discourse Analysis,* edited by David Alan Black, et al., 144–61. Nashville: Broadman, 1992.

Calvin, John. *Calvin: Institutes of the Christian Religion.* Edited by John T. McNeill. Translated by Ford Lewis Battles. Library of Christian Classics, vols. 20–21. Philadelphia: Westminster, 1960.

———. *The Gospel according to St. John 1–10.* Edited by David W. Torrance and Thomas F. Torrance. Translated by T. H. L. Parker. Grand Rapids: Eerdmans, 1996.

Carson, D. A. *The Gospel according to John.* Pillar New Testament Commentary. Grand Rapids: Eerdmans, 1991.

———. "Matthew." In *Expositor's Bible Commentary.* Edited by Frank E. Gaebelein, 8:3–599. Grand Rapids: Zondervan, 1990. Electronic text hypertexted and prepared by OakTree Software, Inc. Version 2.3.

———. "Understanding Misunderstandings in the Fourth Gospel." *Tyndale Bulletin* 33 (1982) 59–91.

———, et al. *An Introduction to the New Testament.* Grand Rapids: Zondervan, 1992.

Clark, John C., and Marcus Peter Johnson, *The Incarnation of God: The Mystery of the Gospel as the Foundation of Evangelical Theology.* Wheaton: Crossway, 2015.

Clem, Eldon. "Translation of Targum Onkelos and Jonathan." OakTree Software, Inc., 2015. Version 7.2.

Clendenen, E. Ray. "'Messenger of the Covenant' in Malachi 3:1 Once Again." *Journal of the Evangelical Society* 62.1 (2019) 81–102.

Cockerill, Gareth L. *The Epistle to the Hebrews.* New International Commentary on the New Testament. Grand Rapids: Eerdmans, 2012.

Cranfield, C. E. B. *Romans.* International Critical Commentary. 2 vols. Edinburgh: T&T Clark, 1975.

Danker, Frederick W., ed. *A Greek-English Lexicon of the New Testament and Other Early Christian Literature.* 3rd Edition. Chicago: University of Chicago Press, 2000.

Davies, W. D., and D. C. Allison. *A Critical and Exegetical Commentary on the Gospel according to Saint Matthew, Volume II.* International Critical Commentary. London: T&T Clark, 1991.

Davis, Ellen F., and Richard B. Hays, eds. *The Art of Reading Scripture*. Grand Rapids: Eerdmans, 2003.

Duguid, Iain. "Messianic Themes in Zechariah 9–14." In *The Lord's Anointed: Interpretation of Old Testament Messianic Texts*, edited by Philip E. Satterthwaite, et al., 265–80. Grand Rapids: Baker, 1995.

Dunn, James D. G. *Christology in the Making: A New Testament Inquiry into the Origins of the Doctrine of the Incarnation*. 2nd ed. Grand Rapids: Eerdmans, 1989.

Eagan, John. *A Traveler Toward the Dawn*. Chicago: Loyola University Press, 1990.

The English Hymnal. London: Oxford University Press, 1933.

Estes, Daniel J. *Psalms 73–150*. New American Commentary, vol. 13. Nashville: B&H, 2019.

Evans, Craig A., and Stanley E. Porter, eds. *Dictionary of New Testament Background*. Downers Grove, IL: InterVarsity, 2000.

Fairbairn, Donald. *Life in the Trinity: An Introduction to Theology with the Help of the Church Fathers*. Downers Grove, IL: InterVarsity Academic, 2009.

Finegan, Jack. *Handbook of Biblical Chronology*. Revised ed. Peabody, MA: Hendrickson, 1998.

Freedman, David Noel, ed. *Anchor Yale Bible Dictionary*. 6 vols. New Haven, CT: Yale University Press, 1992.

Frey, Jörg. *The Glory of the Crucified One: Christology and Theology in the Gospel of John*. Translated by Wayne Coppins and Christoph Heilig. Waco, OX: Baylor University Press, 2018.

Gaffin, Richard B., Jr. "The Holy Spirit," *Westminster Theological Journal* 43.1 (1980) 58–78.

———. "Union with Christ: Some Biblical and Theological Reflections." In *Always Reforming: Explorations in Systematic Theology*, edited by A. T. B. McGowan, 271–88. Downers Grove, IL: InterVarsity, 2006.

Garner, David B. *Sons in the Son: The Riches and Reach of Adoption in Christ*. Phillipsburg, NJ: P&R, 2016.

Garrett, Duane A. *Hosea, Joel*. New American Commentary. Nashville: B&H, 1997.

Gathercole, Simon J. *The Preexistent Son: Recovering the Christologies of Matthew, Mark, and Luke*. Grand Rapids: Eerdmans, 2006.

Green, Chris, ed. *God's Power to Save: One Gospel for a Complex World?* Leicester, England: Inter-Varsity, 2006.

Green, Joel B., and Scot McKnight, eds. *Dictionary of Jesus and the Gospels*. Downers Grove, IL: InterVarsity, 1992.

Green, Joel B., et al., eds. *Dictionary of Jesus and the Gospels*. 2nd ed. Downers Grove, IL: InterVarsity, 2013.

Gregory the Great. "Saint Gregory the Great, Roman Pontiff: Moralia or Commentary on the Book of Blessed Job," http://faculty.georgetown.edu/jod/texts/moralia1.html.

Groothuis, Douglas. *Truth Decay: Defending Christianity against the Challenges of Postmodernism*. Downers Grove, IL: InterVarsity, 2000.

Guthrie, Donald. *New Testament Introduction*. 3rd ed. Downers Grove: Inter-Varsity Press, 1970.

Hamilton, Victor P. *The Book of Genesis, Chapters 18–50*. New International Commentary on the Old Testament. Grand Rapids: Eerdmans, 1995.

Harris, W. Hall, III, "Major Differences between John and the Synoptic Gospels." Accessed 7/18/2018. https://bible.org/seriespage/2-major-differences-between-john-and-synoptic-gospels.

Hess, Richard S., and M. Daniel Carroll R., eds. *Israel's Messiah in the Bible and the Dead Sea Scrolls*. Eugene, OR: Wipf & Stock, 2003.

Hock, R. F. *The Infancy Gospels of James and Thomas*. Santa Rosa, CA: Polebridge, 1995.

Hughes, Philip Edgcumbe. *A Commentary on the Epistle to the Hebrews*. Grand Rapids: Eerdmans, 1977.

Hughes, R. Kent. *1001 Great Stories and Quotes*. Wheaton, IL: Tyndale, 1998.

Jeffery, Steve, et al., *Pierced for Our Transgressions: Rediscovering the Glory of Penal Substitution*. Wheaton, IL: Crossway, 2007.

Johnson, Dennis E. *Triumph of the Lamb: A Commentary on Revelation*. Phillipsburg, NJ: P&R, 2001.

Johnson, Marcus Peter. *One with Christ: An Evangelical Theology of Salvation*. Wheaton: Crossway, 2013.

Joslin, Barry C. "Christ Bore the Sins of Many: Substitution and Atonement in Hebrews." *Southern Baptist Journal of Theology* 11 (2007) 74–103.

Keener, Craig S. *The Gospel of John: A Commentary, Volume One*. Grand Rapids: Baker, 2003.

King, Philip J., and Lawrence E. Stager. *Life in Biblical Israel*. Louisville: Westminster John Knox, 2001.

Kittel, Gerhard, and Gerhard Friedrich, eds. *Theological Dictionary of the New Testament, Abridged in One Volume*. Translated by Geoffrey W. Bromiley. Grand Rapids: Eerdmans, 1985.

Klink, Edward W., III. *John*. Zondervan Exegetical Commentary on the New Testament. Grand Rapids: Zondervan, 2016.

Koester, Craig R. *The Word of Life: A Theology of John's Gospel*. Grand Rapids: Eerdmans, 2008.

Köstenberger, Andreas J. *John*. Baker Exegetical Commentary on the New Testament. Grand Rapids: Baker, 2004.

———. *A Theology of John's Gospel and Letters*. Biblical Theology of the New Testament. Grand Rapids: Zondervan, 2009.

Köstenberger, Andreas J., and Scott R. Swain. *Father, Son and Spirit: The Trinity and John's Gospel*. Downers Grove, IL: InterVarsity, 2008.

Kruger, Michael J. *Canon Revisited: Establishing the Origins and Authority of the New Testament Books*. Wheaton: Crossway, 2012.

Leithart, Peter J. *Deep Exegesis: The Mystery of Reading Scripture*. Waco, TX: Baylor University Press, 2009.

Letham, Robert. *Union with Christ in Scripture, History, and Theology*. Phillipsburg: P&R, 2011.

Levine, Baruch A. *Leviticus*. JPS Torah Commentary. Philadelphia: Jewish Publication Society, 1989.

Levinsohn, Stephen H. *Discourse Features of New Testament Greek: A Coursebook on the Information Structure of New Testament Greek*. 2nd ed. Dallas: SIL International, 2000.

Lewis, C. S. *Mere Christianity*. Revised and amplified ed. New York: HarperOne, 2001.

———. *Miracles*. New York: Macmillan, 1960.

———. "The Weight of Glory." 1949. In *The Weight of Glory and Other Addresses*. Revised ed. New York: HarperCollins, 1980.
Lightfoot, J. B. *Biblical Essays*. London: MacMillan, 1904.
Little, Edmund. *Echoes of the Old Testament in the Wine of Cana in Galilee (John 2:1-11) and the Multiplication of the Loaves and Fish (John 6:1-15): Towards an Appreciation*. Paris: J. Gabalda et Cie Éditeurs, 1998.
Louw, Johannes P., and Eugene A. Nida, eds. *Greek-English Lexicon of the New Testament Based on Semantic Domains*, 2 vols. 2nd ed. New York: United Bible Societies, 1989.
McCullough, Donald W. *Waking from the American Dream: Growing through Your Disappointments*. Downers Grove, IL: InterVarsity, 1988.
McGrath, Alistair. *Thomas F. Torrance: An Intellectual Biography*. Edinburgh: T&T Clark, 1999.
Macgregor, G. H. C. *The Gospel of John*. London: Hodder & Stoughton, 1928.
McGuckin, John Anthony. *Patristic Theology*. Louisville: Westminster John Knox, 2004.
McHugh, John F. *A Critical and Exegetical Commentary on John 1-4*. International Critical Commentary. Paperback ed. London: Bloomsbury, 2014. First published 2009.
McKnight, Scot, and Grant R. Osborne, eds. *The Face of New Testament Studies: A Survey of Recent Research*. Grand Rapids: Baker Academic, 2004.
Maccini, R. G. *Her Testimony Is True: Women as Witnesses according to John*. Sheffield: Sheffield Academic Press, 1996.
Manning, Brennan. *Abba's Child: The Cry of the Heart for Intimate Belonging*. Colorado Springs: NavPress, 2002.
———. *The Ragamuffin Gospel*. Rev. ed. New York: Multnomah, 2005.
Martin, Ralph P., and Peter H. Davids, eds. *The Dictionary of the Later New Testament and Its Developments*. Downers Grove, IL: InterVarsity, 1997.
Metzger, Bruce M. *A Textual Commentary on the Greek New Testament*. 2nd ed. London: United Bible Societies, 1994.
Miller, Paul. "'They Saw His Glory and Spoke of Him': The Gospel of John and the Old Testament." In *Hearing the Old Testament in the New Testament*, edited by Stanley E. Porter, 127-51. Grand Rapids: Eerdmans, 2006.
Morris, Leon. *The Apostolic Preaching of the Cross*. 3rd edition. Grand Rapids: Eerdman Publishing, 1965.
———. *The Cross in the New Testament*. Grand Rapids: Eerdmans, 1965.
———. *The Gospel according to John*. The New International Commentary on the New Testament. Grand Rapids: Eerdmans, 1971.
Motyer, J. Alec. *The Prophecy of Isaiah: An Introduction and Commentary*. Downers Grove, IL: InterVarsity, 1993.
Murray, John. *Redemption Accomplished and Applied*. Grand Rapids: Eerdmans, 1955.
Oswalt, John N. *The Book of Isaiah, Chapters 40-66*. Grand Rapids: Eerdmans, 1998.
Packer, J. I. *Knowing God*. Downers Grove, IL: InterVarsity, 1973.
Pendrick, Gerard. "*Monogenēs*." *New Testament Studies* 41 (1995) 587-600.
Pennington, Jonathan T. *Reading the Gospels Wisely: A Narrative and Theological Introduction*. Grand Rapids: Baker, 2012.
Petry, Ray C., ed. *The Early and Medieval Church*. Vol. 1 of *A History of Christianity: Readings in the History of the Church*. 1962. Reprinted, Grand Rapids: Baker, 1981.

Petterson, Anthony R. *Behold Your King: The Hope for the House of David in the Book of Zechariah.* N.Y.: T&T Clark, 2009.

———. *Haggai, Zechariah and Malachi.* Apollos Old Testament Commentary. Downers Grove, IL: InterVarsity, 2015.

Porter, Stanley E. *Idioms of the Greek New Testament.* 2nd ed. Sheffield: JSOT Press, 1994.

Pritchard, James B. *Ancient Near Eastern Texts Relating to the Old Testament.* Princeton: Princeton University Press, 1969.

Reeves, Michael. *Rejoicing in Christ.* Downers Grove, IL: InterVarsity, 2015.

Ridderbos, Herman. *The Gospel of John: A Theological Commentary.* Grand Rapids: Eerdmans, 1997.

Ryken, Leland, et al. *Dictionary of Biblical Imagery.* Downers Grove, IL: InterVarsity, 1998.

———. *J. I. Packer: An Evangelical Life.* Wheaton, IL: Crossway, 2015.

Schaeffer, Francis. *He Is There, and He Is Not Silent.* Wheaton, IL: Tyndale, 1973.

Schreiner, Thomas R. *Commentary on Hebrews.* Biblical Theology for Christian Proclamation. Nashville: B&H, 2015.

———. *New Testament Theology: Magnifying God in Christ.* Grand Rapids: Baker, 2008.

Silva, Moisés, ed. *Dictionary of New Testament Theology and Exegesis,* 5 vols. Grand Rapids: Zondervan, 2014.

Sklar, Jay. *Leviticus.* Tyndale Old Testament Commentaries. Downers Grove, IL: InterVarsity, 2014.

Spurgeon, Charles H. "Christ the Maker of All Things New." Sermon no. 1328, Metropolitan Tabernacle Pulpit. https://www.spurgeongems.org/vols22-24/chs1328.pdf (accessed 8/27/2018).

Stott, John R. W. *Baptism and Fullness: The Work of the Holy Spirit Today.* 2nd ed. Downers Grove, IL: InterVarsity, 1978.

Stuart, Douglas K. *Exodus.* New American Commentary. Nashville: B&H, 2006.

Tasker, R. V. G. *The Gospel according to St. John: An Introduction and Commentary.* Tyndale New Testament Commentaries. Grand Rapids: Eerdmans, 1960.

———. *The Second Epistle of Paul to the Corinthians: An Introduction and Commentary.* Tyndale New Testament Commentaries. Grand Rapids: Eerdmans, 1958.

Thielman, Frank S. "The Atonement." In *Central Themes in Biblical Theology: Mapping Unity in Diversity,* edited by Scott J. Hafemann and Paul R. House, 102–27. Grand Rapids: Baker, 2007.

Torrance, T. F. *A Passion for Christ: The Vision That Ignites Ministry.* Eugene, OR: Wipf & Stock, 2010.

Treat, Jeremy R. *The Crucified King: Atonement and Kingdom in Biblical and Systematic Theology.* Grand Rapids: Zondervan, 2014.

Turner, Max. "Atonement and the Death of Jesus in John," *Evangelical Quarterly* (1990) 99–122.

Volf, Miroslav. *Exclusion and Embrace: A Theological Exploration of Identity, Otherness, and Reconciliation.* Nashville: Abingdon, 1990.

Wallace, Daniel B. *Greek Grammar Beyond the Basics: An Exegetical Syntax of the New Testament.* Grand Rapids: Zondervan, 1996.

Waltke, Bruce K., with Charles Yu. *An Old Testament Theology: An Exegetical, Canonical, and Thematic Approach.* Grand Rapids: Zondervan, 2007.

Welch, Edward T. *Caring for One Another: 8 Ways to Cultivate Meaningful Relationships*. Wheaton, IL: Crossway, 2018.

Westcott, Brooke Foss. *The Bible in the Church*. 1864. Reprint, Grand Rapids: Baker, 1979.

———. *The Epistle to the Hebrews: The Greek Text with Notes and Essays*. 1892. Reprint, Grand Rapids: Eerdmans, 1974.

Whitacre, R. A. *John*. InterVarsity New Testament Commentary. Downers Grove, IL: InterVarsity, 1999.

White, Ellen G. *The Desire of Ages*. Nampa, ID: Pacific Press, 1898.

Wilkins, Michael J., and J. P. Moreland, eds., *Jesus Under Fire: Modern Scholarship Reinvents the Historical Jesus*. Grand Rapids: Zondervan, 1996.

Williams, M. D. *Far as the Curse Is Found: The Covenant Story of Redemption*. Phillipsburg: P&R, 2005.

Witherington, Ben, III. *New Testament History: A Narrative Account*. Grand Rapids: Baker, 2001.

Wright, N. T. *John for Everyone, Part 1, Chapters 1–10*. Louisville: Westminster John Knox, 2004.

www.ingramcontent.com/pod-product-compliance
Lightning Source LLC
Chambersburg PA
CBHW062045220426
43662CB00010B/1661